UPROOTING
INSTRUCTIONAL
INEQUITY

Also by Jill Harrison Berg

Leading in Sync: Teacher Leaders and Principals
Working Together for Student Learning

Praise for *Uprooting Instructional Inequity*

"Efforts to promote racial equity in schools have frequently ignored or provided little concrete guidance on how to improve the quality of teaching and the learning experiences of students. In this important new book, Jill Harrison Berg shows us how we can impact classroom practices through processes that foster professional collaboration and enhance the efficacy of teachers. Written in a straightforward, accessible style that practitioners will enjoy, this book will be an invaluable resource to all educators who seek to advance equity by making a positive difference for the students they serve."

—Pedro A. Noguera, PhD, Dean, Rossier School of Education, University of Southern California

"In *Uprooting Instructional Inequity*, Jill Harrison Berg helps us level up our understanding and skill around inquiry as a powerful tool for making progress on eliminating gaps in practice that lead to learning and opportunity gaps. She reminds us there are no magic strategies or silver bullets, but there's clearly a road map to change. Berg has shown us a path forward."

—Zaretta Hammond, author of *Culturally Responsive Teaching and the Brain*

"*Uprooting Instructional Inequity* is a thorough and highly practical handbook for practitioners. Based on Jill Harrison Berg's extensive experience leading professional learning, this book provides a road map for designing and facilitating meaningful instructional improvement. Berg goes beyond the usual recommendations as she guides educators to examine systems and beliefs that undermine the achievement of Black and Brown students and other marginalized student groups. Berg is an important voice in the movement to (as she writes) 'get better at learning how to learn together in schools.'"

—Sarah E. Fiarman, EdD, coauthor of *Unconscious Bias in Schools: A Developmental Approach to Exploring Race and Racism* and *Instructional Rounds in Education: A Network Approach to Improving Teaching and Learning*

"Now more than ever, schools and systems need professional learning models and strategies for embedding equity into the DNA of individual and collective educator practices so that each student receives an excellent education. Dr. Berg's book, *Uprooting Instructional Inequity: The Power of Inquiry-Based Professional Learning,* provides a compelling, cohesive, and transformational road map for using collective inquiry to interrogate and dismantle systemic barriers to instructional equity."

—Paul Fleming, EdD, senior vice president, Standards, States & Equity, Learning Forward

"This is the charge: interrogate inequity through inquiry! Easy to say; harder to do. Jill Harrison Berg provides teachers and school leaders with tools and guides to create effective professional development. This is a book I will both teach and use with my colleagues."

—Linda Nathan, cofounder and codirector, Perrone Sizer Institute for Creative Leadership; author of *The Hardest Questions Aren't on the Test: When Grit Isn't Enough*

"Jill Harrison Berg is one of the foremost voices on teacher leadership and offers a blueprint of the work she's put in with thousands of us. To do the work means to interrogate the deep, structural inequities of our day and understand how that gets into our classroom spaces. So many books ask you to change how we do professional learning in this light. This book shows you how to do it."

—José Luis Vilson, NBCT, New York City public school teacher, executive director of EduColor, and author of *This Is Not a Test: A New Narrative on Race, Class, and Education*

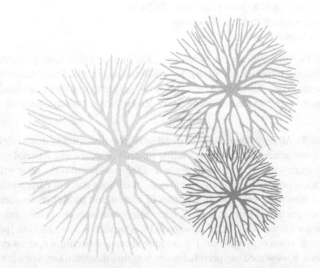

UPROOTING INSTRUCTIONAL INEQUITY

The Power of Inquiry-Based
Professional Learning

JILL HARRISON BERG

Arlington, Virginia USA

2800 Shirlington Rd., Suite 1001 • Arlington, VA 22206 USA
Phone: 800-933-2723 or 703-578-9600 • Fax: 703-575-5400
Website: www.ascd.org • Email: member@ascd.org
Author guidelines: www.ascd.org/write

Ranjit Sidhu, *CEO & Executive Director;* Penny Reinart, *Chief Impact Officer;* Genny Ostertag, *Managing Director, Book Acquisitions & Editing;* Julie Houtz, *Director, Book Editing;* Susan Hills, *Senior Acquisitions Editor;* Mary Beth Nielsen, *Editor;* Thomas Lytle, *Creative Director;* Donald Ely, *Art Director;* Samantha Wood, *Graphic Designer;* Valerie Younkin, *Senior Production Designer;* Kelly Marshall, *Production Manager;* Shajuan Martin, *E-Publishing Specialist*

Author photo taken by Carla Osberg Photography.

All web links in this book are correct as of the publication date below but may have become inactive or otherwise modified since that time. If you notice a deactivated or changed link, please email books@ascd.org with the words "Link Update" in the subject line. In your message, please specify the web link, the book title, and the page number on which the link appears.

PAPERBACK ISBN: 978-1-4166-3069-2 ASCD product #121016   n2/22

PDF E-BOOK ISBN: 978-1-4166-3070-8; see Books in Print for other formats.

Quantity discounts are available: email programteam@ascd.org or call 800-933-2723, ext. 5773, or 703-575-5773. For desk copies, go to www.ascd.org/deskcopy.

Library of Congress Cataloging-in-Publication Data
Names: Berg, Jill Harrison, author.
Title: Uprooting instructional inequity : the power of inquiry-based professional learning / Jill Harrison Berg.
Description: Alexandria, Virginia : ASCD, [2022] | Includes bibliographical references and index.
Identifiers: LCCN 2021036920 (print) | LCCN 2021036921 (ebook) | ISBN 9781416630692 (paperback) | ISBN 9781416630708 (pdf)
Subjects: LCSH: Inquiry-based learning. | Teachers—Professional relationships. | Educational equalization.
Classification: LCC LB1027.23 .B457 2022 (print) | LCC LB1027.23 (ebook) | DDC 379.2/6—dc23
LC record available at https://lccn.loc.gov/2021036920
LC ebook record available at https://lccn.loc.gov/2021036921

31 30 29 28 27 26 25 24 23 22   2 3 4 5 6 7 8 9 10 11 12

Dedicated to my many teachers.

Uprooting Instructional Inequity
The Power of Inquiry-Based Professional Learning

Acknowledgments xi

Introduction 1

This book is a guide for designing inquiry-based professional learning so that it digs at the roots of instructional inequity.

1. Foundations 7

The i3PD Planning Map 24

Download a copy of the i3PD Planning Map at www.ascd.org/i3PDdigitaltools.

Part One: Taking Your Core Components into Account 33

Use Part One of the i3PD Planning Map to explore design considerations important for each element of the instructional core of your learning experience and prepare to make your learning community a vessel for challenging assumptions that might get in the way of uprooting instructional inequity.

2. Content (1A) 35

3. Participants (1B) 46

4. Facilitators (1C) 52

5. Core Assumptions (1D) 58

Part Two: Creating Connections for a Productive Learning Environment 69

Establish strong connections between the core components using Part Two of the i3PD Planning Map so that participants share the commitment, mutual accountability, and trust required for this challenging work and to help you predict contextual factors that may be working against your efforts to uproot instructional inequity.

6. Relevance (2A) 71

7. Rigor (2B) 75

8. Relationships (2C) 80

9. Connections in Context (2D) 90

Part Three: Designing Your Inquiry Cycle & Learning Sequence 99

Design a four-stage inquiry cycle that will engage participants in using evidence to close their instructional gaps and prepare them to use that same evidence to identify ways the system is inequitable by design. Then, prepare to maximize the time and space available and the information you gathered from Parts One and Two to produce agendas for a learning sequence.

10. Setting the Stage (3A) 101

11. Inquiry Cycle Overview (3B) 106

12. Inquiry Stage One: Assess (3B) 116

13. Inquiry Stage Two: Attempt (3B) 126

14. Inquiry Stage Three: Analyze (3B) 134

15. Inquiry Stage Four: Adjust (3B) 140

16. Session Agendas (3C) 147

Part Four: Preparing for Continuous Learning at Three Levels 161

Determine how you will collect and analyze evidence of changes in instructional practice, participant agency, and systemic inequities as well as in your own personal growth as a facilitator, and prepare to build on this learning in future cycles.

17. Collecting and Interpreting Evidence (4A & 4B) 163

18. i3PD in Action 179

Appendixes 185

A. i3PD Digital Tool Collection 187

B. Protocol Families 189

C. Four Sample Immunity Maps 191

D. Norms Construction: A Process of Negotiation 199

E. Sample Completed i3PD Planning Map 203

References 222

Index 225

About the Author 230

Acknowledgments

I love learning. I learned to love learning from my parents, my first teachers, who were both educators themselves and the children of public school teachers. I learned quickly in life that my "why" questions would get a long response, but not an answer. I'd be encouraged to look for patterns, identify connections to what I already knew, or think of something similar to figure it out. These mental models and values about learning were reinforced by my Montessori schooling in early childhood, and then strengthened through the support and challenges of public school teachers.

I became interested in how people learn when, as an undergraduate at Harvard in the 1980s, I took a course with Howard Gardner about a new theory he was working on about multiple intelligences. I wanted to see it in practice and play with these ideas myself, so I went straight from college into teaching. Once I had my own classroom, I often wondered, as I engaged in various inquiry-based professional learning experiences, whether I was learning more from my students than they learned from me. Steve Seidel would come over from Harvard's Project Zero to the Cambridgeport School to engage our faculty in the Collaborative Assessment Conference protocol and help us to see what our students were *really* working on. I pursued the National Board Certification process, which helped me to reflect on the impact of my instructional choices on my students' learning. And my brilliant colleagues from that unique public school were important collaborators for developing unique portfolio routines that pushed my thinking about what should be accepted as evidence of student learning and the role students could play in those decisions.

These experiences led me to more questions and to further study at the Harvard Graduate School of Education. Here, with Susan Moore Johnson and my colleagues on the Project on the Next Generation of Teachers, I found and kept new understandings about the relationship between the problems of teaching as a profession and the issues of inequity we see today. I engaged with rigorous and relevant content that helped me to understand teaching, learning, and schools from the inside out with Richard Elmore. I wrestled with how it might be possible for schools to provide both excellence and equity, and I was inspired by examples of how it's being done with Pedro Noguera. I reflected on the power of teacher teams with Kitty Boles, and key principles for helping teachers learn with Ellie Drago-Severson. And, in reflection on my own learning process, I had transformative learning experiences with Robert Kegan. At the same time, I felt lucky to have my own children enrolled in schools we trust, like Boston's Mission Hill School, where I learned tremendous lessons about leadership from its principal, Deborah Meier.

It wasn't perfectly clear to me, until writing this book, how profoundly the values of inquiry from my home life and these early-career experiences have shaped my beliefs and my approaches to my work in schools since that time. I'm grateful for the many collaborators I've had who have joined me in seeking answers that lead to new questions. A few are important to mention here because of the ways their contributions allowed this book to come together.

In 2011 I was recruited to serve as a faculty member for the Network to Transform Teaching, a seven-year, 10-state project convened by the National Board for Professional Teaching Standards (NBPTS) to apply the principles of improvement science to the problem of ensuring each and every student has an accomplished teacher. The collaborators from this project and the framework from the Carnegie Center for the Advancement of Teaching were invaluable for helping me recognize the power and puzzles involved in taking inquiry to scale in networks. This generated new ideas for me about influencing equity in nested systems, and I was grateful to be able to explore these ideas further with the support and partnership of Liz Homan through the Learning & Leading for Equity Network we created in the Waltham Public Schools.

In 2018, Sonia Caus Gleason invited my partnership in coediting a special equity-focused issue for Learning Forward's journal, *The Learning Professional*. Our lead article, "Come Together for Equity," and the conversations we had with the contributors we'd selected for the issue, were instrumental in shaping my thinking about how educators might learn to advance equity. This led to further and ongoing collaboration with Zaretta Hammond in support of her work to help educators become effective coaches of their students' cognitive independence. My work with her has not only deepened my understanding of culturally responsive practice, but also confirmed my confidence in the role inquiry can play in this unique type of instructional transformation.

As I began to write this manuscript, reflecting with Boston principals Jordan Weymer, Pauline Lugira, Renee McCall, and Christy Connolly—who piloted many of the book's tools or read drafts—helped keep the work grounded. Virtual writing retreats with Melinda Mangin and Cynthia Carver helped keep me accountable and balanced. And loving encouragement from my husband, Erik, and my Sheridan neighbors helped keep me going. Once the finish line was in sight, a mighty team of trusted colleagues generously provided wise feedback that led to essential final touches. I appreciate Aida Sadr-Kiani, Alice Wong-Tucker, Amika Kemmler-Ernst, Dan French, Erik Berg, Megin Charner-Laird, Natalie Lacireno-Paquet, Pauline Lugira, Rosann Tung, Sonia Caus Gleason, Trelane Clark, and Zevey Steinitz for their critical friendship.

Seeds planted by all of these teachers can be found in this book. I am grateful to each and every one of them.

Introduction

The more than 130,000 K–12 schools in the U.S. school system represent a wide variety of programs, pedagogical models, and priorities, but most have one thing in common: They persist in producing unacceptably inequitable results. On average, compared with their white peers, Black and Brown students have a greater chance of leaving elementary school without proficiency in reading, of being moved up from middle school without exposure to basic algebra, and of graduating from high school without being able to compose an effective essay (U.S. Department of Education, 2011a, 2011b, 2015).

The Roots of Inequity

If schooling were a game of chance, some of us would have good reason to refuse to play. In games of chance, the results are supposed to be random; every player is just as likely as another to walk away with a win. Yet in the game of U.S. schools, whether a student will call out "Bingo!" or walk away empty-handed is highly correlated with the color of their skin. A quick look at history shows us that the education game we play today, initially designed almost 400 years ago to groom white boys with the Puritan values and knowledge of the "classics" they would need to become moral and civic leaders in the expanding colonies, has not deviated significantly from its early design despite serving a vastly wider diversity of learners and purposes today (Jeynes, 2007; Rury, 2004).

For much of these 400 years, our education system has conveyed—implicitly and explicitly—that Black and Brown people did not need or deserve a high-quality education, and it did this so thoroughly that traces of this mindset still infect educators' muscle memory today. This legacy affects decisions made at the district, school, and classroom levels in ways we are unaware of, regardless of the color of our skin, and it keeps us from ensuring that the learning needs of each and every student are met, even while we proudly proclaim our aspiration to educate all students. This causes us to create schools in which Black and Brown students are less likely to receive the time and attention of effective teachers; less likely to engage with empowering, rigorous curriculum; less likely to learn in environments with a positive and inviting school climate; and less frequent access to opportunities that stimulate the cognitive development they need to become self-directed learners (Alliance for Resource Equity, 2019; Hammond, 2014). It also causes us to enact school funding formulas that fall far short of ensuring that all students receive what they need to learn (EdBuild, 2019).

Disregard for the effects that historical patterns of systemic racism continue to have on the process and products of education has led many to believe that disparities in achievement by race are a one-dimensional problem. If we want a different result, we tell ourselves, we can simply try a different strategy. For decades, in fact, we've tried to do "something different"—different curriculum, different teachers, different instructional strategies, different assessments, different student groupings, and so on (Fullan, 2007; Sarason, 1996). Those who are paying attention have noticed that "different" doesn't necessarily mean "better" and that the problem is far more complex than that.

Inequity in a New Light

The year 2020 brought with it a public health crisis that cast new light on these long-standing racial inequities, revealing their complexity. Some schools were more likely than others to enter the COVID-19 pandemic with the effective systems of collaboration, communication, and instructional technology needed to manage the required pivots (Kraft, Simon, & Lyon, 2020), but these schools were not equally distributed across U.S. zip codes, and, on average, Black and Brown students were at a greater disadvantage than their white peers (Dorn, Hancock, Sarakatsannis, & Viruleg, 2020). Technology was a saving grace for many students who were able to continue learning online or whose family members could work from the safety of home, but the financial means and infrastructure needed for connectivity were not equally available to all (Stelitano et al., 2020).

The events of 2020 made it clear that racial inequity is a problem of societal proportions that affects all aspects of the system. This fact came into view not only in the health care system (through race-based patterns of preexisting conditions and access to quality health care), but also in the justice system (with the murders of George Floyd, Breonna Taylor, and too many others) and in the electoral system (through voter suppression). Notably, none of these problems were new in 2020. The pandemic created greater awareness of these inequities while deepening them, as the fear and trauma of losing loved ones or managing food, job, and housing insecurity during this crisis clearly affected the population disproportionately by race.

Taking Action from Three Angles

What we witnessed in 2020 is not only upsetting individually, but also galvanizing at scale. It has raised the sense of urgency for action from individual-level angst to collective-level agency and gives reason to be hopeful that now is a good time for collective action that can make a real difference. This book is for educators who are ready to do things differently together and who are looking for guidance on how.

Educators are not to blame for the current state of affairs, but we are well-positioned to be part of the solution. We've got to do more than just try different strategies though; we have to do "different" differently. Instead of merely changing our practices, we must start to change our processes. Instead of changing what we do as individuals, we must change how we make decisions about what we do and create a new ethos that values doing it *together* (Berg & Gleason, 2018).

Schools already have the time, attention, and funds dedicated to change. They make regular investments in professional development, but the quality of those experiences varies greatly. Some educators experience professional development (PD) as an "event" where they come together, learn new tips and tricks, and then return to their classrooms to individually decide whether and how to make changes. Others engage in inquiry-based learning, in which they draw on various forms of evidence to strategize about how to level-up their teaching practice. But even if these investments do support some teachers in shifting their own practice, they won't make a dent in the system.

What if individuals came together with more than just changes in their own practice in mind? The occasion of educators committing their expertise, experiences, and perspectives to shared problems of practice is a potent opportunity to consider larger changes to the system.

This book provides the design principles and tools that educators need to facilitate new or existing inquiry-based professional learning experiences so that they will advance instructional equity from three angles. First, it supports teachers in improving the quality of their instructional decision making in ways that are essential to equity. Second, it prepares facilitators to become transformational leaders who support participants in becoming greater agents of their own learning in service of equity. Finally, it engages teachers in creating a culture committed to identifying and uprooting systemic barriers to equity. This is i3PD.

What Is i3PD?

i3PD is professional learning that advances instructional equity from three angles:

1. It supports teachers in improving the quality of their instructional decision making in ways that are essential to equity.

2. It prepares facilitators to support participants in becoming greater agents of their own learning in service of equity.

3. It engages teachers in creating a culture committed to identifying and uprooting systemic barriers to equity.

Schooling today is a game of chance, but it shouldn't be. Instead of merely increasing students' chances of success, we need to change the game. We want a game that is designed so that all students, no matter where they start, what they bring, or how they learn, can receive what they need to shout "Bingo!"—and walk away with the prize of an excellent education.

A Look at the Book

This book will change your expectations of what professional learning is and get you started in creating a professional learning revolution in your school. It is a comprehensive planning guide for designing i3PD, an inquiry-focused professional learning cycle in which educators will interrogate inequity through inquiry to support both individual and organizational learning. If you are a principal or teacher leader planning school-based professional development, a department head laying out the year's meetings, or other education leader organizing a new community of practice, you may benefit from starting at the beginning and reading straight through.

However, you may already be in the middle of the year or in the position of facilitating time with colleagues where the agenda is not fully your own. Perhaps you are the leader of your grade-level team meetings, a mentor for a cohort of novice teachers, or a member of your school's instructional leadership team. In these cases, you may initially want to use the book's planning tools to document what you are currently doing, then use what you know about your colleagues and your context to choose which i3PD elements to bring in over time.

Whether you decide to read straight through or jump around, the following overview will help you, as facilitator, plan your journey. Your journey should begin with Chapter 1, **Foundations**, which establishes the approach and the rationale of the book—why and how inquiry-based professional development can be an effective engine for interrogating inequity. This chapter also provides a grounding of crucial terms and key ideas that prepare you for the primary frame of the book—the i3PD Planning Map.

The book's four main parts align with the four sections of the i3PD Planning Map, which you can find beginning on page 24, and in the i3PD Digital Tool Collection outlined in Appendix A and available at **www.ascd.org/i3PDdigitaltools**. Be sure to copy or download this tool to have at your side as you move through the book. You'll find each chapter is coded with the part number and section letter to help you orient yourself to the i3PD Map.

In **Part One: Taking Your Core Components into Account** (Chapters 2–5), you will establish a solid foundation for your improvement cycle by describing and analyzing the three components of the instructional core: content, participants, and facilitators. The decisions you make about how these three components will interact will determine the quality of the learning experience, so taking time to understand them is important. In the final section of Part One, you will consider the three core components in context and make some predictions about how participants' assumptions, mindsets, and mental models might support or limit the success of their efforts to influence instructional equity. These insights will help you design an i3PD planning process that can do more than change practice; it can shift how participants are thinking about their work.

Part Two: Creating Connections for a Productive Learning Environment (Chapters 6–9) directs your attention to the links between the three core components. It's essential to create a *relevant* and *rigorous* learning experience and cultivate *relationships* within the community of learners so that participants feel safe and ready for the challenge of changing their practice. The chapters in Part Two will help you articulate a clear and compelling purpose with focused and challenging objectives for the improvement cycle; envision the outcome and establish criteria for success; and predict existing or prospective interpersonal connections that can be assets for engagement and trust building. At the end of Part Two, you will consider your work in context and make predictions about how existing systemic structures and policies may support or limit the success of your plans to influence instructional equity. In this way, you prepare participants so that they not only avoid getting hung up on these issues, but also organize to reform them.

The preparations laid in Parts One and Two come together in **Part Three: Designing Your Inquiry Cycle and Learning Sequence** (Chapters 10–16). Here you will plan out each of the four stages of your improvement cycle based on decisions you made earlier about the content: the focus of learning and the inquiry question you will bring to it. You'll strategically consider the time and space available to you so that you can maximize these factors as assets to support participants' learning. You will then plan out your series of agendas in a way that helps participants to capitalize on one another's expertise and experience as they engage in the work. You will design these with thoughtful attention to the welcome and wrap-up of each session.

Part Four: Preparing for Continuous Learning at Three Levels (Chapters 17–18) guides you to think through the evidence you will collect throughout the cycle and decide how you will analyze it in view of emerging new insights about inequity. These insights can inform the next cycle and help you take your facilitation skills to the next level. This section also shares a glimpse of what i3PD looks like in action and provides ideas and inspiration to get you started.

The five appendixes at the end of the book provide additional resources, including a list of the tools and templates featured in the book that are available digitally (see Appendix A or go to **www.ascd.org/i3PDdigitaltools**) and a sample of a completed i3PD Planning Map (Appendix E).

1

Foundations

Today it is abundantly clear that we, as a profession, do not yet know what we need to know to ensure that all students get the education they deserve. Many students do develop mastery of critical competencies, learn to investigate questions with passion and skill, produce clever and beautiful products of their learning, and put their hard-won knowledge and skills to use in meaningful ways that help them achieve their dreams. But these outcomes are not widespread, and the demographic patterns that describe who succeeds are not random. Students with Black and Brown skin, some of whom are from the same few zip codes, speak languages other than English at home, or are from families with a low income, and some of whom are not, are less likely to attain the education they need to achieve these outcomes. We are failing these students because of our inability to address inequity.

Educators do not want to leave children behind. If we knew what to do, we would already be doing it. We need to *learn* our way to more equitable schools. Yet too many of today's professional learning experiences engage educators in merely trading ideas that largely haven't worked, given the fact that they have led us to produce the inequitable results we see today. What we really need to do is grow new ideas that can produce greater shifts.

One might ask, isn't that the role of education research? Education research can play an important role in ensuring educators build on prior knowledge even while they question it; better understand the social, political, and geographic contexts in which they work; and identify potentially promising practices (National Research Council, 2002). But best practices offer only possibilities because of the enormous variation in classroom conditions. What works with my constellation of learners might not work with yours. What works in my small, tight-knit community school may not work in your large, comprehensive one. What works on Tuesday might not work on Friday. These contextual variations are not adequately accounted for in traditional research, and educators know that in schools, variation is the rule, not the exception. We need to narrow the gap between research and practice, and to do so, we need to get better at learning how to learn together in schools.

Many educators are already committed to doing so. They help one another interpret and respond to formative assessment results, unpack the misconceptions represented in a student's response and address them, or codesign unit plans based on identified patterns of performance in common writing prompt responses. In lines of inquiry such as these, teachers collaborate colleague-to-colleague in ways that benefit those individuals. But we cannot achieve an ambitious goal like educational equity through an effort focused merely on individual change. We need a more deliberate and more timely system for learning together from the test kitchens of our own classrooms about what we need to start and stop doing as a community of professionals. We need professional learning experiences that can help us get smarter collectively and finally start making the systemic changes our students need us to make to confront educational inequity.

This book will guide educators in amplifying the power of collaborative inquiry as an engine for identifying, interrogating, and addressing instructional inequity throughout their schools. The goal of i3PD is to engage educators in advancing equity by helping them elevate inquiry as a catalyst for needed individual and organizational change.

Unpacking Equity and Inequity

The Latin root *aequus*—meaning level, even, or just—has given us the terms *equity* and *equality*, two different words with distinct meanings. The distinction between the two has to do with whether we're taking the circumstances of the situation into consideration while making judgments about what is "even" or "just." If we are not, we have equality; if we are, we have equity. The *Oxford English Dictionary* (1989) explains that "a decision 'in equity' was 'one given in accordance with natural justice, in a case for which the law did not provide adequate remedy, or in which its operation would have been unfair.'"

While you consider this Latin word, *aequus,* and its meaning (level, even, or just), conjure up the image of a large balance or scale (see Figure 1.1). The divergence in meaning between equity and equality comes from whether or not we account for tare weight. That is, when we want to trade a pound of water for a pound of sand, should we account for the

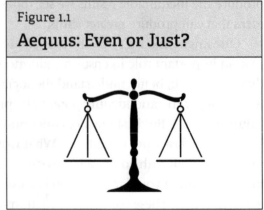

Figure 1.1

Aequus: Even or Just?

container the water is in? By the law of the scale, there is *equality* when the scale balances. There is *equity* when we consider the context of the question, recognize that "the law did not provide adequate remedy," and determine that "natural justice" requires subtracting the weight of the container.

It wouldn't occur to us to blame the water or think it inferior because it needs a container. In truth, the need for the container has less to do with the water and more to do with the characteristics of this particular flat-plated scale. Other objects might have different requirements for being measured by this scale. A marble might need a container underneath it to keep it from rolling, whereas a frog might need to be contained on all sides. In each case, we could achieve equity by accounting for the tare weight of the container. Thinking more expansively, we could consider designing a new scale with built-in buckets or boxes that would be appropriate for a wider array of objects. Further, we could question whether the scale is the right tool at all. We could even reexamine whether comparing the two really accomplishes our goal and innovate to create a system that would more adaptably meet the needs of each and every object.

In today's schools, we want to achieve equity. But our education system in the United States was not originally built to educate each and every student. It's a scale built with a particular purpose. The first semblance of our U.S. school system appeared in the colony of Massachusetts in 1635, when Boston Latin School was established. Modeled after a school in England, it was designed to ensure white male students could provide both moral and intellectual leadership to the developing settlements. In the following decade, more schools were established throughout Massachusetts to further perpetuate the Puritan values of personal responsibility and self-control and to ensure the colonists' male children would be able to read the Bible and perhaps even meet the entrance requirements of Harvard University. Eventually schools proliferated throughout the colonies. Puritan values were pushed into the background as reading, writing, and math skills came to the fore due to the cultural influence of the rise of capitalism and its need to build capacity for the Industrial Revolution (Goldin, 1999; Jeynes, 2007; Rury, 2004).

Black, indigenous, other people of color, and women were systematically excluded from these schools. In fact, by the 1830s, many states had gone one step further by passing laws to prohibit enslaved people from learning to read (Angulo, 2016). When Horace Mann, the "father of public education," began advocating for universal education in the 1850s, his rationale—that the United States needed qualified voters to elect qualified governors—further reinforced assumptions about the priorities and population that U.S. schools should serve (Mann, 1855). Thus, for these first 200 years and more, formal U.S. schools were institutions for cultivating sensibilities about what is right, wrong, and true, and what we want for the country— from the perspective of white, voting-eligible males for white, future-voting males.

Meanwhile, the majority of the population (that is, nonwhite nonmales) had a range of other priorities. Native Americans actively passed on their wisdom, traditions, and language through elders, people of African descent learned trades and histories through apprenticeship, and women built their talents and faculties through homeschooling. Interestingly, in the 17th century, Native Americans outnumbered whites on this continent; by the end of the 18th century (the height of the slave trade), Africans outnumbered whites in some parts of the South; and in the 19th century (due to immigration patterns and the American Civil War), women outnumbered men. Yet the prevailing form of schooling today—in fact, compulsory today for all people, regardless of race or gender—is the one established by and for one narrow purpose and population.

Now as we approach the 400th anniversary of the establishment of that first school, whose purpose, structure, and values became an early model for others throughout the U.S. education system, it is interesting to watch society puzzle over why students from historically marginalized groups are less likely to attain the education they need to succeed. It is compelling to speculate what U.S. schools might be like today if the purpose, structure, and values of Native Americans', Africans', or women's education had not been marginalized, but, instead, had prevailed. For over a century, we have tried to make an increasingly diverse array of learners fit a mold of schooling that was built for a narrow selection of students, where success is measured by putting every student on the same scale. It is a fundamentally inequitable system.

The fact is, we don't yet know what to do differently. As products of the system ourselves, we cannot easily see what mindsets have to shift, which of our practices we need to abandon or adjust, or how a system that is grounded in more balanced cultural assumptions might work.

The good news is that our system of schooling continues to be an institution that cultivates our sensibilities about what is right, wrong, and true and about what we want for the country—and educators have begun to realize that we *are* the system. Increasingly, we represent a wider diversity of perspectives; we recognize that it's our job to teach the way our diverse students learn, not *their* job to learn the way we teach; and we are willing to go outside the box to do what it takes to rebalance the scale for students from historically marginalized groups.

The answers are not going to be handed to us. We need a way to do some research and development in schools.

Taking an Inquiry Stance

Where historical assumptions and cultural norms have perpetuated the idea that all students are basically the same, it might have seemed appropriate to assume that what works for one student should work for others and that when it doesn't, something must be wrong with the student. Further, it might even suggest that when those patterns persist among groups of students, something is inferior about those groups.

This line of reasoning has several problems. First, even when students were more homogeneous, schools never worked for everyone. Students who did not learn what the teachers were teaching had other options within schools, such as vocational education, or outside of schools, where dropping out opened the door to agricultural, manufacturing, or creative lines of work. One size has never fit all.

Second, regarding the student as the dependent variable in the experiment of teaching and learning is highly problematic. If we teach something and find that students don't learn, the problem is *not* the student; it's the teaching. The teaching practice must change to suit the student. We can be so sure of ourselves when implementing best practices, including ones we grew up with in our own education experience, that we don't see them as variables in the equation. From a moral point of view, we need to take responsibility when our professional practice comes up short of meeting students' needs and stop blaming the victims or making judgments about their characteristics.

Third, this line of reasoning elevates unfair observations of individuals in ways that contribute to and reinforce forms of oppression of whole groups of people. It supports problematic power structures—such as racism, classism, sexism, and other isms—in that it advances the idea that certain groups are inherently inferior or superior to another.

Fourth, it diminishes the status of teaching as a profession. Teaching is a much more complex interaction than simply cause and effect: "I'll teach it and watch it work." Effective teachers are consummate professionals who are passionate about drawing on the latest advances in professional knowledge and using that information skillfully to inform the complex decisions they have to make in situations where the outcomes cannot be easily predicted (Johnson, 2005; Metzger, 1987). In fact, teachers must do this at a blindingly rapid rate, which some have estimated to be as frequent as a dozen decisions per minute (Ball, 2018). When we underplay the complexity of teachers' work or allow others to do so, we forfeit the agency we have in making a bigger difference for students; we discredit the importance of the decisions with which we have been entrusted; and we jeopardize the confidence and support we might otherwise receive from administrators, other education leaders, and the public to use our voices and specialized expertise to create stronger schools (Schon, 1987).

Teaching is not simple stuff. Teachers must stay on their toes to make the best decisions they can for their students every day, even while the situation is never the same twice. And when our teaching does not lead to the student learning results we expect, effective teachers don't respond with anger, blaming, and name calling. We get curious, and we take an inquiry stance.

The Power of Inquiry

When we think of *inquiry* in education, we might recall the project-based learning units that engage students in exploring their own questions or teachers' action research projects in which they dig into a particular problem of practice. These forms of inquiry contain the key idea of inquiry—a systematic investigation—but they might imply that inquiry is a once-and-done project. Inquiry might be something that we *do*, but, more important, it's a way of *thinking* about what we do. It's not an end in itself or even a means to an end, but a habit of mind required for continuous improvement.

Inquiry is a process of identifying important questions, slowing down to take a fresh look at evidence, seeking to understand new ways of seeing that evidence, identifying implications for action, and trying them out while remaining attentive to what's working, in what way, and under what conditions. It's the process of being diagnostic in our professional practice, something the demands of equity require us to get better at. It's a habit of mind we must cultivate individually, as well as a habit of work we should establish collectively (Cochran-Smith & Lytle, 2009).

In collaborative inquiry, educators commit their time and attention to helping one another identify and close a gap between the results their current practice produces and the results they wish to see. They lend their diverse perspectives to understanding this practice gap from every angle, tap their varied experiences or relevant research to propose a plan to close it, and put this plan into action while helping one another see both intended and unintended effects. Members then examine results together, such that the process leads not only to closing the targeted gap but also to a deeper understanding of the changes and the conditions under which they are effective, and this leads to stronger decision making beyond the case at hand.

Today, individuals and teams at all levels of the education system engage in inquiry practices that vary widely in structure and formality. Although many educators have been introduced to inquiry as a schoolwide initiative that has a series of prescribed steps to follow, such as lesson study, instructional rounds, peer observation, or student data inquiry cycles, others with inquiring minds might do so on their own in or outside of school by pursuing such inquiry-based professional learning experiences as National Board Certification, action research projects, or critical friends groups for looking at student work.

Inquiry, in all its varied forms, always has the same bones. At its core, inquiry is a habit of mind—the disposition to systematically investigate things to try to make them better—and this thinking process includes four general stages (see Figure 1.2):

- **Assess.** We evaluate the current and contextualized status of our undesired outcomes and set our sights on where we would like those outcomes to be.
- **Attempt.** We rethink existing routines as we identify new, informed ways to influence the outcome, and we carry them out while monitoring for changes.

- **Analyze**. We examine the evidence of impact to understand what conditions contributed to changes and capture emerging new lines of inquiry.
- **Adjust**. We reflect on what other changes are necessary and what we will commit to doing about them to take our practice to a higher level.

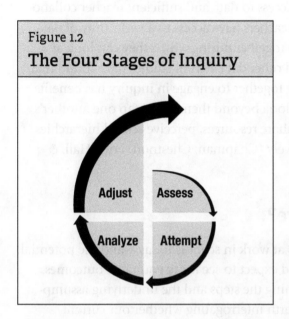

Figure 1.2

The Four Stages of Inquiry

One reason inquiry is powerful is because it forces us to slow down and look at the evidence. We spend most of our lives with our brains on autopilot, making assumptions about what we think we see and what we think it means. It tends to be enlightening—if not downright disorienting—to stop and check those assumptions. In inquiry, we find ourselves putting words to previously unnamed teaching and learning connections, which helps make our assumptions and tacit knowledge explicit and makes it possible to interrogate them.

Another reason for the power of inquiry is that it turns experience into expertise. As John Dewey reminds us, we don't learn from experience, we learn from *reflecting* on experience. An effective inquiry cycle is designed to do more than achieve results for the cycle at hand; it is designed to reveal insights about how and why we're obtaining the results we get and thus inform our practice going forward. That is, it doesn't just change our practice; it changes our practice by changing how we *think* about our practice.

The power of inquiry is further amplified when we collaborate with others. The hard work we put into articulating our instructional decisions has a multiplier effect in a community of educators because it cultivates both shared language and relational trust (Love, 2009). That is, the more we talk about teaching and learning, the more we are able—effectively and affectively—to talk about teaching and learning. Just think about how many of our knottiest problems go unaddressed simply because we cannot or dare not articulate them! Through collaborative inquiry, we build the skill and will for talking out our professional challenges together.

In addition, collaborative inquiry is a powerful way to grow professional capital. When teachers let one another into their professional practice and collaborate in honing the quality of their instructional decisions, they benefit from the wisdom of their colleagues' experience (Hargreaves & Fullan, 2015). In circles of collaborative inquiry, teachers feel both supported and accountable as they experiment with practices beyond their usual repertoire and reflect on the effects of those experiments. As a result, students benefit from the professional expertise of more than just that one teacher to whom they have been assigned.

Although collaborative inquiry has long been recognized as a potent way to deepen teachers' knowledge and improve their instructional practice, it has traditionally been stalled by a lack of timely access to data and sufficient teacher collaborative time. In today's schools, however, teachers have access to a wide array of data, and they commonly have protected time together during which they can look at student work, one another's practice, and other data. Recent studies have found that the investment teachers make in working together to engage in inquiry has benefits that pay off in spades: Teachers begin to look beyond themselves, tap one another's expertise, develop a common language, share resources, perceive school hierarchies as flatter, and collaborate more productively (Chapman, Chestnutt, Friel, Hall, & Lowden, 2016).

What Are We Learning Here?

Considering the scale at which inquiry is at work in schools today—and the potential promise of inquiry for equity—we should expect to see more equitable outcomes. This not being the case, it's worth examining the steps and the underlying assumptions in existing inquiry processes. It's worth interrogating whether our current inquiry routines adequately account for tare weight and other variations at play.

Looped Learning

The questions we tend to ask in our inquiry cycles represent *single-loop learning*. We are eager to see results, and so we focus our questions on whether or not we are getting those outcomes. Where we are not, we look for clues that can tell us what needs to change for us to obtain them. We might, for example, examine student work samples or spreadsheets of achievement data and engage in elaborate protocols to uncover patterns associated with those results.

The fact is, we already know the answers. We've been observing our outcomes long enough to know that we're not getting the results we want and to recognize that the patterns are systemic: Outcomes can largely be predicted by race, zip code, and other demographic factors. Incorporating new approaches into our instructional practices, honing our practice to become more skillful, spending extra time with students, or holding ourselves to higher expectations for students are important shifts, but they cannot on their own make up for a substantive difference in such an inequitable system. We need to also strengthen our muscles for questioning at deeper levels.

Double-loop learning looks at the underlying policies and processes causing the patterns in results. We're concerned about the outcomes, but we're focused on influencing those by changing the processes (Duffy, 2014). Thus, instead of asking, "Did we get the results we wanted?" we ask, "*Why* are we getting these results?" We are interrogating how our current policies and processes might support or inhibit our practices and desired outcomes. From this perspective, we might question assumptions we've previously taken for granted about student assignment, teacher qualifications, curricular procurement policies, or even what counts as "results."

It takes a bit more time—which admittedly is at a premium in schools—to engage in a reflective process that requires us to not only do the work, but also think together about how we're doing it in this way. Too often, we don't make the time needed to do this, or we fail to protect that time when time runs short. It also takes a measure of courage to push back against existing organizational routines when input has not necessarily been solicited and to advocate for change without having the positional authority to do so. But when we neglect to do these things, we are inadvertently working against the outcomes we say we want, and we fail to identify or correct the patterns that reinforce inequities, and thus we need to protect the space for it.

In *triple-loop learning*, we commit to thinking about our thinking. We question why we—individually and collectively—have come to understand things the way we have (Tosey, Visser, & Saunders, 2012). By doing so, we are able to inquire into how our systems have come to be designed to produce the outcomes they produce, to recognize our own part in creating and perpetuating those systems—and to play a key role in transforming them.

We make sense of the world by using our personal experiences to develop schema or mindsets that help our brains process efficiently. We often become emotionally attached to these mindsets, embracing them unconsciously or consciously as beliefs, even as part of who we are. They shape what we see and don't see and lead us to certain conclusions about what practices are "right" or even possible. For example, people who grow up around generosity, share. People who've been taught to believe they can achieve, strive. We don't tend to question it.

At the same time, society develops collective mindsets (Quinn, 2005). These often take the form of cultural norms and expectations and just like individual mindsets, we embrace these both consciously and unconsciously, often without question. We assume—and take for granted that others also assume—that it is in our best interest if we all do so. Most of us with a driver's license, for example, consciously agree to learn and obey traffic rules and don't think to question them. Many of us born in the last century unconsciously learned and obeyed distinct gender roles and didn't think to question those either, even though we should have. Triple-loop learning invites us to question the very foundations of what we've accepted as important, possible, or permissible.

Collective mindsets, just like individual mindsets, are not universal, however. Our distinct personal experience and cultural perspectives can lead us to dramatically different conclusions about what is important, possible, and permissible. Is it important to show respect to elders? If so, does respect mean looking them in the eyes or averting our gaze? Because everyone doesn't experience collective mindsets in the same way, we must be attentive to whether the assumptions we hold for ourselves should apply to others. In collaborative inquiry, we're able to help one another see hidden assumptions. We must take a critical look at the assumptions and shape new mindsets together.

If we can work together to interrogate the beliefs and mindsets underlying the current culture of inequity in our schools, we can open the door to changing more than just what we produce (our outcomes) or what we do together (our processes). We can become a powerful force for transforming shared mindsets and the culture of schooling so that equity is at the center.

If we were challenged to make time and create will for double-loop learning, then creating space for triple-loop learning may feel near impossible. It all may sound like a lot of extra work. In fact, it's futile *not* to do so. If we try to change our outcomes by merely changing our individual practices without considering the hold our organizational policies and our culture have on those practices, change will be neither effective nor sustained. By the same token, if change is merely pursued from a top-down perspective through new policies or imposed expectations, individuals with unchanged practices or unaligned beliefs will have neither the skill nor the will to meet them (Berg & Gleason, 2018). Because changes in practice happen at the individual level, changes in policy happen at the organizational level, and changes in culture happen at the intersection of the two, the challenge is to establish a routine capable of influencing change, or learning, at all levels simultaneously. So, let's look at individual learning and organizational learning in schools.

Individual Learning

In effective schools, students are not the only ones learning. Effective schools are invested in adults' learning, and one important component of that is professional development, defined as "structured professional learning that results in changes in teacher practices and improvements in student learning outcomes" (Darling-Hammond, Hyler, & Gardner, 2017, p. 2). A recent meta-analysis of three decades of studies found effective professional development has seven essential elements (Darling-Hammond et al., 2017). Such experiences

- Are content focused,
- Incorporate active learning,
- Support collaboration,
- Use models of effective practice,
- Provide coaching and expert support,
- Offer feedback and reflection, and
- Are of sustained duration.

This research emphasizes that professional learning for educators must be about more than just picking up new strategies. It must be active, collaborative, and reflective. To be sure, having a full toolkit of strategies is important, but too often we focus on expanding that toolkit at the expense of deepening teachers' skill in using the tools. The goal of professional learning *might* involve expanding one's repertoire of strategies or extending one's knowledge and skill, but it *must* provide educators with opportunities to integrate these strategies and skills into their processes of instructional decision making so they can collaboratively examine their effect on students and reflect on implications for their practice. In this way, teachers learn to make stronger decisions for their current and future students.

Organizational Learning

Individual learning is necessary but not sufficient to embed new thinking and practices. Organizational learning is "the deliberate use of individual, group, and systems learning to embed new thinking and practices that continuously renew and transform the organization in ways that support shared aims" (Collinson & Cook, 2007, p. 8). When individuals engage in collaborative dialogue and make shared discoveries about common problems, they stimulate new ways of thinking and practicing within the group that can lead to learning at a systems level. Instead of merely asking, "What should I do differently to achieve equity?" the shared dialogue and discoveries cause a change in the collective mindset that leads them to wonder together, "How must we reform our structures and policies if we want them to produce equity by design?" And instead of responding by creating workarounds to try to operate within a system that wasn't designed to produce these outcomes, we might ask, "How should we think about this differently to achieve equity?"

This work does not have to involve every individual in the organization, but ideally it involves individuals from many parts of the organization (Romme & Van Witteloostuijn, 1999). By virtue of their roles, all have a unique view of the problem, their own perspectives on what is needed, and a particular vantage point for influencing the way the organization works. In particular, it's important that titular leaders—be they school administrators, teacher leaders, or others who have influence in school-level decision making—are learning alongside teachers and are open to change.

Organizational learning thrives when individuals see how their own personal goals and values align with the organization. When this happens, they feel invested in taking the organization to new heights, they feel empowered to take greater risks, they feel responsible for contributing to decision making, and they feel compelled to push for fresh perspectives in service of the greater organizational goal (Collinson & Cook, 2007). Coordinated individual and organizational learning can best be supported by transformational leaders who inspire followers to commit to a shared vision and goals, challenge them to be innovative problem solvers, and develop their leadership capacity through both challenge and support (Bass & Riggio, 2006).

The change we seek—organizational transformation—is anchored by both behavioral and cognitive change of individuals. To achieve this, we must develop new routines for interrogating how the ways we think affect what we do, how what we do collectively creates our systems, and what we need to change to replace existing systems with ones designed with equity in mind. We can build routines that promote this change when we understand *collaborative inquiry*.

Collaborative Inquiry as an Engine for Equity

In collaborative inquiry, participants engage in authentic, evidence-informed dialogue about how, when, and how well their actions are producing the outcomes they say they want. In the process, educators' diverse perspectives combine to accelerate their ability to meet the needs of each and every student in front of them. When done effectively, the culture of challenge and support created by the structure of the inquiry cycle empowers them to commit to being collaborative problem solvers and leads to new solutions with the potential to transform how the school works.

In this way, collaborative inquiry is professional development that develops the profession. As Cochran-Smith and Lytle (2001) wrote,

> a legitimate and essential purpose of professional development is the development of an inquiry stance on teaching that is critical and transformative, a stance linked not only to high standards for the learning of all students but also to social change and social justice and to the individual and collective professional growth of teachers. (p. 46)

Collaborative inquiry, then, is an ideal engine for generating the changes needed for equity. It represents an important departure from most current professional development that features theoretical ideas from an external "expert" or the exchange of the same old strategies that have led us to the inequitable outcomes we now have. Collaborative inquiry, when facilitated with equity in mind, starts with what our students need us to learn and ensures coordinated individual and organizational changes needed to achieve those results.

Our students need us to do at least four types of learning to avoid common threats to instructional equity. They point to four types of inquiry models (see Figure 1.3).

Knowledge Gap Inquiry

Fact: Some students are not benefiting from instruction informed by the highest standards of professional knowledge available.

Inquiry question: *How thorough is our knowledge about this instructional practice?*

Figure 1.3

Four Inquiry-Based PD Models

	Knowledge Gap Inquiry	Implementation Gap Inquiry	Teaching–Learning Gap Inquiry	Expectations Gap Inquiry
Threat to Equity	Some students are not benefitting from instruction informed by the current knowledge base for this practice.	Some students are not experiencing skillful instruction or quality implementation of this practice.	Some students are not being taught in a way that responsively improves their learning processes.	Some students receive instruction that has low expectations for the quality of their learning products.
Practice Gap	What to do.	How to do it skillfully.	How to do it responsively.	How to do it effectively.
Inquiry Question	*How thorough is our knowledge about this instructional practice?*	*How skillfully are we implementing this instructional practice?*	*How responsively are we making implementation choices about this instructional practice?*	*How authentically are we estimating our effectiveness with this instructional practice?*
Evidence	Teachers' instructional repertoire	Teachers' instructional implementation	Students' learning processes	Students' learning products
Sample Practices	• Instructional Walkthroughs • Educator Assessments	• Instructional Rounds • Lesson Study	• Data Cycles • Looking at Student Work (LASW) Protocols	• Perspective Protocols* • Refining Protocols*
Individual Learning Outcomes	*We will be able to . . .* make decisions informed by a wider breadth of the knowledge and skill base for this professional practice.	*We will be able to . . .* engage in high-quality implementation of this professional practice.	*We will be able to . . .* strategically and appropriately make decisions about this professional practice that strengthen students' learning processes.	*We will be able to . . .* recognize and raise artificially low expectations about what we accept as quality student work products in context of this instructional practice.
Organizational Learning Outcomes	*We will be able to . . .* identify internal barriers to equity (collective mindsets) and external barriers to equity (structures and policies) and take action together to reform them.			

*See Appendix B for a description of protocol families.

Knowledge gap inquiry is what we do when we use established standards of professional knowledge to identify gaps in our own knowledge of teaching. Today's knowledge base has evolved organically through the professional consensus and education research of a homogeneous group of thinkers. Although there is much we need to question critically and much we still don't know, we must not overlook all this knowledge base has to offer because operating without attention to core knowledge of teaching and learning can lead to malpractice. Educators can identify gaps in their professional knowledge through peer observations, instructional walkthroughs, or performance assessments that are guided by locally selected standards for professional practice. These may include implementation rubrics, state licensure standards, accomplished teaching standards from the National Board for Professional Teaching Standards, or competency checklists produced by professional associations, universities, nonprofits, or district-based sources.

Implementation Gap Inquiry

Fact: Some students are not experiencing instruction that is skillfully implemented.

Inquiry question: *How skillfully are we implementing this instructional practice?*

Implementation gap inquiry is concerned less with educators' knowledge and more with educators' skill. Instead of looking to external sources for standards of quality, this model of inquiry engages educators in calibrating their conceptions of effective practice with one another. It involves educators observing one another at work and thinking together about descriptions or videos of that practice so they sync their understandings of what a practice looks like when implemented skillfully. Peer coaching conversations, lesson study, and instructional rounds are examples of this form of inquiry in which educators compare and model their visions of high-level practice with one another.

Teaching-Learning Gap Inquiry

Fact: Some students are not being taught in the way that improves their learning processes.

Inquiry question: *How responsively are we making implementation choices about this instructional practice?*

Teaching-learning gap inquiry focuses educators' attention on the gap between the *observed impact* and the *desired impact* of their teaching on their students. It is important to note that we are interested not only in their learning outcomes—which can be academic, socioemotional, or behavioral—but also in their processes: how students produce those outcomes. In teaching-learning gap inquiry, educators are concerned about how they will adapt their instructional practice to be responsive to their students with attention to both what and how those students are learning. Examples of this type of inquiry might include student data cycles or looking at student work.

 Expectations Gap Inquiry

Fact: Some students are not supported to meet high expectations.

Inquiry question: *How authentically are we estimating our effectiveness with this instructional practice?*

John Hattie's (2009) studies of factors that influence student learning have heightened educators' attention to the importance of "knowing thy impact." Expectations gap inquiry represents a form of inquiry that provides checks and balances on educators' estimations of their own impact. It is too easy to pass a student whose work does not meet expectations, and it's even more common to overlook whether we've effectively supported students to meet the expectations. In this type of inquiry, educators get better at recognizing the gaps between what they say they expect from students, what they are accepting, and the support they are providing to meet those expectations. Perspective protocols such as ATLAS and Collaborative Assessment Conference help us see and address gaps in our expectations and solicit new insights and perspectives, whereas refining protocols such as Tuning and Slice are designed to refine or improve our practice. (See Appendix B, "Protocol Families," for more information about types of protocols.)

Most of us already engage in some of these forms of collaborative inquiry in our schools and beyond, by requirement and voluntarily, as part of scheduled routines and as individual events. This book aims to elevate how each of these forms of inquiry stands to address a major threat to instructional equity and to prepare you to facilitate collaborative inquiry with colleagues in such a way that it effectively tackles those threats.

To be sure, there are plenty of other threats to equity and other models of inquiry. This book will focus on these four common models as windows into the systemic barriers to equity that, once identified and addressed, can lead to improvement throughout the system.

i3PD

This book introduces the i3PD Planning Map, a template designed to guide readers in facilitating a collaborative inquiry process through which they can work with colleagues to interrogate inequity through inquiry. See the i3PD Planning Map at the end of this chapter for a blank version of the template or go to

www.ascd.org/i3PDdigitaltools for a digital version. Make or print a copy for easy reference as you move through this book.

In i3PD, participants formally and systematically investigate how—despite their best intentions—their teaching currently produces educational inequity. As a result, they make necessary changes and use clues from their individual investigations to work collectively on improving equity throughout the school. The process supports the success of changes in practice by attending to the requisite changes in our structures and policies, as well as in our individual and collective mindsets.

This book guides professional learning leaders to answer three guiding questions:

- How do we bolster our **colleagues'** abilities to interrogate gaps in their own instructional practice that pose a threat to instructional equity and to make changes that improve the quality of their instructional decision making through inquiry?
- How do we expand our confidence as **facilitators** and our competence as transformational leaders who can successfully support participants to assume roles as agents of their own and their schools' organizational learning through inquiry?
- How do we support the **school** (or other context) to become a learning organization whose members can interrogate and eliminate systemic barriers to equity through inquiry?

The i3PD planning process can serve either as a planning guide to improve the ability of existing inquiry-based professional development experiences to effectively interrogate inequity, or as a way to engage a community in establishing new inquiry-based practices. In either case, i3PD aims to influence the abilities of participants, facilitators, and the school. And because a goal of i3PD is to identify and influence systemic barriers, it is ideal if the participants work within the same school (or other shared context) and commit to sustained engagement over time (for example, not fewer than four sessions).

i3PD is for you if you are ready to see your school move beyond year-to-year changes that have a marginal effect, if you're willing to learn alongside your colleagues as you take risks to assume greater agency over inequity, and if you're eager for deeper change. It works because of three key features:

- **i3PD is teacher-powered work.** When teachers are in the driver's seat of inquiry-based professional collaboration, they stand to have outsized influence because of their subject-specific expertise, the passion that comes from their rich knowledge of students and families, and their relatively nonhierarchical relationships with colleagues. They use these perspectives to ask the questions that need to be asked, examine important insights about what might be getting in the way of student progress, and draw out their colleagues as collaborators willing to engage with honesty. As such, collaborative inquiry that gives teachers a role in shaping the journey has special power to support their readiness for the challenge of interrogating inequity.

- **i3PD taps evidence to ask deeper questions.** When we engage in inquiry-based activities, we collect various forms of data to investigate a particular question, yet we often leave much of that data and the insights gleaned from them on the cutting room floor. In i3PD, educators mine evidence for insights about what factors contributed to achieving a given set of results. Schools are systems: Examining evidence of inequity in one part of the school can reveal important clues about how the system is designed to produce that same result across the entire building, and in i3PD we're attentive to that.

- **i3PD is a catalyst for cultural change.** When participants in collaborative inquiry discover patterns of inequity that persist across classrooms, they are motivated to think even more deeply about the provenance of the routines and policies that enable those patterns. How have our unexamined priorities, collective mindsets, and shared hidden assumptions shaped those routines and policies? When educators build time into inquiry cycles to reflect together on what their current policies and practices reveal about their individual and collective mindsets, they take away new collective commitments about what they—as a school—need to start or stop doing.

This book will be your guide as you design or re-envision inquiry-based professional learning experiences in a way that turns inquiry into an engine for increasing instructional equity.

The i3PD Planning Map

PART ONE: Core Components

1A. Content

Focus of Learning	Practice Gap
	We will interrogate potential gaps between participants' current practice and (choose one)
	☐ Practice informed by the current knowledge base for this practice.
	☐ Professional standards for quality implementation of this practice.
	☐ Practice that responsively matches teaching to students' learning processes.
	☐ Practice that authentically achieves high expectations for students' learning products.

1B. Participants

The Cohort and Their Context	Questions	Insights and Implications
What do you know about the participants?	What do you wonder about the participants?	
What do you know about the students they work with from historically marginalized groups (i.e., Spotlight Students)?	What do you wonder about their Spotlight Students?	

1C. Facilitators

Your Role	Your Goal(s)	Cofacilitation Notes

1D. Seeing the System: Core Assumptions*

Improvement Goal	Behavior Inventory (Doing/Not Doing)	Hidden Competing Commitments	Big Assumptions
1. What do our Spotlight Students need us to improve?	2. What are we doing and not doing that work against our goal of improving our practice for our Spotlight Students?	3A. What might be worrisome about doing the opposite of the things in column two?	4. What do our hidden commitments suggest about how we might see the world and ourselves (i.e., our collective mindset)?
		3B. What self-protective, hidden commitments stand behind our worries?	

Insights and Implications

Source: Adapted from *Change Leadership: A Practical Guide to Transforming Our Schools*, by T. Wagner et al., 2012, San Francisco: John Wiley & Sons. Copyright 2012 Minds at Work.

PART TWO: Creating Connections

2A. Relevance

Purpose	Outcome-Based Objectives
• We believe each and every child deserves…. • Teachers' ability to *[name the instructional practice]* is essential to that because…. • Closing this instructional practice gap is important for these specific participants, at this time, in this setting because….	If this series is successful,

2B. Rigor

Process Objectives	Evidence of Impact
As individual participants, you will support one another to • **Assess:** Identify gaps in your own instructional practice (your knowledge, implementation, strategic use, or expectations of that practice) that currently contribute to inequitable outcomes. • **Attempt:** Design a response to the gap and a system for documenting change as you take action to close it. • **Analyze:** Interpret evidence of change, identify challenges to change, and integrate insights into your professional practice. As a community, we will • **Adjust:** Reflect on patterns across our lines of inquiry to identify relevant systemic factors that inhibit equity and organize our efforts to make the changes they require.	

2C. Relationships

Clarifying Role Expectations	*Strengthening Trust: Respect and Personal Regard*

Community Agreements	*Strengthening Trust: Competence and Integrity*

2D. Seeing the System: Structures and Policies

Local Structures and Policies	*Contextual Conditions*

PART THREE: Inquiry Cycles and Learning Sequence

3A. Setting the Stage

Time	Space	Insights and Implications
Date: Time:	Location: Venue setup:	

3B. Inquiry Cycle Map

Stages	Key Components	Implementation Notes	Timing Notes
Assess: Capture current reality	**Standard** How will participants define the professional standard of this instructional practice?		
	Status How will participants identify the gap between this standard and their current practice? How will they identify what contextual factors might contribute to that gap?		
	Success Target How will participants establish a target for improved practice?		

Attempt: Plan and implement changes	**Dig** How will participants gain new knowledge to assist them in closing the gap and meeting the success target?	
	Decide How will participants decide what they will start doing, continue doing differently, and stop doing?	
	Do and Document How will participants track what they actually do, the effect of these changes, and the contextual factors that matter?	
Analyze: Examine and interpret evidence	**Identify** How will participants characterize the effect of the change they have made?	
	Interpret How will participants interpret what the evidence says about the conditions that have supported or limited their change in practice?	
	Infer How might participants determine what they have learned and might need to learn next?	

(continued)

PART THREE: Inquiry Cycles and Learning Sequence—*(continued)*

3B. Inquiry Cycle Map

Stages	Key Components	Implementation Notes	Timing Notes
Adjust Commit to changes	**Structures** How will participants illustrate the ways that existing structures and policies currently function as systemic barriers to equity?		
	Suppositions How will participants uncover the collective mindsets that have produced our current system of inequitable structures?		
	Seismic Shift How will participants identify the strategic moves they need to make to create a seismic shift in the system?		

3C. Session Agendas

Duplicate this agenda template for the number of sessions involved.

Time	Key Topics	Minutes	Implementation Notes	Materials and Handouts
--	Prework			
X:00	1. Welcome			
	Relevance			
	Rigor			
	Relationships			
	2. Inquiry Cycle Work			
	3. Wrap-up			
	Relevance			
	Rigor			
	Relationships			
X:30	Adjourn			

PART FOUR: Continuous Learning

4A. Multiple Sources of Evidence

Data Sources	Research Question 1	Research Question 2	Research Question 3	Research Question 4	Collection Routine	Review Routine
	In what ways have participants made changes to practice and improved instructional decision making to close those gaps?	To what extent have participants demonstrated confidence, commitment, and capacity as agents of their own learning in this series?	In what ways have participants identified systemic barriers to equity and coordinated efforts toward eliminating them?	To what extent have you advanced toward your personal goal established in 1C? ___ ___ ___		

4B. Analyzing Data

Data Sources	Who	When	How

Note: An editable version of this figure is available in Word format as part of the Digital Tool Collection. See Appendix A for more information.

Part One

Taking Your Core Components into Account

In this section you will use Part One of the i3PD Planning Map to explore design considerations important for each element of the instructional core of your learning experience and prepare to make your learning community a vessel for challenging assumptions that might get in the way of uprooting instructional inequity.

2

Content (1A)

When I want to bake a cake, I set out the ingredients and take stock of what I've got. Understanding the properties of my ingredients and how they work together gives me confidence to take some risks to improvise a little and, in some cases, surprise myself with next-level results. In i3PD, what we're going for is next-level results. We're going to need to do some improvising, so we need to know the basic ingredients.

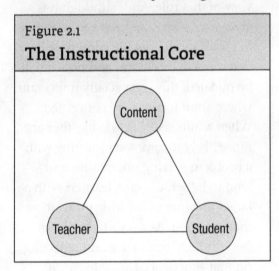

Figure 2.1

The Instructional Core

Content

Teacher   Student

Teaching and learning have three basic ingredients or core components: the content, the teacher, and the student. Learning happens when the student interacts with the content, and the teacher plays a key role in determining what content and what type of interaction the student will have with that content. If we want to improve student learning, we have to pay attention to these three core components, how they influence one another, and the ways in which a change in one calls for changes in another. This nexus of the content, student, and teacher is called the *instructional core* (Cohen & Ball, 1999; Elmore, 1996; Hawkins, 2002) (see Figure 2.1). This chapter will guide you in making decisions about the content of your i3PD plan, but first let's have a look at the instructional core through the lens of adult learning.

The Instructional Core and Adult Learning

Effective teachers design tasks and activities with keen attention to how their instructional decisions will lead to meaningful engagement of students with rigorous content. Effective school and district administrators ensure that change efforts—from policy shifts to training to resource allocation—are felt inside the instructional core and that increases in one element (content rigor, student engagement, or the teacher's knowledge and skills) are matched with parallel attention to the others. Research has found that schools and systems that have succeeded in making improvements to the instructional core demonstrate a positive effect on student learning (see Loughland & Nguyen, 2016; Rincón-Gallardo & Fleisch, 2016).

Once we understand the concept of the instructional core, we can innovate and apply it to *adult* learning (see Figure 2.2). Adults are a peculiar type of student. Their many years of experience as students lead them to have their own unique and deeply entrenched routines for thinking about the world. Meanwhile, the "teachers" in the adult learning context are often the peers of these "students," producing a whole new dynamic. Adult learners bring a wide diversity of life experiences and deep funds of knowledge to the learning experience that potentially rival those of the "teacher" and signal the need for a new view of that role. And, although it is always important to keep assumptions in check about how the content will be determined, by whom, and how it will be pursued, this is especially important where adult learners are concerned. When adults seek knowledge, they are more likely to approach learning with a problem-solving orientation and tend to be self-directed learners with a larger measure of intrinsic motivation than children. As a result, they learn best through experience and reflecting on that experience (Knowles, 1990; National Research Council, 2000).

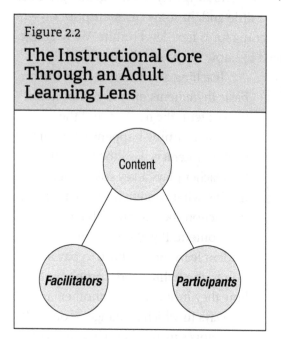

Figure 2.2

The Instructional Core Through an Adult Learning Lens

Content

Facilitators

Participants

The i3PD planner uses the framework of the instructional core to erect a strong foundation for designing inquiry-based professional learning experiences but proposes some new terms.

To start, I use the term *facilitator* for the teacher. The facilitator is not the "sage on the stage" but rather a "guide on the side." The facilitator is tasked with ensuring that each member has the experience they need to learn and that all are empowered to share their expertise and experience to benefit their colleagues' learning. The term *facilitator* suggests a less hierarchical relationship than *teacher* might and invites dialogue that is open, curious, and possibly even critical in both directions.

I use the term *participants* for the adult learners in this framework for several reasons. First, the term *students* might be confusing because participants engage in inquiry cycles that often involve examining evidence of products or performances from the students in their classrooms. I reserve the term *student* for these younger charges for clarity's sake. Second, to use the term "student" or "learner" for the nonfacilitator members of the learning community might misguide members into thinking that the facilitators are not learners too. (In i3PD, the facilitators are learning to become effective as transformational leaders, and ideally, they engage in inquiry alongside their participant peers.) Finally, the term *participant* connotes engagement. Using this active term invites members to put their whole selves into the learning task and signals their role as engaged collaborators.

In K–12 classrooms, the *content* is often dictated by standards and policed by assessments. Where adults are concerned, by contrast, there should be greater latitude for the learners to be the decision makers of their own learning. Even though the focus may be determined in advance based on school goals or district priorities, the inquiry-based structure of the i3PD learning experience means the participants have a voice too. They will use evidence from their own practice about what is not working and what they feel they need to learn to make their own meaningful choices about how to explore that content.

This last point is crucial to the goal of uprooting instructional inequity. Too often our schools don't have a space for exploring fresh ideas. We need new routines in which we can experiment with pushing beyond what hasn't worked and, in doing so, create the professional work habits necessary for a stronger profession. This isn't just "a PD" or a "professional learning experience." We're initiating an improvement cycle that can keep going and going and going and change the way we work.

Beginning the Journey

Chapters 2, 3, 4 and 5 will launch your planning journey and guide you in completing Part One of the i3PD Planning Map. If you have not already done so, be sure to make a copy of the planner to have with you as you go through the book. In addition, you will find an annotated version of this section of the planner at the end of Part One on page 66 and an example of a completed planner in Appendix E. In this first part of the planner, you will establish a solid foundation for your improvement cycle by committing a critical eye to each key component of the instructional core (content, participants, and facilitator) and to how the collective mindset in your context views them.

Specifically, in section 1A of the planner, you will make important decisions about the content for this improvement cycle while ensuring room for participants' voices. In section 1B (Chapter 3), you will gather and review what you know about your participants to identify characteristics of this cohort that will have implications for your planning. Section 1C (Chapter 4) requires you to reflect on your own involvement: what you bring to the community, what you hope to leave with, and how you will engage the participants to own the individual and organizational learning that equity demands. And because our work in the instructional core aims to change practices that have previously proven themselves to be challenging to change, section 1D (Chapter 5) introduces an exercise to draw your attention to ways collective mindsets in the context might inadvertently be at work against efforts to change.

What Will the Learning Focus Be?

Identifying the focus of learning for a shared PD experience can be tricky. Individuals naturally have their own unique learning needs, yet collaborating to pursue shared learning about an instructional practice can be both a richer experience for participants and more efficiently supported by the facilitator. Directing our collective attention to a shared practice has an additional benefit in i3PD: We are able to look across the evidence from our lines of inquiry to identify relevant systemic factors that currently support or limit this practice from advancing equity and organize our efforts to make changes.

You may capture your focus initially with a wide-angle lens. That is, you may broadly define an area of instructional practice that you know represents a shared concern or an established priority so that you can later invite participants to help define more specific practices within it. The topic is often predetermined by school or district priorities. Ideally those priorities have been determined in evidence-informed ways, even while they may be influenced by partnerships and grant opportunities. These topics will be appropriate for the i3PD planning process if claims that our students need us to learn them are professionally credible and if they point to changes in teachers' instructional practice.

Following are examples of broad areas of instructional practice that are commonly identified as school or district priorities. They are too broad to be the focus of an improvement cycle because they refer to a wide toolkit of theories, approaches, practices, and strategies:

- Trauma-Informed Instruction
- Differentiated Instruction
- Culturally Responsive Teaching
- Academic Conversation

You'll want to focus closer in by choosing a specific instructional practice from that toolkit. Following are examples of practices that teachers might employ within the broad areas above. These practices are only as good as the quality of the decisions educators make about when and how to employ them:

- Clarity
- Scaffolding
- Feedback
- Accountable Talk

Or you might prefer to define an even narrower focus. Will this investigation be restricted to a certain strategy, student group, or subject? Following are some focused examples:

- Establishing clear language objectives with English learners
- Creating appropriate scaffolds for students approaching middle school math tasks
- Drawing on students' funds of knowledge for effective writing conferences
- Using questioning strategies in early childhood science classrooms

Narrowing to this extent would make it easier for participants to support and learn from one another. They could read more specific articles and collaborate more intentionally. On the other hand, it is important that the topic feel directly relevant to all. Where participants have a wide range of teaching assignments, a narrow focus will not do. Will all participants explore and experiment with the same feedback strategy (for example, conferencing), or will each participant choose their own feedback strategy (for example, feedback during instruction, grading, peer feedback)?

Choose the size of your focus and write your instructional practice in section 1A of the i3PD Planning Map. The challenge is to keep your focus as narrow as possible but still wide enough to be relevant to the prospective participants (whom you will get to know better in section 1B). Within these parameters, participants will have some voice in directing their i3PD journey as they engage individually in their own cycle of inquiry and collectively in identifying implications across cycles for school change. There's no one right way to engage in these practices; each of these areas requires teachers to make implementation decisions that depend on their own context. In i3PD, participants will engage in parallel experiments while helping one another make stronger decisions. Experimenting in practice and reflecting with colleagues not only expand the ways we understand an instructional practice, but also keep us accountable for the effect of our practice on our students.

What Gap Will We Interrogate?

At the root of compelling professional learning is a puzzle, problem, or disorienting dilemma. If we truly believe all students can learn—and recognize that in current reality some students are not yet doing so—it should draw us in with care and concern, tugging at our emotions so that we're compelled to inquire about what we can learn to make stronger instructional decisions.

Teachers make hundreds of decisions each hour, and the quality of those decisions determines whether and how to meet the needs of each and every student. Among the many decisions teachers make are four salient ones:

- What to do
- How to do it skillfully
- How to do it responsively
- Whether we're doing it effectively

Inquiry-based professional learning strengthens teachers' abilities to get better at making these decisions. Each of these types of decisions digs at the roots of instructional inequity in its own way and calls for a unique model of inquiry.

Knowledge Gap Inquiry: Interrogating Decisions About What to Do

Teaching has a vast and complex professional knowledge base informed by both research and practice. Teachers acquire this specialized knowledge base over time through teacher preparation programs, professional learning experiences, and their own investigations; it is not mastered quickly. The existence of this knowledge base is one of the main features that defines teaching as a profession, yet the lack of an effective process for how to develop and share that knowledge base holds us back.

Current conceptions about our knowledge base have emerged over time through professional dialogue about research and practice, albeit while leaving many voices out. This professional consensus informs perceptions of a continuum of practice that runs from what we consider to be "state-of-the-art" on one end to malpractice on the other, while leaving a large grey area in the middle.

For contrast, we could look to the field of medicine. New diagnostic tools, vaccine treatments, and surgical procedures may be invented in Boston, Cleveland, or Los Angeles, and within a short time they become the standard of care throughout most of the United States. In the education profession, however, we have not yet developed systems for sharing new developments or routines for learning about advances in our own field. As new tools and approaches in education are developed and found to be effective, they do become the standard of care in some parts of the country. The schools they *don't* reach, however, are not random; they can be predicted by zip code.

How many of our schools today are still using outdated practices? And if effective new approaches were available, how would your school even know about them? If we don't create norms and venues in our schools for routinely identifying, testing, and integrating advances into our practice, how can we be sure we are not engaging in malpractice?

In **knowledge gap inquiry**, we are interested in guiding teachers to interrogate gaps between the knowledge base on the targeted practice and their current practice. We are committed to identifying things we don't know we don't know. In this model of inquiry, teachers measure themselves up to a locally accepted professional standard or have others evaluate them against those standards. In doing so, they identify gaps in practice about which they were previously unaware and discover new or updated elements of practice to add to their repertoire. In this way, knowledge gap inquiry helps teachers expand and update the pool of practices and ideas they draw from when deciding what to do to meet the needs of each and every student.

Implementation Gap Inquiry: Interrogating Decisions About How to Do It Well

Too often we toss aside ideas as failures, not because they have no value but because we have poorly implemented them. This is especially true in education where, because of our tremendous sense of urgency and exacerbated by high-stakes accountability, we scale things up before we learn to do them well. We often try something new rather than take the time to examine the conditions supporting or limiting success and build new knowledge about implementation quality. Yet, it is the mark of a true profession to be engaged as both producers and consumers of our knowledge base and to be the arbiters of quality.

In medicine, doctors train in multiyear residencies, working alongside one another to hone skillful implementation of core professional practices. In education, however, we too often work in isolation. We can spend a long time leaning on the way we've always done things, not knowing if we're doing it well, and we can overlook the value of essential practices because they didn't seem to work when we implemented them poorly. We cannot afford to limit our repertoire when it comes to meeting the needs of each and every student. To meet a wide array of needs, we must have all the tools in our toolkit, and we need to become skillful at knowing how to use each tool well.

By working together in cycles of inquiry, we gain new perspective on what good teaching looks like and how to do it well. **Implementation gap inquiry** models provide structure for teachers to look to one another as they sync their understandings, raise the standard of practice, and become more skillful in their implementation of an instructional practice.

Teaching-Learning Gap Inquiry: Interrogating Decisions About How to Do It Responsively

Each one of our students is unique. They bring different funds of knowledge, cultural perspectives, driving passions, and background experiences. They may call for varied starting points, instructional approaches, and modes for demonstrating mastery. There's no magic algorithm that can point unfailingly to the right course of action. Teachers, then, must make judgments about whether, when, and how to apply the instructional practices in their repertoire as they engage students in the learning process. All true professions require judgment calls such as these.

In medicine, doctors have to make a judgment call when faced with a laceration. Do they use stitches, staples, glue, or simply a Band-Aid? Guidelines are helpful, but with so many variables no single rule applies. Professional judgment is required and developed through experience. Professional learning in teaching, similarly, should focus not only on expanding our repertoire, but also on providing the opportunity to sharpen our diagnostic abilities. Some schools put this kind of work front and center; there, teachers hone their ability to make instructional practice decisions that are responsive to the specific learning needs of individual students.

Because we're interested in equity, we're interested in more than just whether students have learned what they've been taught; we're interested in whether they can learn things they *haven't* been taught. To avoid reproducing the current inequitable system, we need students to learn their way far beyond the current system. Thus, equity-minded educators need to be more strategic and more skillful in helping students build the learning competencies, information processing skills, and work habits they need to be self-directed learners. Students need teachers who can teach the way students learn and who can teach them how to learn, not teachers who expect them to learn the way teachers teach.

When we notice patterns of underperformance in our results, we need to change how we're having students interact with content and do something different. But what? The **teaching-learning gap inquiry** model guides us in using observations of student work and of students at work to address a gap between the results we achieve and the results we desire from our teaching practice. Teaching-learning gap inquiry enables teachers to change their practice so that they are more responsive in the instructional choices they make for their students.

Expectations Gap Inquiry: Interrogating Decisions About Whether We're Doing It Effectively

We teach so students can grow, develop, and learn. This is important, not just for our students' sakes, but also for the betterment of our world and the well-being of humankind. Like all true professions, education deals with matters of urgent importance.

There's little doubt that doctors deal with matters of urgent importance. Their efforts not only deal with life or death, but also influence the quality of our lives and the timing of our deaths. In recognition of the consequential nature of their work, these professionals are supported with what they need—training, time, tools, and resources—to do whatever it takes to get their job done well. Educators, however, especially those serving Black and Brown students, too often find supports lacking, and the gap between their impact and their hopes for their impact can feel overwhelming. The easy way out is to lower expectations or overestimate our impact instead of figuring out how to improve our impact.

It's important, then, for teachers to remain on the lookout for sagging standards: gaps between what they say they're achieving and the results they're actually producing. In the **expectations gap inquiry** model, we hold a mirror up for teachers to see the effect of their instructional practice from multiple angles and to collaborate to increase it. We support teachers to get a second opinion and potentially change or expand their view of the effect their professional decisions are having—and could be having—on student learning. In the same way that implementation gap inquiry involves checks on teachers' claims of quality teaching practice, expectations gap inquiry serves to sync understandings of quality student work.

Students Show the Way

If you're not sure which of these four types of practice gaps you will investigate, let the students decide. That is, you can consider the decision in the context of the students who stand to benefit most from this change. Use a variety of evidence to identify between three and five students from historically marginalized groups who have not yet responded to the teaching they're receiving. We're not looking at *all* students because our eye is on equity, not equality. And we don't want to focus on *most* students or *more* students because when we do that, the students who are left out are too often the ones who have already been left behind in other ways. Throughout this process we'll keep a *spotlight* on the students in our classrooms who most need us to change our practice. We'll call them our Spotlight Students.

As you consider your Spotlight Students, ask yourself:

- Are they benefiting from instruction informed by the highest standards of professional knowledge available? If not, pursue knowledge gap inquiry.
- Are they experiencing instruction that is skillfully implemented? If not, pursue implementation gap inquiry.
- Are they demonstrating improvement in their learning processes? If not, pursue teaching-learning gap inquiry.
- Are they meeting high expectations? If not, pursue expectations gap inquiry.

If the answer to one of the above is "no," in section 1A of the i3PD Planning Map indicate the practice gap in the right-hand column.

If the answer to *more than one* of the above questions is "no," you should narrow it down to one by looking more closely at the distinctions between these models. Two of them (the knowledge gap and expectations gap) define the gap against a professional standard, whereas the other two (the implementation gap and the teaching-learning gap) define the gap through dialogue within a community of practice. That is, in the first two, participants will consider an established professional standard; in the latter two, participants will collaborate to define the standard. The models have another distinction. Two look at effects through changes in teachers' practice, whereas the other two define success by looking at the effect of those changes on students' learning processes, products, or performances. You can explore these distinctions in Figure 2.3. You can also refer to Figure 1.3 in the Foundations chapter to help you compare and contrast the four inquiry models.

If you don't see a match for what your participants need or expect, the i3PD process may not be for you. You may have a goal in mind that does not immediately call for changes in practice. For instance, you might simply aim to deepen knowledge of content or pedagogy through book study, learning circles, content courses, or demonstration lessons. Alternatively, you might aim to help teachers hone a skill through planning a unit or lesson, designing common formative assessments, creating instructional materials, or conducting a curriculum review. These are worthwhile PD experiences, but they are not the focus of this book. They are learning activities that might bolster changes in practice, and, as such, they might each be incorporated as components of i3PD, but they do not *require* changes in practice.

Still unsure? Don't worry. Inquiry is a cycle. Pick one place to start and know that you can cycle back. Focusing on gaps in our own practice can feel deficit-focused, like a real downer, and participants may be overwhelmed, intimidated, frustrated, defensive, or in denial. Yet when they approach this with a growth mindset and the support of peers, they will find their attention to this gap will provide some creative tension that will draw them into the challenge of closing that gap.

This is the first level of inquiry in the i3PD process: How do we bolster colleagues' abilities to interrogate gaps in their own instructional practice that pose a threat to instructional equity and make changes that improve the quality of their instructional decision making through inquiry?

Figure 2.3

Inquiry-Based PD Models: Defining the Gap and Defining Success

		Defining Success	
		Change in Teachers' Instruction	*Change in Students' Work*
Defining the Gap	*Success is defined by a professional standard.*	**Knowledge Gap Inquiry** What does **the professional standard** suggest ***teachers*** should be doing? What is the gap between this standard and my current practice? If I succeed in closing the gap (by expanding my knowledge), how do I expect **my instructional repertoire** to change?	**Teaching-Learning Gap Inquiry** What does **the professional standard** suggest ***students*** should be doing? What is the gap between this standard and the results of my current practice? If I succeed in closing the gap (by teaching more responsively), how do I expect my **students' learning processes** to change?
	Success is defined by colleagues in the community of practice.	**Implementation Gap Inquiry** What do **we believe** ***teachers*** should be doing? What is the gap between this standard and my current practice? If I succeed in closing the gap (by teaching more skillfully), how do I expect **my instructional implementation** to change?	**Expectations Gap Inquiry** What do **we believe** ***students*** should be producing? What is the gap between this standard and the results of my current practice? If I succeed in closing the gap (by improving my support for students to meet high expectations), how do I expect the quality of **my students' learning products** to change?

3

Participants (1B)

In this chapter, you will capture and reflect on what you know about your participants and the students they serve, and you will lay plans to collect any additional information you need to invite the active and equity-focused engagement of each participant.

This improvement cycle will not be a "sit 'n git." There's no room for passive learning here. You'll need to learn about your colleagues so that you can help them embrace their role as coinvestigators of research on their own practice conducted in a community convened by you. In i3PD, engaged participants are committed to (1) improving equity through changes in their practice, (2) honoring their role as coauthors of the learning experience, and (3) being critical friends who assume responsibility for pushing colleagues' thinking. Admittedly, this is a higher level of participant commitment than most professional learning experiences require. To achieve this, you will need to gather information that can inform your invitation to participate.

What Do You Know? What Do You Wonder?

If you're expecting a short list of known participants, collect their names and roles. If you're expecting a longer list, gather their names and descriptive data in a spreadsheet to link to your i3PD plan.

You will also want to gather and link or summarize student demographic data from the context. We're working to make changes with underserved students from historically marginalized groups in mind. The data you collect will help you to know who these students are so that you can help participants stay focused on them. Keep these students in the spotlight throughout i3PD, knowing that growing your practice in ways that make a difference for them will make a difference for all learners.

Next, take note of any additional information you feel is relevant about the individuals or the cohort. Describe and reflect on what you know about the participants in terms of their predispositions to be concerned about the content, prepared to accept their role as coauthor, and ready for critical friendship.

Engagement with Content

Are participants concerned about how this practice currently contributes to inequity?

- What do participants already know about this practice and its relationship to inequity?
- What is their range of relevant experience with this practice?
- To what extent do they have what they need to engage in this practice?
- To what extent are they aware of which students in their classrooms experience the effects of historical marginalization?
- In what ways do they talk about inequity in their classrooms?

Engagement as Coauthors

Are participants ready to accept their role as engaged participants with a shared responsibility for shaping the learning experience?

- To what extent have they chosen to be here?
- To what extent have they participated in collaborative professional learning communities before?
- To what extent are they willing to risk sharing an independent opinion?
- What is the range of their relationships with authority? Do they prefer following rules or making rules?
- To what extent are they willing to see beyond "right" and "wrong," that is, to see multiple perspectives?

Engagement as Colleagues

Are they prepared to be critical friends to colleagues in the community?

- What range of titles do they hold? What power dynamics might be at play?
- What is the range of their teaching expertise and experience in terms of student demographics, grade span, subjects, programs, and so on?
- What is the range of demographic diversity in terms of race, gender, and other identities?
- What level of familiarity and trust do they have with one another?
- What level of familiarity and trust do they have with you?

Add this information in the first column in section 1B ("What do you know…?"). Sometimes you won't find out who the individual participants are in advance. In that case, use the middle column ("What do you wonder…?") to list what you want to know about the participants and their students and any other questions you may have.

Based on what you do know, try to predict their readiness to be active participants in this learning community. If you're unable to uncover at least a few strong reasons for participants to lean into this improvement cycle, then use your collection of "wonder" questions to gather information that can help you *build* their commitment as active participants.

How proactive you are in gathering information about your participants will depend on your familiarity with the group and the expected duration of the relationship. That is, preparing to lead professional learning with colleagues at your own school will look different from preparing to lead a new districtwide cohort to which participants have been assigned. The longevity of the community and the sorting method, (for example, self-selected or required participation) will determine whether you're able to designate presession or in-session time to gather information about your participants. These factors can affect whether participants are invested in learning about one another, which will be important when we lay the groundwork for fostering relationships of trust in section 2C of the i3PD Planning Map.

If you're working with a self-selected community of learners, use the registration form or application to pose questions based on your "what do you wonder?" list. Open-ended questions might be worthwhile if the community will be together for a sustained amount of time, but short-answer questions may provide a sufficient snapshot for more short-term professional learning. When there's no opportunity to connect with participants in advance, polling tools may enable you to glean the information you need quickly. If you have the time, having participants interview one another may be worthwhile, especially if they can capture notes in a form that you can access later on.

It's important to not collect information you will not use. It's annoying for your participants and makes it harder for you to pay attention to the information you *do* need. If you decide to collect information, preface your request by telling the participants how you plan to use it. Doing so honors the time you've asked them to put in, while also holding you accountable for using the information.

You can also gather information in ways that don't involve bothering the participants. You can solicit answers to your "wonder" questions from key leaders, such as teacher leaders or administrators, and you can discover relevant information such as student demographics, outcome disparities, and local priorities by exploring school webpages, district websites, or state-level report cards that are posted online.

Insights and Implications: Communicating and Planning

We want to ensure participants approach this learning experience eager to jump in and embrace the types of engagement that i3PD invites. After reflecting on the information you've gathered, return to the third column in section 1B and capture your *insights* about how engaged you predict this cohort to be with content, as coauthors, and as colleagues. You'll also want to capture here your initial thoughts about the *implications*—that is, how you'll encourage the positive dispositions you see and cultivate the ones you don't. You can begin to do this through clear communication and planning.

Communication includes messages you send before and during the series, as well as your promotion of the learning opportunity. Your communication serves to clarify expectations, which creates an important foundation for trust. When we know what to expect from one another, we are more attentive to noticing when those expectations have been met, and we more quickly develop positive discernments about one another's integrity.

Planning includes building time into your agenda for the types of interaction that reinforce these expectations and strengthen trust. You might provide an overview of the series or inquiry cycle to highlight these cultural expectations, engage participants in opportunities to coconstruct what these expectations will mean in practice, or share responsibility for collective accountability of these expectations.

Following are some different ways to embed expectations in your communication and planning.

Engagement with Content

- **Communicate what this is.** "In i3PD, you will make changes in practice."
- **Communicate what this is not.** "Some professional development experiences are designed to give you new ideas or expand your thinking. Although i3PD may do these things, it is structured as an opportunity to guide you in testing and reflecting on changes in practice."
- **Clarify the focus** (i.e., the targeted instructional practice) and how it was selected. Walk through a cycle of inquiry so participants understand the theory of change and see the engagement it requires.
- **Elevate the promise of the practice.** Guide participants in learning or exploring the potential of the targeted instructional practice. Provide testimonials of impact.
- **Activate prior knowledge/experience.** Ask participants to share current understandings and prior (positive and negative) experiences with the practice; remind them we don't know what we don't know, and we owe it to our students to become as knowledgeable and skillful as possible.

Engagement as Coauthors

- **Communicate what this is.** "In i3PD, participants share responsibility for shaping the learning experience. They must make decisions about when and how to apply and evaluate the instructional practice, as well as when and how to deepen their knowledge about the practice."
- **Communicate what this is not.** "This is not an experience in which you will be fed information and assessed by an evaluator. In i3PD, you will hone routines for expanding your practice and monitoring the results."
- **Use nonhierarchical language.** Use language that signals your position as a learner and an adjacent member of the group, and avoid terms that suggest top-down leadership.
- **Provide a preview.** Provide an agenda overview and highlight the kinds of decisions participants will be responsible for making, individually and collectively.
- **Clarify community agreements.** Identify any existing (explicit or implicit) norms and coconstruct your own community agreements about the structures and culture needed to do this work together.
- **Reinforce a culture of a growth mindset.** Use challenges as opportunities to remind participants that you are learning to do this together and that their feedback (and ideas on how to address those challenges) is both expected and essential to improving the experience.

Engagement as Colleagues

- **Communicate what this is.** "i3PD is designed to leverage colleagues in the learning community as assets for one another's learning."
- **Communicate what this is not.** "This is not 'parallel play,' in which learners each do their own thing and pat one another on the back. In i3PD, participants depend on one another to push their thinking."
- **Model expectations.** Practice and point out the routines you've established for colleagues to engage in discourse, disagree agreeably, and safely challenge one another's thinking.
- **Provide a preview.** Point out places in the learning series and in the inquiry cycle where we'll depend on one another as critical colleagues.
- **Elevate one another's expertise.** Use connecting activities that help participants learn about one another's areas of expertise and experience.
- **Engage participants as experts.** Encourage participants to answer one another's questions, share resources, and communicate directly among the group for support.

Recognizing that your work of gathering data about your participants may still be underway, make some notes now in section 1B, and be sure to come back to review and revise this section before planning the agenda in Part Three. You want to be sure participants understand that you are not merely offering an opportunity for them to question the content, weigh in as coauthors of our methods, and ask critical questions of their colleagues. You are communicating these as *expectations of participation* that determine the power of the i3PD learning experience.

This is a tall order, especially in contexts where educators have grown accustomed to professional learning experiences that require little more than going along for the ride. We're asking participants to climb up into the driver's seat.

Therefore, **in the second level of inquiry in i3PD**, we ask the following question: How do we expand our own (facilitators') confidence and competence as transformational leaders who can successfully support participants to assume roles as agents of their own and their schools' organizational learning through inquiry?

4

Facilitators (1C)

Many of us are accustomed to traditional teaching and learning roles in which the teacher is the keeper of an established knowledge base and the students are the receivers. In i3PD, we disavow this mental model. Here, the third key element of the instructional core, the "teacher," is a facilitator charged with providing a process (an inquiry cycle) through which participants can question, strengthen, and expand the knowledge base, not blindly follow or reinforce existing assumptions about what they know and should do.

This is a new kind of role for many and, as such, it requires facilitators to be a student of sorts, too. As facilitators engage in their own cycle of inquiry, they will focus on interrogating how to be confident and competent transformational leaders of this learning experience. Section 1C of the i3PD planner ("Facilitators") will guide you in exploring your role; planning an inquiry cycle focused on your own facilitation; and, for those working in a team, laying plans to coordinate cofacilitation.

What Is Your Role?

The i3PD experience calls on you to be a "transformational leader." In this role, leaders "inspire followers to commit to a shared vision and goals for an organization or unit, challenging them to be innovative problem solvers and developing followers' leadership capacity via coaching, mentoring, and provision of both challenge and support" (Bass & Riggio, 2006, p. 4). In other words, transformational leadership is leadership that inspires and supports individuals within an organization to coordinate their efforts in working together to build something greater than what we have now. It requires us to reconsider where we've been and learn as we go because our goal is not something we already have seen before, and, in the process, it changes how we work with one another. It doesn't just get the job done; it results in organizational learning (Senge, 2006). In our case, the shared vision is equitable schools, and our method for challenging and supporting our "followers" as leaders in problem solving for equitable schools is inquiry.

The literature on transformational learning is clear about what behaviors are crucial to transformational leadership, and the i3PD structure supports you in enacting some of them. Transformational leaders stimulate their followers intellectually, encouraging them "to be innovative and creative by questioning assumptions, reframing problems, and approaching old situations in new ways" (Avolio & Bass, 2002, p. 2). The i3PD inquiry cycle process will give you the structure to stimulate innovation and creativity in these ways. However, additional leadership behaviors are needed to ensure a culture in which followers will want to do so.

Transformational leaders also establish relationships of individual consideration with and among followers. They communicate in ways that ensure followers feel heard, supported, and challenged based on their individual needs for achievement and growth (Bass & Riggio, 2006). This combination of challenge and support fuels both participants' success and their sense of success, which results in empowerment or collective efficacy, and it fosters a culture of commitment to the vision the participants share. Throughout i3PD inquiry cycles, participants will document their progress in inquiry maps that make their progress visible to all so that it can be challenged, celebrated, interrogated, and supported.

Two additional behaviors are typically seen in transformational leaders. Transformational leaders engender trust such that followers have respect, personal regard, and confidence in their competence and integrity. As a result, followers have faith in their leader and in one another. In addition, and possibly by extension, transformational leaders inspire others to take risks with them in service of the shared vision (Bass & Riggio, 2006). Followers want to work with the leader and with one another for the good of the group. To demonstrate these two behaviors, you'll want to be transparent about the experience and expertise you bring (and don't bring) to the role and communicate clearly about what participants can expect of you.

Leader versus Facilitator

The terms *leader* and *facilitator* are frequently used synonymously, but they have a subtle distinction (Eller, 2004). Generally, *leader* implies a more hierarchical relationship with group members where the authority rests with that individual. *Facilitator* implies a more egalitarian relationship that, at its extreme, vests all authority with the group and places responsibility on the facilitator only for galvanizing it.

In i3PD, we use the term *facilitator*, but in your setting, you should clarify what that will mean. You may assume more of a hierarchical leader-like role in some areas. Perhaps your participants will have no role in setting the goal. Perhaps you bring a wealth of relevant content knowledge that will position you as more of a leader to the team. Perhaps time is insufficient for participants to set the conditions of the learning community, and it makes more sense for you to do that.

With recognition that many use these terms interchangeably, the chart shown in Figure 4.1 amplifies the distinction between these two terms to throw them into contrast. Compare the left and right columns, then take special note of the tasks that they share. After reviewing the chart and reflecting on how you will define your role, turn to section 1C of the i3PD Planning Map and use ideas from the chart to help you articulate your role as facilitator so that you can clearly communicate to participants the role that they can expect you to play.

Now that you've reflected on and articulated your role as the facilitator, you may feel daunted about filling it! For your own sake and for the sake of your participants, identify (and celebrate) the knowledge, skills, dispositions, and experiences you bring to this role. Think about how you will communicate your strengths. Then note areas in which you'd like to strengthen your practice in preparation for filling out the middle column of section 1C.

What Do You Hope to Learn?

Your participants are not the only ones learning here. Every time you facilitate a group, it's an opportunity to focus with intentionality and receive feedback on an area in which *you* want to grow.

You may already have set a goal for yourself. If not, review Figure 4.1 to help you think about what your participants will need you to be able to do if you are to succeed in being a transformational leader and identify one or two aspects of your own practice that you will focus on during this learning experience. You may recognize, for example, that you have participants who do not already know one another, and you'll need to establish trust among members; or you may recognize that you are not yet aware of your own leadership style and strengths. Identify resources to help you strengthen your skills in these areas, such as knowledgeable colleagues, books and articles, or podcasts and videos. Assess the current reality of your practice in this area, then use the resources you've identified to set a target to aim for.

You're going to take action toward your goal as you facilitate, so think about evidence you can collect to help you monitor your progress. You can think creatively about what you will accept as evidence that you have been successful in improving in this area, but, at a minimum, you should plan to add to the session exit slip a question that can provide you with regular feedback on your goal. (You will develop the exit slip in section 4A.) Throughout the series and at the end of it, you can review and analyze the evidence you collect and identify new implications for adjusting your facilitation practice.

Figure 4.1

Leaders vs. Facilitators

Leaders will...	Facilitators will...
• Establish the vision.	• Support participants to establish a shared vision.
• Set the goals.	• Support participants to set the goal.
• Serve the needs of the organization.	• Serve the needs of the team.
• Are concerned about the integrity of the product or outcome.	• Are concerned about the integrity of the process.
• Control the conditions of the meeting.	• Invite participants to help shape the conditions of the meeting.
• Seek members' trust.	• Seek to establish trust among members.
• Bring crucial content knowledge.	• Do not need to be well-versed in the content knowledge; they draw out content knowledge from the group.
• Do most of the talking.	• Ensure participants do most of the talking.
• Secure resources, including research, funding, and partnerships.	• Organize participants to secure resources needed, including research, funding, and partnerships.
• Track progress of the work.	• Support the group to track progress of the work.
• Have a higher level of authority than group members.	• Do not have a higher level of authority than group members; authority is not necessary (or helpful) in their role.
• Work to get buy-in.	• Strive toward consensus building.
• Have the final authority in decision making.	• Support decisions made by the group.

Both will...	

- Communicate the vision.
- Help maintain group focus on the goal.
- Be responsible for the integrity of the work.
- Plan meeting agendas.
- Manage and communicate logistics (time, space, materials).
- Support participants to make connections to related goals and priorities.
- Read the group and manage interpersonal dynamics.
- Depersonalize anger and negativity.
- Communicate with clarity, tact, and transparency.
- Support evidence-based decision making.
- Acknowledge and celebrate progress.
- Know their own work style, leadership style, strengths, and challenges.

How Will You Work Together?

Cofacilitating with another educator can be a win-win situation. You can be there for each other as supporters in strengthening your facilitation practice, and participants can benefit from a greater range of experience, expertise, and perspectives. These possibilities can become probabilities through planning.

Cofacilitators should reflect individually on their responses in the first two columns of section 1C ("Your Role" and "Your Goal(s)") and share and compare their thinking. Then ask yourselves how you will leverage each other's strengths.

It's possible to step on each other's toes and get on each other's nerves if cofacilitators have not worked out their dance steps in advance. Will you divide roles strategically based on your strengths and then tag-team by passing the "mic" back and forth? Will you assume differentiated roles, with one providing information and the other facilitating participant engagement? Or perhaps one of you will lead throughout, and the other will play a supporting role. It's a bad idea to assume you share an understanding about how you'll cofacilitate. Make time to talk it out.

As the series progresses, you'll need agreements to synchronize your efforts. Perhaps within a session one of you will notice time is running over, you missed something important, or a correction is in order. Some are happy to have the partner chime in; others might appreciate a hand signal or a note. What about between sessions? One of the benefits of cofacilitation is having a partner with whom to debrief, analyze exit slip data, and plan adjustments to the subsequent session. Will you set aside time to meet immediately after each session, designate a regular meeting time, or simply connect electronically?

Cofacilitators should not assume they both have the same idea in mind. Use this space in the third column of section 1C to work out the plan for sharing facilitation.

Seeing Beyond What We Thought We Knew

It's worthwhile to pause here and look across the work you've done in sections 1A, 1B, and 1C of the i3PD Planning Map to deepen your understanding—and possibly your appreciation for—the three core components: content, participant, and facilitator. Your efforts are shaped by what you think you know about the content and participants. And the participants' willingness and ability to engage are influenced by what they think they know about the content and you. So, although making predictions about these core components can be helpful, this final section challenges you to consider how your predictions may be incomplete or possibly wrong.

When we enter into an inquiry cycle with an open mind about how we might be wrong, none of the three core components emerges unchanged. The participants are empowered to take an active role in engaging with the content and with you (and one another) to solve this puzzle. And the content actually changes, too, as we see beyond what we thought we knew and possibly even create new knowledge. This is a distinctive goal of i3PD: probing for new knowledge so that we can create more equitable schools.

And this brings us to the third level of inquiry in i3PD: How do we support the school (or other context) to become a learning organization whose members can interrogate and eliminate systemic barriers to equity?

5

Core Assumptions (1D)

Because we exist within a system that is currently producing inequitable results and because schools' change efforts thus far have largely proven the system to be immune to change, it's important to zoom out beyond our focus on the instructional core and look at influences that might counterbalance our efforts to disrupt inequity. In this section, we'll identify how the assumptions, mindsets, and behaviors at work in our context might work against our efforts to establish equity—and how to design our i3PD experience as a test kitchen for challenging them.

You and your participants are not blank slates. You each bring expectations about how the world works that are shaped by years of drawing conclusions about cause and effect in your own life experiences. These expectations are mental models that shape how you understand the world and what you think is possible. But we are all social beings, so others who share these experiences, whether in your family, community, or workplace, influence those mental models (your assumptions); your attitudes about those mental models (your mindsets or commitments); and how you apply those mental models (your behavioral strategies) (Duffy, 2014).

Over time, mental models shared within a community become part of that community's culture, but some voices and perspectives end up lending more weight than others. As a result, the collective mindsets that develop are not perfectly matched with all of the various mindsets of the individuals within them, just as a scale is not designed to equitably weigh all objects. As time goes by, however, the attitudes and behaviors we develop in response to these mindsets become habits, making them rather impervious to change and making the resulting inequities seem intractable.

One way in which change can gain a foothold, however, is through a disruption or a disorienting dilemma (Mezirow, 1981). Normally, when we encounter experiences that don't make sense to us, we like to explain them away. We shrug off the anomaly and move on. A disorienting dilemma is an experience that feels so significantly unaligned with your mental models that you *can't* shrug it off. It triggers you to question your assumptions and opens a window of opportunity to change them, all while society's collective mindset is working against you, pushing your thinking back into widely accepted norms—that is, until society begins to budge, too.

In 2020, everything began to budge. The convergence of health, political, and social crises stretched individuals and the communities in which they live on a scale that left no one unscathed. To be sure, the tragedies ran deep and must not be discounted, but at the same time—and perhaps even because of them—we should see them as a ripe opportunity to gain leverage for social change.

We can illustrate this point with just one example. Throughout the past century, educators' efforts to propose novel ways to think differently about time in learning have stalled as a result of our collective mindset—our deeply rooted assumptions about where and when school happens. When COVID-19 rolled in, social distancing requirements led to a rise in remote learning and challenged our definitions of "going to school." It exposed longstanding assumptions that have shaped our laws and policies. In a remote learning environment, state laws built to regulate the minimum number of hours of seat time per year were hard to apply. Homework policies made no sense because *all* work was completed at home. Structures that schools provided to support children to be ready to learn, such as meals, social services, and health check-ins, had to be reconfigured. The pandemic produced a disorienting dilemma that has opened up a new appetite for change in the structure of schooling at a societal scale.

What we want to budge today is *instructional inequity*. We need to make space to question what we think we know. If we want to truly change the results we produce, tinkering with our practices or even reforming the structures and policies that guide them is insufficient. We need to do these things while also becoming more aware of how our collective mindset currently influences what we think we know and commit to reversing the influence.

In i3PD, you can shake things up and make a dent in the collective mindset at your school. You'll be looking together at a shared problem of practice from multiple angles and with diverse perspectives within a safe space. While doing so, you have the perfect opportunity to guide your colleagues in questioning how our current mindset might unwittingly be holding us hostage, renegotiate that mindset among the diverse perspectives of your participants, and push back with a collective effort to reform some of the mindsets that have made your school immune to change.

Exploring Immunity to Change

Because our shared mindsets and mental models have a stranglehold on the ways we've become accustomed to seeing and doing things—and, more significantly, to *not* seeing and *not* doing things—we need to identify the commitments and assumptions that shape our collective mindset and that inadvertently keep us from achieving the changes we seek. We're lucky in i3PD to be working with individuals who share a context. That means our professional learning series can double as a safe space for testing existing assumptions, overcoming the limitations of some assumptions, and growing a network of roots for a new collective mindset that can spread far beyond this group.

To do this, we'll use the Immunity Map pictured in Figure 5.1, based on the Immunity to Change Framework (Wagner, Kegan, Lahey, Lemons, Garnier et al., 2012). This map is a thinking exercise designed initially to support individuals as they identify and test the hidden assumptions that cause them to inadvertently work against themselves. We will use it here in a slightly different way. Instead of exploring our *own* immunity to change, we will be making *predictions* about the participants in your improvement cycle. Understanding that you may not yet know these participants well and that even if you did, you could never fully predict their responses, review what you *do* know about them (revisiting section 1B as necessary) and do your best to put yourself in their shoes and mindsets as you proceed through this thinking exercise. We will use the Immunity Map to imagine assumptions that may be influencing the *collective* mindset in the participants' shared context.

Set aside approximately 45 minutes to go through this exercise. You may want to duplicate Figure 5.1 or access the digital copy as a worksheet. Later you can copy the key ideas into section 1D ("Seeing the System: Core Assumptions") of your i3PD planner.

Improvement Goal

In section 1A ("Content") of the i3PD Planning Map, you picked an instructional practice and made predictions about the type of practice gap that is currently having an adverse impact on equity. You chose a gap that was limiting the learning experience of students from historically marginalized groups, your Spotlight Students. You committed to getting better at one of the following:

- Providing these students with instructional practice that is informed by the highest standards of professional knowledge available (knowledge gap inquiry).
- Providing these students with high-quality implementation of this practice (implementation gap inquiry).
- Ensuring your implementation of this practice supports these students responsively to improve their learning processes (teaching-learning gap inquiry).
- Ensuring your implementation of this practice supports these students authentically to meet high expectations (expectations gap inquiry).

Figure 5.1

Immunity Map

Improvement Goal	Behavior Inventory (Doing/Not Doing)	Hidden Competing Commitments	Big Assumptions
1. What do our Spotlight Students need us to improve?	2. What are we doing and not doing that works against our goal of improving our practice for our Spotlight Students?	3A. What might be worrisome about doing the opposite of the things in column two?	4. What do our hidden commitments suggest about how we might see the world and ourselves (that is, our collective mindset)?
We are committed to getting better at. . .	We are. . . We are not. . .	We are scared of. . . We are afraid that. . . We worry about. . . 3B. What self-protective, hidden commitments stand behind our worries? We are committed to. . .	We assume that. . .

Source: Adapted from *Change Leadership: A Practical Guide to Transforming Our Schools*, by T. Wagner et al., 2012, San Francisco: John Wiley & Sons. Copyright 2012 Minds at Work.

Note: A fillable PDF version of this figure is available as part of the Digital Tool Collection. See Appendix A for more information.

Copy your improvement goal in the first column of the Immunity Map. Note that this goal is really a no-brainer—of course we want this. The reason for this goal is not because we haven't previously thought of it or weren't committed deeply enough to it. We're picking it because we're stuck. Fueled by our commitment to get better at it, we're now going to invest in discovering why we're stuck.

Behavior Inventory

Although we may be committed to our improvement goal in word, we're stuck because we have conflicting commitments in deed. We're saying one thing and doing another in ways we don't realize. The way to become conscious of these competing commitments is by using those deeds or behaviors as clues.

In column two of the Immunity Map, put yourself in the participants' shoes and brainstorm from three to five examples of things you might be doing that unintentionally work against your improvement goal. You're not interested (now) in circumstances outside your control that might get in the way of achieving the goal, but in how you get in your *own* way. This will include things you're doing or not doing that contradict your goal or make it less possible—or even impossible—to fulfill.

For example, if you're pursuing a line of inquiry to close a gap in participants' knowledge base (knowledge gap inquiry), you may reflect and recognize that you pull "best practices" from anywhere without vetting the sources. You might also identify things you're *not* doing that you would expect to see yourself doing if you were going to ensure the instruction you bring to students is not outdated. For instance, maybe you don't maintain connections with sources of professional knowledge, such as attending conferences, joining professional associations, and engaging in professional reading.

Hidden Competing Commitments

Now look over those behaviors you just listed and ask yourself what might be scary to participants about doing *the opposite* of these things. For example, what might be scary about tapping only sources that have been backed by research and professional associations? What might be scary about vetting the resources you find? Try to picture yourself doing each of these opposite behaviors and capture what goes through your head. At the top of column three, document the concerns that worry you enough to make you squirm. Maybe you don't actually know how to find and evaluate professional resources; perhaps you're worried about exposing your lack of knowledge. If you've done this with honesty, you'll have a list that makes you so uncomfortable that you might hesitate to show it to anyone.

One pitfall to avoid here is naming things outside your control. Time, materials, resources, the structure of the school day, access, permission, and other factors may be in play. Write those down on a sticky note and keep them for later. We'll explore structures and policies in section 2D. But do not use these as an excuse to avoid claiming responsibility for your role.

Each of the worries at the top of column three represents an effort to protect yourself from something. In the bottom of column three, brainstorm the self-protective commitments that lead to these worries. Remember, you're not alone. In your context, you've adopted some common "smart" behaviors to mask things that you perceive would be unacceptable to others: For example, you're committed to not revealing our weaknesses; or to protecting a certain image of yourself as a professional. These commitments compete with the commitment in the first column—your improvement goal—and counterbalance efforts for progress. They are the keys to unlocking immunity to change.

Big Assumptions

When we look at our competing commitments and reflect on what assumptions we must be holding to make us feel we have to protect ourselves in these ways, we reveal how we're viewing the world and ourselves. Brainstorm as many assumptions as you can and capture your thoughts in column four of the Immunity Map. For example, perhaps you assume that rocking the boat will have dire consequences for teachers. Perhaps you assume that teachers are powerless to influence the intractable systems and structures in place. Look over your list of assumptions: Do these help explain why teachers do and don't do the things you noted in column two? These assumptions point to cultural norms that would make it impossible to make lasting progress on our improvement goal. We need to prove them wrong, and to do so safely. With some strategic planning, the safe space you create in your i3PD community will enable you to test the truth of these assumptions and possibly enable you to change your column-two behaviors. Maybe you *can* rock the boat. Maybe you're *not* powerless!

Approach the Immunity Map as a thinking exercise that can help you make some predictions about the mental models your participants might bring to the improvement cycle. There are no right answers, and there is no formal endpoint. You can come back and revisit as you get to know your participants. You may find it helpful to review the four sample Immunity Maps shown in Appendix C or to delve into one of the readings recommended there.

Mindset Shifts

Now that you have predicted some assumptions that may be driving your brain to make decisions that work against what you say you're working for, we will turn this challenge into an opportunity. We will prepare to challenge your participants to test some of these assumptions. Pick one or two of them and compose a question that begins with "How might we…?" Following are four examples:

Assumption 1: We assume that educators should know everything and that if others see we don't know everything, they will judge us incompetent. Is this true?

Experiment: *How might we create an i3PD environment that enables participants to explore the costs and benefits of exposing what they don't know?*

Assumption 2: We assume that authentic conversations about the quality of our teaching are too risky, time consuming, and challenging to be worth the effort. Is this true?

Experiment: *How might we create an i3PD environment in which teachers explore the pros and cons of difficult conversations?*

Assumption 3: We assume that student achievement is more important than students learning to become independent learners. Is this true?

Experiment: *How might we create an i3PD environment that enables participants to test whether these are mutually exclusive?*

Assumption 4: We assume that finding racial patterns in our student learning data is a problem. Is this true?

Experiment: *How might we create an i3PD environment in which we look at identifying racial disparities as keys to addressing them?*

If you can design your i3PD communities so that they double as laboratories for testing your assumptions, you might be able to create a small but critical mass of community members who are prepared to be catalysts for shifting mindsets throughout the context.

This exercise has helped you predict some of the collective mindsets that may be in the way of change efforts, and it should have heightened your attention to how scary this work may feel for your participants. With this new awareness, you'll be better prepared to support them. For now, simply capture your improvement goal, competing commitments, and "how might we" questions in section 1D of the i3PD planner so that you can revisit them later on in the process.

At the same time, take note: Participants' assumptions may get in the way of their ability to achieve the results they say they want in ways you haven't predicted here. They may have interpersonal baggage, prior experiences, or cultural backgrounds with which you are unfamiliar, making it hard for you to make predictions about their behaviors and assumptions. You may want to revisit this exercise after your series begins and after you've had a chance to know them better. In addition, remember that you're a learner too. You might try this exercise again while reflecting on an improvement goal you've struggled to make progress on. What are *you* committed to getting better at, and what competing commitments have been getting in your way?

In Part One you explored each of the core components of your learning experience—the content, participants, and facilitators—and made predictions about assumptions that could get in the way of participants' ability to make the changes they say they want to make. The i3PD Planning Map is designed to support you in capturing the design considerations from these insights so that you can refer to them when planning the learning sequence. An annotated version of Part One of the planner appears on the next page. Use the annotations to reflect on a past or current PD experience you've had or led.

- Did it interrogate a practice gap? How did it aim to address instructional inequity?
- In what ways was it responsive to the characteristics of the cohort and the students they serve?
- Was it facilitated or led, and how did that work for you?
- What competing commitments went unaddressed or were challenged?

You'll find this annotated map to be a useful reference whether you're ready to plan your own i3PD, or simply eager to use new understandings about the Core Components to bolster existing professional development.

The i3PD Planning Map: Part One—Annotated

PART ONE: Core Components

1A. Content

Focus of Learning		Practice Gap
What instructional practice will be the focus of learning? Clarify the boundaries within which you aim to invite participant exploration (e.g., topic, subject area, student population).		*What practice gap will we interrogate? Choose one of the below.*

We will interrogate potential gaps between participants' current practice and (choose one)

- ☐ Practice informed by the current knowledge base for this practice.
- ☐ Professional standards for quality implementation of this practice.
- ☐ Practice that responsively matches teaching to students' learning processes.
- ☐ Practice that authentically achieves high expectations for students' learning products.

1B. Participants

The Cohort and Their Context	Questions	Insights and Implications
What do you know? Describe the cohort and their students. *If possible, add links to the participant roster below and data on students served.*	*What do you wonder? What else do you need to know to help you earn their engagement as active, equity-focused participants?* *How will you gather this information?*	*What insights and implications do you want to hold on to while communicating about and planning this improvement cycle?*

1B. Participants

What do you know about the participants?

What do you wonder about the participants?

What do you know about the students they work with from historically marginalized groups (i.e., Spotlight Students)?

What do you wonder about their Spotlight Students?

1C. Facilitators

Your Role

- *In what ways will you be leading and in what ways will you be facilitating?*
- *What assets (e.g., knowledge, skills, dispositions, experiences) do you bring to this group?*

Your Goal(s)

- *Which one aspect of your facilitation will you focus on with intentionality?*
- *How will you monitor results?*

Cofacilitation Notes

If cofacilitating, how will you work together?

- *How will you leverage each other's strengths?*
- *How will you coperform this work?*
- *What norms and signals will help keep you in sync?*

(continued)

🌿 The i3PD Planning Map: Part One—Annotated—(continued)

1D. Seeing the System: Core Assumptions *

> *You may want to complete this using the Immunity Map shown in Figure 5.1 and copy the highlights here.*

Improvement Goal	Behavior Inventory (Doing/Not Doing)	Hidden Competing Commitments	Big Assumptions
1. What do our Spotlight Students need us to improve? *What are we committed to getting better at in this PD experience?*	2. What are we doing and not doing that work against our goal of improving our practice for our Spotlight Students? *What are some of the obvious things you would expect someone with this improvement goal to be doing or not doing?*	3A. What might be worrisome about doing the opposite of the things in column two? *Identify some of the "good reasons" we don't do the things in column 2.* 3B. What self-protective, hidden commitments stand behind our worries? *The fears in 3A are terribly uncomfortable to admit and read. What commitments lie at the roots of these fears?*	4. What do our hidden commitments suggest about how we might see the world and ourselves (i.e., our collective mindset)? *What unstated cultural norms might be at play in this context?*

Insights and Implications

> *How might you make your i3PD experience a space in which participants can free themselves of these Big Assumptions or experiment with the opposite of them?*

Source: Adapted from *Change Leadership: A Practical Guide to Transforming Our Schools*, by T. Wagner et al., (2012), San Francisco: John Wiley & Sons. Copyright 2012 Minds at Work.

Part Two

Creating Connections for a Productive Learning Environment

In Part Two of the i3PD Planning Map, you will establish strong connections between the core components so that participants share the commitment, mutual accountability, and trust required for this challenging work and to help you predict contextual factors that may be working against your efforts to uproot instructional inequity.

6

Relevance (2A)

In Part One of this book, we established a strong foundation for this improvement cycle through keen attention to each aspect of the instructional core: the content, the participants, and the facilitators. In Part Two, we build on that foundation with a look at the relationships among those core components (see Figure 6.1). By predicting and elevating participants' connections to the content, we strengthen the **relevance** of the learning experience. By strategizing about our responsibility as facilitator for providing support and accountability for strong content, we ensure **rigor** in the learning experience. And by investing time in how trust will be built between ourselves as facilitators and the participants, as well as among them, we cultivate productive **relationships** that are essential to the learning experience. You'll find that the annotated version of Part Two of the i3PD Planning Map on page 96 will be a helpful guide as you work through Chapters 6–9.

In this chapter, we'll start by examining **relevance** (section 2A of the planner). To do so, we're going to articulate connections between the content and the participants: Why might these participants need to engage with this content? Starting with the "why" keeps us grounded and gives us something to return to when things get rough. It also creates solidarity for our shared mission because it helps

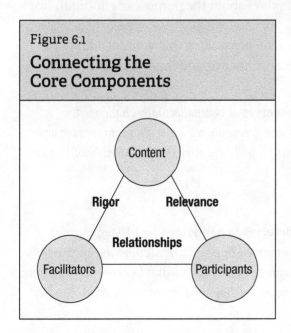

Figure 6.1

Connecting the Core Components

Content

Rigor   Relevance

Relationships

Facilitators   Participants

participants see how their personal goals are in sync with our shared purpose (Berg, 2018). "Why?" is a question we can answer at multiple levels. We're going to address it from both a high altitude, defined by our lofty ideals and core values, and as a low altitude, grounded in what we know about the needs of the students in front of us.

Purpose: The High-Altitude Why

We will begin by connecting the work ahead to a larger vision of the purpose of education and to key values and ideals that members of this learning community share. It's an opportunity to connect the dots among the work we're about to take on, why we've chosen this career in the first place, and why our families send their beloved children to our school. The aim is to ensure that participants recognize the ways in which their own personal driving motivations align with the purpose of this improvement cycle.

You've already identified a perceived gap in practice as the focus for change. Perhaps you're looking at appropriate scaffolding supports for your Spotlight Students to meet high expectations in writing and you're concerned by a potential gap between participants' current practices and conceptions of quality implementation of this practice. Now we'll contextualize this gap in the higher calling of what each student deserves. If your community of learners already shares a common vision embraced by everyone in your school, district, or professional association, you can connect to this. If not, articulating global values about the purpose of education from your own perspective will work.

Section 2A in the planner offers three sentence starters that you can adopt or adapt to contextualize learning goals into an authentic and important shared purpose. The first two may look like this:

- **We believe each and every child deserves** *to be intellectually challenged.*
- **Teachers' ability to** *strategically use and gradually release scaffolds to support writing mastery* is essential to that because *it will help strengthen students' abilities to be independent learners.*

Or, like this:

- **We believe each and every child deserves** *to be prepared for lifelong learning.*
- **Teachers' ability to** *make decisions informed by a wider breadth of the knowledge and skill base on differentiating instruction* is essential to that because *it will ensure students are supported with the best-known methods of ensuring each gets what they need for success.*

Write down some of your ideas in section 2A of the planner. When you prepare your session agendas later in section 3C, use these notes to think about how to help participants connect these dots. Offer your thoughts on these connections when sharing the session purpose and objectives, or, if time allows, engage participants in identifying their own connections or elaborating on yours.

Purpose: The Low-Altitude Why

You've identified why students generally need this change, but honestly, many changes are likely to benefit your students right now. Why is closing this particular gap in your instruction so important for these specific children, at this moment in time, within this unique setting?

Take some time to reflect on what you know about these participants and the student populations they work with that have been historically marginalized, starting with what you captured in section 1B ("Participants"). Revisit the source of your hunches that this instructional change was needed in the first place. Reflect on what you know about what participants and students are doing or not doing. Consider what else they may be experiencing or not experiencing.

Take into account, too, the current time and location. What else is going on concurrently for these participants and students that might make this an opportune time to address this gap? Perhaps there is a new curriculum adoption underway in the district, a grant-funded opportunity for new resources, or key personnel changes that will bring new expertise and experience. You can use shifts in the system such as these to strategically help make this a particularly high-leverage move right now.

Adopt or adapt the third sentence starter listed in section 2A of the planner to capture your thoughts. Here are some examples:

- **Closing this gap is important for these specific participants, at this time, in this setting because** *only 67 percent of the Black students who received As and Bs in 9th grade English in our school passed our state's English language arts assessment, whereas 93 percent of white students who received As and Bs in the same cohort scored proficient or above on the same test. Our district supporting teachers to create new common formative writing assessments provides a timely opportunity to help teachers shed over-scaffolding practices.*
- **Closing this gap is important for these specific participants, at this time, in this setting because** *40 percent of the students in our district are from Haitian families who speak Creole at home, yet they currently represent 89 percent of the students who are advancing to middle school without grade-level proficiency in math. The district has recently adopted a new math curriculum, and we want to be sure that as we learn to implement it, we do so with keen understanding of the role our knowledge of students must play in effectively differentiating instruction within this new curriculum.*

If you are less familiar with your participants and their context, you might not be able to reach this level of detail. You'll be surprised, however, at how much you can learn from exploring publicly available data, perusing school and district websites, and conversing with local administrators.

Identifying and articulating these compelling high-altitude and low-altitude statements of purpose will help you frame the relevance of the work and convey its urgency as you begin communicating with participants.

Outcome-Based Objectives

The i3PD experience is designed to support changes in practice to advance equity at both an individual and organizational level, and participants will benefit from knowing these twin goals. From a backward-planning point of view, we can articulate the outcome-based objectives of an i3PD series this way:

1. Individual participants will (choose one)
   - close their knowledge gap: They will be able to make decisions informed by a wider breadth of the knowledge and skill base for this instructional practice.
   - close their implementation gap: They will be able to engage in high-quality implementation of this instructional practice.
   - close their teaching-learning gap: They will be able to use this instructional practice more strategically and appropriately to strengthen students' learning processes.
   - close their expectations gap: They will be able to recognize and raise artificially low expectations about what they accept as quality student work products in context of this instructional practice.

2. Our community of participants will be able to use inquiry results to identify systemic barriers to equity and take action together.

Capture these draft objectives in the second column of section 2A of your i3PD planner ("Outcome-Based Objectives"). If you're working with the digital version of the tool, you can edit this language to reference your specific practice gap and to suit your audience and context.

7

Rigor (2B)

Another important "why" concerns the effect of the changes on student learning. Who wants to put in the effort if we're not going to make a difference? Painting a vivid picture of the difference we aim to make can not only be motivating, but also practically useful for backward planning. Remember that it is not your responsibility as facilitator to be the expert in all of the content. However, it *is* your responsibility to ensure the experience is rigorous: that the outcome-based objectives for the content are high and worthwhile and that we have a plan to meet them. To help you fulfill your role in ensuring both support and accountability for rigorous content, in this section you will describe the intended outcomes of this improvement cycle and identify forms of evidence to use to monitor results.

Process Objectives

The outcome-based objectives we identified in the previous section described what we'll leave with. The process objectives we'll identify now articulate what we aim to do within this series to achieve these outcomes. They enable participants to preview the four-stage inquiry process with a bifocal view of individual and organizational change. We can state the objectives of i3PD as follows:

As individual participants, you will support one another to

- **Assess.** You will identify gaps in your own instructional practice (your knowledge, implementation, strategic use, or expectations of that practice) that currently contribute to inequitable outcomes.
- **Attempt.** You will design a response to the gap, as well as a system for documenting change as you take action to close it.

- **Analyze.** You will interpret evidence of change, identify challenges to change, and integrate insights into your ongoing professional practice.

As a community, you will

- **Adjust.** You will reflect on patterns across our lines of inquiry to identify relevant systemic factors that inhibit equity, and you will organize efforts to make the changes they require.

These process objectives are listed in section 2B of the planner ("Rigor") because i3PD targets practice gaps through this four-stage inquiry process. Later, in Part Three, you will plan out each of the inquiry steps of your learning series in detail. After you do so, you should return to this section of the planner and adjust the language here to increase the specificity of your objectives and paint an even clearer picture of the learning path. Doing so will help your participants understand in what specific ways you will be inviting them to engage in the learning. They will be better prepared to engage with new ideas, feelings, and actions and to begin thinking about how this experience will support them in making changes in their practice.

Evidence of Impact

What would you accept as evidence that this improvement cycle had the results you intended? Certainly, in the end we want to have an effect on student learning and growth. We also hope that participants will have positive feelings about the improvement cycle and that they might have expanded their knowledge and skills for engaging in ongoing cycles of inquiry. We'll address the need to monitor for these ancillary outcomes in Part Four when we turn our attention to evaluating this improvement cycle. The primary and more significant outcome of inquiry-based professional learning is *a specific change in teachers' practice*. As such, it's helpful to visualize this change and keep it front and center in our planning.

The sources of evidence that might be appropriate for your inquiry cycle depend on what type of inquiry you're pursuing—that is, what practice gap you are addressing and what type of change you aim to inspire. You have already selected a practice gap in section 1A. Following are some examples of data sources that might serve as evidence of change.

📚 Knowledge Gap Inquiry

If you're aiming to address a perceived gap between the **knowledge base** of instructional practice and current practice, then you're looking for data that show that teachers can make decisions informed by a wider breadth of the knowledge and skill base for this professional practice. Here are some examples of such data:

- **Teachers' self-reports and reflections** can be useful, especially when they are built from evidence—that is, from annotated lesson plans, classroom transcripts, or videos of instruction.
- **Instructional observations** might be captured through low-inference classroom transcripts documented by colleagues or by the teacher using video.
- **Student artifacts**, such as work products or videotaped performances, might serve as evidence that new learning on the teacher's part has influenced their professional practices.

Implementation Gap Inquiry

In education, sometimes we end up throwing out great ideas or deeming them ineffective, not because they are objectively worthless, but because we implemented them poorly. It's important, then, to occasionally inspect the quality of implementation. Here, we're not talking about the effect on students, but simply about whether the teacher has implemented the practice skillfully and with fidelity to performance indicators of that practice. In this form of inquiry, then, we want to address gaps between **established standards of quality implementation** and current practice. To do so, we need data showing that teachers can engage in higher-quality implementation of this instructional practice. Consider the following forms of data:

- **Teaching logs** are one way for teachers to capture their own data and their reflections on changes in quality. In such a medium, they can describe each instance of implementation, look for changes over time, and reflect on their own or with the support of implementation rubrics about whether those changes represent positive improvements.
- **Observations of teaching** are essential to an examination of implementation quality. We need to see the micromoves that compose the practice, regardless of whether we measure these moves against an established checklist of quality indicators or use them to engage in our own critical conversations about what we believe represents quality.
- **Artifacts** may be useful for capturing changes in practices that produce objects over time. For example, we might compare teachers' progress-monitoring pages, whole-class conversation charts, or samples of feedback that teachers have provided to students.

Teaching-Learning Gap Inquiry

You might see a need for helping teachers address gaps between the influence their instructional practice has on **students' learning processes** and the influence they aim for it to have. That is, participants might need to improve their ability to make better decisions about *when and how* to employ an instructional practice for the specific students in front of them. In this case, you'll want to identify data sources that show that teachers have strategically and appropriately matched the implementation of this instructional practice to student needs in ways that influence both how and how much they learn. The following data sources can help:

- **Student interviews** are essential to understanding how students make sense of their work. By repeatedly asking students over time to describe the steps they took or explain the decisions they made about how to proceed, we get a window into changes in their thinking routines.
- **Observations of students at work**, whether live or through video, draw teachers' attention to students' microroutines: their order of approach, the sequence of their gaze, the sources of help to which they turn, and more. Such observations can document and track changes over time. They also provide clues about whether and how the context has influenced the students' performance.
- **Student work**, whether products or performances, whether live or through video, can be useful, too. Such qualitative data are essential for looking beyond *whether* students have performed to understanding in *what ways* they have done so. Observations of students and their work can also help teachers identify invaluable prompts for student interviews.

Expectations Gap Inquiry

It's human to see only what we want to see. When there is a high bar to meet, it's easier to lower expectations or deceive ourselves into believing we've met it than it is to put the work in to achieve it. Therefore, there may be a need to support teachers to develop their ability to effectively recognize and address gaps between **expectations of quality student work** and the student work they accept in their current practice. In this case, we need data that show whether or not the work teachers are currently accepting from students meets high expectations, and we need others to help us see what lies beyond our own filtered gaze. Consider the following:

- **Triangulated student work**, whether quantitative or qualitative, is essential for making judgments about what students know and are able to do. By triangulating multiple forms of evidence—such as a journal entry, an essay, and writing from a content area—teachers can crosscheck the judgments they have made about student work quality and what students know.
- **Student interviews** are another way to crosscheck judgments. If we believe our practice has had a certain effect, we might be able to test that assumption by looking together with students at the work and asking about what they perceive to be the influences that led to changes in their work.
- **Stakeholder interviews** enable teachers to hear how students, their families, the students' other teachers, and even colleagues who don't know the students

interpret the evidence of student outcomes and the influences that produced them. We may think we see change, and we may believe that change represents improvement. But do the others—those who bring different perspectives and levels of attachment to the question—come to the same conclusion?

Use the guidance above to help you consider what you will accept as evidence that change has occurred and to determine whether that change is an improvement. Think about how and when participants will collect these data throughout the improvement cycle. Then, in section 2B of the i3PD Planning Map ("Rigor"), identify the data you'll collect as evidence of impact, as well as your initial thoughts about how and when you might collect this evidence. For example, if you're focusing on improving appropriate writing scaffolds for your Spotlight Students, you might decide to have teachers keep a reflection journal, organize peer observations, and gather the notes teachers have taken during writing conferences, and you'll want to inform them of this in advance. You'll find your notes helpful when you complete your data collection plan as part of Part Four: Continuous Learning.

8

Relationships (2C)

We've challenged participants to be honest about inequities occurring under their watch, to identify crucial gaps, and to make necessary changes in their practice. Under what conditions might they accept and persist in this challenge? It's up to you to establish and nurture relationships that will ensure the safe and collaborative learning community needed to earn their eager engagement. For this we'll direct our attention to relationship building among participants as well as between participants and facilitators as we design deliberate moves to strengthen trust and clarify role expectations within the team.

Strengthening Trust

The i3PD experience may involve putting some frightening requests to participants, such as to experiment with something they're not sure will work; replace well-worn mental models with potentially uncomfortable new ones; acknowledge they have been doing something incompletely, wrong, or ineffectively; and possibly let go of an existing professional practice that has a longstanding place in their repertoire. You have detailed some of these fears in section 1D ("Seeing the System: Core Assumptions") of the planner. If participants do not have a reason to trust, they are likely to hold themselves back with caution instead of engaging with vulnerability and curiosity—and the goal of changed practice becomes unattainable. Thus, strengthening trust is not just a "nice-to-have" component of your professional learning community. It's a nonnegotiable necessity (Bryk & Schneider, 2002; Tschannen-Moran, 2014).

Our readiness to trust—that is, our willingness to make ourselves vulnerable— is influenced in part by whether we feel others have respect for us as humans and personal regard for us as individuals. When assessing whether we feel respected, we wonder, "Do I feel seen and heard?" When determining the level of personal regard, we ask, "Am I confident others will be open to accepting and respecting my uniqueness?" Others cannot have respect or personal regard for us if they don't have opportunities to know us.

In section 1B you identified some key information about your participants and possibly laid plans to gather additional material. Currently, you're the only one with this information. Right from the start, you can help participants connect over characteristics they have in common and make visible the range of expertise they collectively contribute as assets to our new community. As the work gets going, you can create role-alike groups, pair individuals strategically by interest, and tap those with specialized expertise as consultants to the group. You can also use this information to inform ways you'll demonstrate vulnerability yourself. For example, given what you know about the participants, think about what they might like to know about you and your experiences and share these stories as you introduce yourself. What do participants know more about than you? Be transparent about that and clarify where you hope to learn from them.

In addition to providing embedded interactive opportunities for participants to strengthen respect and personal regard, set aside time in which relationship building sits squarely in the foreground. This helps initiate an important cycle: As participants take small risks to make themselves vulnerable and share a bit about themselves, positive responses from colleagues can help them feel seen, heard, and regarded, causing them to respond in kind. Repeated positive exchanges will ease their vulnerability so that they'll be willing to stick their necks out even further and share from a deeper and more vulnerable place. In the end, the risk is worth the reward: Opportunities that require greater vulnerability have greater payoff by confirming for participants that they are in a relationship of respect and personal regard (Kochanek, 2005), and unlocking participants' willingness to learn deeply.

If participants have no or a low level of familiarity with you or one another, you'll want to begin with some low-risk ways to build respect and personal regard. You might create opportunities for acknowledging commonalities and shared values in ways such as these:

- Reflect with others about the school's strengths and about what those strengths say about us as a community.
- Invite participants to share good news from their classrooms, such as a student who made a breakthrough, a student who made you laugh, or new ideas you're excited about trying.
- Ask an open-ended question all can answer—for example, Why did you enter teaching? Who was your favorite teacher and why? What brings you to this i3PD series? What kind of student are you? Look for common themes in responses.

In addition to recognizing our sameness, you'll want to celebrate our differences. You can create opportunities for participants to learn about and acknowledge one another's uniqueness by engaging in activities such as these:

- Ask participants to discuss a special talent they have—for example, language ability, carrying a tune, having a green thumb.
- Do an activity to help participants discover one another's work styles, such as Compass Points (an exercise in understanding preferences in group work) or Continuum Dialogue (which requires participants to physically stand on a link according to where they place themselves between two statements). Discuss ways in which we contrast and complement one another.
- Invite participants to show positive regard for one another by writing a note of appreciation to another participant or posting their remarks on a bulletin board or padlet.

If participants are already familiar with one another, you might move quickly from some initial low-risk activities into higher-risk ones, such as these that strengthen respect:

- Critically reflect on community agreements: In what ways are our actions really aligned to our school vision? Which of our norms has been hardest for us? Identify the themes, but discuss the outliers.
- Ask participants to identify one identity they hold in life, such as student, teacher, parent, neighbor, female, African American, and so on. With that one identity in the forefront, have everyone answer the same question: When does your school stress you out as a _____? In your opinion, what is the best thing about your school as a _____?
- Ask an open-ended question everyone can answer: What would you like to change about the teaching profession? Can you tell us about a student you struggled to reach? What would you like us to know about you as a learner? Look for contrasts and similarities in the responses.

You might also engage participants who have established familiarity with each other in activities such as these, which deepen personal regard with a bit more heat:

- Present a collection of objects, such as office supplies, small toys, or dollar store items. Invite participants to take turns picking an object and gifting it to another participant, sharing their rationale for doing so.
- Ask each participant to identify one aspect of the community that has helped them make deeper changes in practice and one thing they need from the community to help them continue to do so.
- Discuss a current event or charged incident that occurred in the group (or on the news) and map the range of reactions.

As the facilitator, you have the responsibility of kicking things off and getting a cycle of positivity going while gradually turning up the heat when you see participants are ready.

Look back at section 1D of your i3PD planner ("Seeing the System: Core Assumptions") to recall the types of mindset shifts that you have predicted might be needed and reflect on the vulnerability this will require. In section 2C ("Relationships"), make some notes about the preexisting level of respect and personal regard within the community (including details about how you see yourself in those terms) and identify a few ideas for strengthening those that you would like to return to when planning the series.

Clarifying Role Expectations

Before participants will be willing to really share what's hard, confusing, or even unacceptable to them about their own practice, they need a reason to trust in others' competence and integrity. They need to have confidence that others will be willing and able to respond appropriately. Although they may not know it, their conceptions of what is "appropriate" depends on their expectations of the roles involved. Leaders of professional learning, therefore, must clarify what participants can expect from them as facilitators and what participants can expect from one another.

As new learning communities come together, participants may have a variety of ideas about their roles—for example, whether they're expected to sit and listen, encourage others, ask questions, offer advice, or argue—and about your role as leader, including whether you'll be offering expert advice, coaching them to make their own discoveries, or facilitating collegial exchange. If participants expect others to perform one role but then experience a different one, they are liable to make negative judgments about their colleagues' competence and integrity. It's a worthwhile proactive move, then, to create space for making explicit our commitments to one another and for educating one another about the perspectives, experiences, and expertise that we're able to draw on to make good on those commitments.

i3PD is designed with specific expectations in mind, grounded in the literature on dialogic education among adult learners (Vella, 2002). The expectations for both facilitators and participants are laid out in Figure 8.1.

This framing of the expectations may be a shift from what members of your learning community are used to. It proposes that participants should count on facilitators for defining a learning path informed by participant needs and for keeping them safe as they explore the new ideas, feelings, and actions that the learning path requires. It further proposes that participants and facilitators share responsibility and accountability for connecting the learning path to significant work in practice, reflecting in action to ensure continuous improvement of teachers' practice and of the series, and sustaining the types of relationships needed to do this together. Finally, it clarifies the unique role participants play in determining the success of their own and their colleagues' learning. Their learning will emerge from their collaborative dialogue about the experiments they have designed to pursue in their practice.

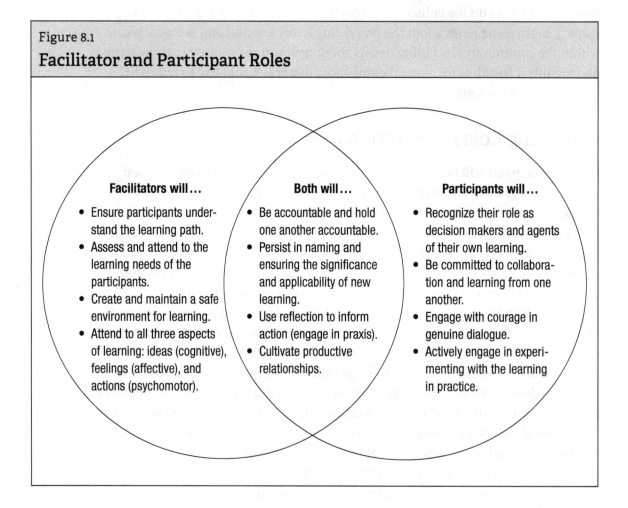

Figure 8.1

Facilitator and Participant Roles

Facilitators will...

- Ensure participants understand the learning path.
- Assess and attend to the learning needs of the participants.
- Create and maintain a safe environment for learning.
- Attend to all three aspects of learning: ideas (cognitive), feelings (affective), and actions (psychomotor).

Both will...

- Be accountable and hold one another accountable.
- Persist in naming and ensuring the significance and applicability of new learning.
- Use reflection to inform action (engage in praxis).
- Cultivate productive relationships.

Participants will...

- Recognize their role as decision makers and agents of their own learning.
- Be committed to collaboration and learning from one another.
- Engage with courage in genuine dialogue.
- Actively engage in experimenting with the learning in practice.

This is a tall bill to fill. Facilitators and participants alike must have confidence in one another to fill it. We can foster such confidence by engaging in some of the following lower-stakes activities that help us learn about one another's role-relevant competence and record of integrity:

- Collect in advance, compile, and distribute a page of brief written bios from participants.
- Survey participants about their self-perceptions of competency with regard to key areas of expertise relevant to your series; share data displays at the first session.

- Invite pairs of participants to interview each other about their areas of professional expertise that can be an asset for the group. Each member then introduces their partner to the group.
- Ask participants to share resources relevant to our inquiry focus by contributing to an annotated list for the group's use.
- Structure connecting activities to include interdependent roles, such as facilitator or note taker; acknowledge everyone's part in the result.
- Call on volunteers to take on minor tasks for the group (such as bringing snacks or creating a summary of group thinking) and acknowledge task completion.
- Publicly appreciate collaborative contributions that participants spontaneously make in service of the group through shout-outs or sharing.

Over time, as we see evidence that our colleagues can be invaluable resources for helping us be more effective for our students, we'll become more willing to expose ourselves and to engage in such higher-stakes activities as these:

- Use protocols that call for participants to push one another's thinking, such as providing warm and cool feedback.
- Make space for participants to share how they're putting their reflections into action and what they're learning from that.
- Call on volunteers to take on substantive tasks for the group (such as facilitating a connecting activity or teaching a mini-lesson) and acknowledge task completion.
- Ask volunteers to participate in a fishbowl feedback conversation about their inquiry cycle.
- Invite participants to bring videos of their teaching practice to share in the session.
- Invite candid exit slip feedback about how the experience could better meet their needs.

These higher-stakes activities are the reason for i3PD. We cannot hope to influence practice, mindsets, and systems without making ourselves vulnerable to share our prickliest problems and without investing in helping one another see new perspectives, push others' thinking, give others' the courage and support to try something new, and help one another make sense of what happened. Use section 2C of the i3PD planner ("Relationships") to decide how you will clarify roles and how you will support participants as they strengthen trust in one another's competence and integrity. You might even choose to review Figure 8.1 as a group to decide together what the facilitators will do and not do and to adjust expectations to suit your learning community.

Note, too, that mutual respect, personal regard, and confidence are built through *positive* exchanges. If participants' efforts to put themselves out there and build connections are snubbed, they will protect themselves from the risk of future disregard. If collaborative efforts reveal that colleagues can't be counted on, for example, for good advice or follow-through, it's unlikely that participants will rely again on their competence or integrity. As the facilitator, you're responsible for keeping participants safe. If you fail to act when there's a breach of trust, whether inadvertent or intentional, participants may lose trust in you.

Remember that when we trust, we're willing to make ourselves vulnerable with the expectation that others will act *appropriately*. Where there's a breach of trust, there's often misunderstanding about what is appropriate. In this case, you can use what you know about the participants to find a dignity-preserving way to identify the discrepancy and hammer out a shared understanding. The proactive move, however, would be to support the community of participants in negotiating up front what they can and can't expect from one another and to secure participants' commitment to holding one another accountable for these group agreements.

Community Agreements

If your learning community is school or district based, you likely already have formal agreements or informal norms that shape expectations about how members will interact with one another. Where norms are not named through explicit agreement, they emerge just as authoritatively through patterns of behavior exhibited in the majority of the group. Such implicit norms not only create tension for individuals who are not part of the dominant culture, but also tend to have a low bar, set at the lowest behaviors seen within the group. If we're interested in equity, we need to replace implicit norms with negotiated agreements that are clear to all and that are designed to ensure everyone receives what they need to feel safe and learn. Many protocols exist for developing community agreements, such as that provided in Appendix D ("Norms Construction: A Process of Negotiation").

Whether you make time to establish new agreements from scratch or adopt preexisting ones is of little consequence. The agreements themselves are far less important than individuals' understandings of those agreements and whether their understandings are in sync.

All learning communities that come together for i3PD should engage in the exercise shown in Figure 8.2. It helps members share their interpretations of local norms in the context of this specific work we're about to do.

The first part of the activity ("Consider the norms…") ensures all have the same movie playing in their heads when we talk about a safe learning environment. The second part ("What would you like someone to say or do….") focuses on what should happen if someone violates the agreement—and this helps you share responsibility for maintaining that agreement. This may be unnecessary with a community that has a short amount of time together. However, where community members have a long-term commitment to working together, it's prudent to invest time in ensuring shared responsibility for safeguarding norms.

Creating deliberate ways to build and safeguard trust—and not just leave it to chance—increases the likelihood that participants will quickly develop the kind of relationships needed to productively push one another's thinking. The more they connect around their common challenges while recognizing the ways in which each participant can help them address those challenges, the more they become invested in tackling those challenges together and willing to embrace the types of mindset shifts required.

But teachers do not work in isolation. Their classrooms are within schools, districts, and states where preexisting structures and policies may inadvertently work against these changes. In the next chapter, we look at the ways in which those structures and policies may work against you—and how you can prepare to effectively push against them.

Figure 8.2

Making Agreements About Community Norms

The objectives of this learning community are...

Copy from section 2A of the i3PD Planning Map.

Each team or learning community includes its own combination of individuals with unique perspectives, learning styles, work preferences, and cultural experiences.

Therefore, these norms might look different within each team and members should take time to clarify and agree upon them.

In Part A:

1. Copy each of your existing or proposed norms into its own row of the first column below.
2. Invite members to describe their personal expectations of each in the second two columns.
3. Compare and contrast responses, then discuss and edit to reflect team agreements.

In Part B:

1. Invite each member of your team to add their name to a row in the first column.
2. Provide time for members to independently reflect on and record their personal preferences for support and accountability in the second two columns.
3. Invite members to recognize and note one another's personal preferences and to bookmark this page for future reference.

Part A: Consider the norms in the context of the objectives of this community:

How should they be enacted to allow you to do your best work?

Community Norm	What might this look or sound like to you?	What do you believe this norm suggests we should *not* do?

Part B: Who should do what when an agreement is broken?		
Name	**What would you like someone to say or do when you violate an agreement? Who should do this?** *Note: Think beyond the facilitator.*	**What would you like someone to say or do if this becomes a chronic problem?** *Note: Think beyond, "Remind me."*

Note: A fillable PDF version of this figure is available as part of the Digital Tool Collection. See Appendix A for more information.

9

Connections in Context (2D)

Thus far the focus has been on amplifying reasons for participants to commit to this work, invest in its outcomes, and support one another to achieve them. However, many other individuals have an influence on those outcomes. They and their predecessors have contributed to the establishment of structures and policies that reinforce deeply embedded mindsets that perpetuate our current inequitable outcomes. These structures and policies not only resist change, but also make us resistant to change. In this chapter, we'll identify a few dimensions of those systems as potential focus areas for our systems-level inquiry.

How Context Matters

One challenge to changing the system is really *seeing* the system. We don't see it because we live in it, so we tend to take it for granted. And we don't talk about it because we don't have good language for pointing to the complexities that make up the system that produces education outcomes. In theory, school and district leaders have established the current structures and policies to ensure systemic support for teaching and learning. In practice, however, evidence suggests that our structures and policies often serve some students less effectively than others and that the students they disadvantage typically are from historically marginalized groups (Alliance for Resource Equity, 2019). Our policies and structures currently produce a situation in which students from low-income families are less likely to attend adequately funded schools (Morgan & Amerikaner, 2018); Black and Hispanic students are less likely to feel safe at school (Alvarez & Bachman, 1997); and students of color are less likely to have teachers in their classrooms or characters in their books that look like them (Lindsay, Blom, & Tilsley, 2017).

As national attention is drawn to the ways that U.S. school systems are inequitable *by design*, the knowledge base is growing on how context matters in school quality (Blankstein, Noguera, & Kelly, 2016; Johnson, Kraft, & Papay, 2012; Leithwood, Harris, & Hopkins, 2019; Massachusetts Consortium for Innovative Education Assessment, 2018; Quintero, 2017; University of Chicago Consortium on School Research, n.d.). The chart presented in Figure 9.1 draws from this literature to suggest a menu of the types of structures and policies that might support or limit your efforts to advance equity. Our inquiry cycle may give us insights to reimagine some of them anew.

Look over the 18 dimensions displayed in Figure 9.1 with your own context in mind. Sometimes preexisting structures and policies that educators have come to take for granted stand in the way of changes they say they want. Consider the types of policies that exist in your setting in each domain, as well as the offices or individuals involved in the support and accountability for each.

Consider the effect of these structures and policies on different groups of students and on different sectors of your faculty; who makes decisions and how about resource allocation tradeoffs; and what's required in terms of communication and coordination to align these systems so that they are in sync. These reflections will help you recognize the interdependence of these systems and appreciate how complex the system is.

But here's the good news: The same inquiry cycles we engage in to improve our instructional practice can also yield invaluable data and insights about systemic barriers that challenge our change efforts—and they may even provide the clues needed to help eliminate them.

Identifying Dimensions of the System to Explore

Depending on the instructional practice you're targeting for improvement and possibly the type of practice gap you're looking to close, some of the dimensions will be more directly relevant than others. Pick two or three dimensions that represent policy areas on which your change depends, and note your choices under "Contextual Conditions" in section 2D of the i3PD planner. We'll share these with participants as potential focus areas for our collaborative goal of identifying and reforming relevant systemic barriers to equity.

Next, brainstorm some of the local structures and policies that would be worth a closer look in each dimension. For example, if you want your instructional practice to regularly include strong decisions about how you're using student profiles to inform culturally responsive math instruction, you should keep an eye on how you can prepare the culture and climate for the changes this work requires. You might look at

- **Schoolwide Expectations and Agreements.** In what ways might rebalancing cultural perspectives in math classrooms conflict with schoolwide norms and district policies and send confusing mixed messages to students?

Figure 9.1

Equity in Context: Sample Structures and Policies

We know that our schools are currently designed to produce the inequitable results we get. To untangle this problem, it can be helpful to know where to start looking for systemic inequities in our context and to consider ideas about what equitable systems might look like.

What systems does your school have in place in each of the following six domains? How do the structures and policies of your school create conditions for advancing (or limiting) equity?

	Dimensions	Sample Structures and Policies for Advancing Equity
Domain 1: Culture and Climate Supports	1A: Schoolwide Expectations and Agreements	• Soliciting and addressing stakeholders' perspectives on expectations and whether we're meeting them. • Recognizing and celebrating accomplishments. • Agreeing on and reinforcing expectations about how we treat one another.
	1B: Ownership, Engagement, and Collegiality	• Fostering students' sense of belonging. • Helping students make connections between learning and their postsecondary goals. • Preparing students to be independent learners with the skills needed for self-efficacy and self-advocacy.
	1C: Physical, Emotional, and Intellectual Safety	• Ensuring each and every student feels physically, emotionally, and intellectually safe. • Responding to student endangerment. • Using restorative practices that strengthen relationships and repair harm.
Domain 2: Teaching Supports	2A: Curriculum	• Reviewing and updating materials to ensure they meet standards for quality (e.g., standards-aligned, research-based) reflecting the diverse languages, cultures, and histories of students. • Supporting teachers to make evidence-informed decisions around differentiated implementation of a curriculum. • Evaluating and replacing or adapting curricular materials for bias.
	2B: Instruction	• Offering a variety of instructional approaches to meet students' needs. • Providing teachers with efficient access to instructional support materials, including instructional technology, data systems, and planning tools. • Ensuring teachers have adequate time and access to relevant colleagues to support effective instructional planning.
	2C: Assessment, Grading, and Feedback	• Providing grades that are based on authentic demonstrations of students' knowledge and skill and reducing the adverse impact of bias. • Ensuring students receive feedback that is clear, growth-oriented, and timely. • Empowering students to monitor their own academic progress and personal growth.

	Dimensions	Sample Structures and Policies for Advancing Equity
Domain 3: Learning Supports	3A: Student Supports and Interventions	• Ensuring that students who require special services receive them with quality (e.g., English language support, special education, social services, or mental health support). • Intervening when evidence indicates teachers' instruction is not reaching students. • Educating students and families about how they can get help when needed.
	3B: Extended Learning Opportunities	• Providing after-school, summer, and vacation programming. • Ensuring partners have the information they need to provide personalized and aligned supports to the school's students. • Evaluating the programming to ensure it is high-quality.
	3C: Student-Teacher Relationships	• Providing opportunities for students to build and maintain strong relationships with adults. • Reducing student social-emotional stress and supporting students to manage it when it occurs. • Supporting teachers to engage families as partners.
Domain 4: Structural Supports	4A: Facilities	• Providing, maintaining, and being accountable for a safe, clean, and well-maintained learning environment. • Using and sharing indoor and outdoor spaces flexibly. • Making it easy for teachers to use external facilities to enhance teaching and learning (e.g., buses, permissions, partnerships).
	4B: School Schedule and Programming	• Ensuring time, space, subjects, and students are organized and grouped to maximize teaching and learning. • Ensuring students' schedules do not limit their access. • Providing access to online and other alternative learning modes.
	4C: School Partnerships	• Connecting students to external after-school, summer, and vacation programming. • Identifying and tapping community assets to strengthen students' connections to content. • Providing career pathway exploration opportunities (e.g., internships, externships).
Domain 5: Professional Capacity	5A: Professional Learning Resources	• Providing access to the professional knowledge base (e.g., education research, professional literature, networking). • Identifying and tapping internal expertise among the faculty. • Protecting time for teachers to reflect on the effect of their own strengths, challenges, and perspectives on student learning.
	5B: Hiring/ Personnel Processes	• Ensuring the hiring of diverse and qualified personnel. • Providing adequate substitute coverage when needed. • Using insights from exiting personnel to improve working conditions.
	5C: Teacher Collaboration	• Providing sufficient time for teacher collaboration (e.g., push-in, pull-out, release, after school). • Ensuring educators have time and support for building productive relationships with one another and learning of each other's strengths. • Creating and maintaining a culture of deprivatized practice and peer learning.

(continued)

	Dimensions	Sample Structures and Policies for Advancing Equity
Domain 6: Leadership Supports	6A: Principal Leadership	• Fostering and maintaining productive working relationships with and among the faculty. • Ensuring professional growth and career advancement of all staff. • Ensuring the quality of the instructional program (e.g., adequate staffing and resources, progress monitoring, addressing issues, removing distractions).
	6B: Governance/ School-Level Decision-Making Structure	• Including stakeholder voices (teachers, families, students, community) in decisions, and as owners of school improvement efforts. • Ensuring ready access to relevant information. • Communicating about school-level decisions.
	6C: Influence of Family and Community Voice	• Ensuring that the voices and values of families and the local community inform the vision of the school. • Holding school accountable to family and community for meeting that vision. • Providing systems that allow all to participate in the language and mode that is comfortable for them.

Figure 9.1

Equity in Context: Sample Structures and Policies—(*continued*)

- **Teacher Collaboration**. How might existing professional norms about collegiality support or limit the work of establishing a schoolwide student profiles routine?
- **Teaching Supports for Curriculum, Instruction, and Assessment**. To what extent might the insights from student profiles call for changes in curriculum, instruction, and assessment tools or for new investments in professional learning?

Let's say you want to focus on teaching academic vocabulary to English language learners. In that case, you might need to ensure that the school day is structured with ample instructional time and learning supports for these students. You might look at

- **School Schedule and Programming**. To what extent are these students receiving their required instructional support minutes?
- **Hiring/Personnel Processes**. Do students have teachers who look like them? Do students have teachers who are highly qualified?
- **Student Supports and Interventions**. Are systems in place to ensure that we can identify students who need supports and offer them appropriate interventions?

Our aim here is to pay attention to the ways that the changes in classroom practice advocated in our inquiry cycle might bump up against the system beyond teachers' classrooms. We can then use these observations to look for structures and policies that are inappropriate for equity or that compete with the equitable out-comes we say we want. We'll sleuth them out and organize ourselves to uproot them.

This chapter has given you an opportunity to do some advance thinking about potential pitfalls to your work and to predict some dimensions your participants may want to focus on. In this way, you'll be better prepared to support their inquiry with examples. And the earlier chapters of Part Two directed your attention toward ways of strengthening the connections between the elements of the instructional core so that the learning experience will maximize relevance, rigor, and relationships.

You'll find an annotated version of Part Two of the planner on the next page. You can use the annotations to reflect on past or current PD experiences you've had or led, to lay plans for creating stronger core connections in upcoming professional development, or to help you plan Part Two for a new i3PD series. Next, in Part Three, we'll build on the foundation of strong core components in Part One and the plans to build critical connections among them in Part Two to design the inquiry series and plan how it will unfold across the time span available to you.

The i3PD Planning Map: Part Two—Annotated

PART TWO: Creating Connections

2A. Relevance

Purpose	Outcome-Based Objectives
Why are we doing this? Record the high- and low-altitude "why."	*What will participants be able to do after this series?*

Purpose

- We believe each and every child deserves…

- Teachers' ability to *[name the instructional practice]* is essential to that because…

- Closing this instructional practice gap is important for these specific participants, at this time, in this setting because…

Outcome-Based Objectives

If this series is successful,

1. Individual participants will (choose one)

   ☐ close their knowledge gap: They will be able to make decisions informed by a wider breadth of the knowledge and skill base for this instructional practice.

   ☐ close their implementation gap: They will be able to engage in high-quality implementation of this instructional practice.

   ☐ close their teaching-learning gap: They will be able to use this instructional practice more strategically and appropriately to strengthen students' learning processes.

   ☐ close their expectations gap: They will be able to recognize and raise artificially low expectations about what they accept as quality student work products in context of this instructional practice.

And

2. Our community of participants will use inquiry results to identify systemic barriers to equity and be able to take action together.

2B. Rigor

Process Objectives	*Evidence of Impact*

Process Objectives:
What will we do in this series to accomplish this purpose? We will engage in a four-stage inquiry process with a bifocal view of individual and organizational change.

Evidence of Impact:
What will you accept as evidence that this inquiry cycle has had the intended effect? How and when will you collect this evidence?

As individual participants, you will support one another to

- **Assess:** Identify gaps in your own instructional practice (your knowledge, implementation, strategic use, or expectations of that practice) that currently contribute to inequitable outcomes.
- **Attempt:** Design a response to the gap and a system for documenting change as you take action to close it.
- **Analyze:** Interpret evidence of change, identify challenges to change, and integrate insights into your professional practice.

As a community, we will

- **Adjust:** Reflect on patterns across our lines of inquiry to identify relevant systemic factors that inhibit equity and organize our efforts to make the changes they require.

2C. Relationships

Strengthening Trust: Respect and Personal Regard	*Clarifying Role Expectations*

Strengthening Trust: Respect and Personal Regard:
What is the preexisting level of respect and personal regard? How will you strengthen it?

Clarifying Role Expectations:
How might participants react to role expectations? What will you do to engage them in dialogue about those expectations?

(continued)

The i3PD Planning Map: Part Two—Annotated—(continued)

Strengthening Trust: Competence and Integrity	*Community Agreements*			
What is the preexisting level of confidence in one another's competence and integrity? How will you strengthen it?	Will you use existing agreements (if so, link to them here) or will you create new ones? How will you develop shared understanding and responsibility?			

2D. Seeing the System: Structures and Policies

Contextual Conditions	*Local Structures and Policies*			
Which domains and dimensions of the context are most likely to support or constrain the professional practice you are targeting?	For each, identify examples of local structures and policies that may be worth a closer look and potential data sources we could collect.			

Part Three

Designing Your Inquiry Cycle & Learning Sequence

In Part Three, you will design a four-stage inquiry cycle that will engage participants in using evidence to close their instructional gaps and prepare them to use that same evidence to identify ways the system is inequitable by design. Then, you will prepare to maximize the time and space available and the information gathered from Parts One and Two to produce agendas for a learning sequence.

10

Setting the Stage (3A)

In this chapter, we'll pay attention to how aspects of time and space that are out of your control might influence the choices you make about participants' interaction with content and how these might, in turn, influence what *is* within your control: the ways you use time and space for maximizing engagement of your participants with the content.

Because we aim to change practice, participants need sufficient time to explore new ideas, experiment with them in their classrooms, and then reflect on results and implications for their practice. This requires at least four professional learning sessions and, ideally, involves more sessions than that. Thus, you are not planning an event, but rather a *learning series*.

Whether you have multiple one-hour sessions with your participants, fewer extended day-long sessions, or something in between, the basic structure of a welcome and wrap-up with inquiry cycle work in between will provide a supportive framework participants can count on for all of them.

Many of your planning decisions, such as which connecting activities to use or which portions of the inquiry cycle to work on in each session, will depend on the needs of your participants and where you are in the sequence. But the reality of time and space also influences what's possible and how people experience it.

In theory, your topic may be compelling enough to engage your participants, but in practice, if timing and location are not working for you, they're working against you. The problem is that these factors are often fixed, not flexible. Will your professional learning experiences take place early in the morning when folks are fresh or at the end of a long school day? Will you have all-day retreats or a series of one-hour sessions? Will they fall in quick succession or with weeks in between? Will they be held in a basement, a sunlit room, or online? This chapter draws your attention to factors such as these.

Time

There's never enough time for professional learning, and busy educators don't want to waste the little time they have. It's important, therefore, to maximize every minute of the time available to you. You might start your planning by analyzing the kinds of time you *do* have.

Look at the given attributes of that time—time of day, session duration, series duration, and frequency—to predict potential challenges and take note of unforeseen opportunities. For example, if you're not confined to a certain set of dates, consider potential opportunities to align with other school rhythms: Can you sync with the formative assessment cycle and use that data? Are there one or two questions you might have teachers ask during family conferences to engage family perspectives as data? The ideas in Figure 10.1 for analyzing time may help.

These attributes of time may affect your content choice if they influence the evidence available for your inquiry cycles or the extent of participants' opportunities to experiment with changing their practice. For example, the writing samples you want to look at may not be available until after the series ends, and classroom observations of instruction are challenging to arrange during standardized testing season. It's helpful, therefore, to identify parameters of time that might be important *before* you begin planning your inquiry cycle. In section 3A of the planner, identify anything that is fixed about the date, time, and location. Then capture some notes about the special characteristics of the kinds of time you have so that you'll remember what you need to be attentive to when you begin your planning. Of course, if some of these attributes of time are flexible because your series has not yet been scheduled, you can use your reflections to design the ideal size and shape of time.

Space

The purpose of learning in community is interaction, so it's worth thinking deliberately and in advance about the ways space will enable or constrain participants' interaction. In addition, our brains need oxygen and frequent breaks, so it's important to find creative ways to move.

- **Think beyond the chair.** It's invaluable for participants to check their understandings with others and help one another discover questions they have. Short on space? Have participants simply stand and find someone they have not been sitting with to connect in new configurations.
- **Think beyond the room.** For a longer period of interaction, participants can leave the room. A change in scenery can create readiness for changing mindsets. You can create a mini-retreat feeling by inviting participants to set up a circle of chairs somewhere new. You can also invite them to pair up and take a walk while they talk over a prompt you've provided.

Figure 10.1

Analyzing Kinds of Time

		Opportunity/Challenge	Strategic Moves
Time of Day			
Early morning or middle of day		Participants may be more likely to feel fresh and ready to engage with new or challenging ideas. They may also be distracted by what they have to do next.	Consider designing a note-catcher that can help participants stay focused and that they can reference to reground themselves in session learning.
End of day		Participants' minds are in gear and already thinking about teaching and learning. They may be physically, emotionally, and mentally fatigued.	As you plan your series, build in time to begin with opportunities to reflect on the day and connect those reflections to session learning. Be sure to include energizers and movement routines.
Session Duration			
Full day		Participants can have an immersive experience and go deeper than usual. Participants may be distracted by what is going on beyond them (at home or school). Participants may become fatigued.	As you plan your series, build in sustained time for interaction and discussion. Create agreements about checking email and messages during breaks. Include opportunities for movement.
Short sessions (< 1 hour)		Participants might be more focused. You have less time to warm-up and connect.	As you plan your series, think about how you'll chunk the work into focused segments. Introduce a running note-catcher that participants can use to easily review past progress and build on it. Build in alternate ways of reinforcing relevance, rigor, and relationships, such as through asynchronous activity between meetings, so that they can hit the ground running during the sessions.
Series Duration			
Long term (> 1 semester)		Participants have a reason to invest in one another. They have the potential for deeper, more sustained change. Their attention, passion, and commitment may wane over time.	As you plan your series, foster interdependence within the group by developing routines that share ownership of the group's learning. For example, have participants plan and lead connecting activities, embedded protocols, or minilessons on skill. Be sure to communicate the plan and report on progress throughout.

(continued)

Figure 10.1

Analyzing Kinds of Time—(*continued*)

	Opportunity/Challenge	Strategic Moves
Series Duration		
Short term	Participants may be focused; there's no room/time to get lost. They may not invest in building relationships that are deep enough to push one another's thinking.	As you plan your series, use participants' interest in the outcome as leverage to help them see the value of building relationships to get there faster.
Gap Duration		
Long spaces in between sessions	Participants have plenty of time to experiment in practice and reflect between meetings. When reconnecting, they may require more time to get back into the work.	As you plan your series, think about how you will provide support and accountability for using the gaps between meetings as time to practice and reflect. Provide opportunities to connect asynchronously, (e.g., set up an email list or interactive Google Doc).
Short spaces in between sessions	Participants have less time for their attention to stray between meetings. There may not be enough time to collect data or see the effects of the learning in between sessions.	As you plan your series, think about how using cases or modeling might enable you to practice or prepare for inquiry stages when participants have not yet engaged in necessary prework themselves.

- **Think hybrid.** The COVID-19 pandemic has vastly expanded our familiarity with online tools in a way that promises to transform our interactions for good. Incorporating online tools in a face-to-face meeting or fresh new tools and apps within a virtual meeting can help spice things up and take conversations to a new level.

Analyze the space available to you and consider what you've got to work with. Figure 10.2 may help you imagine creative ways to use your space, whether it's physical, virtual, or a combination. Capture your initial ideas in section 3A of the i3PD Planning Map.

Keep in mind these possibilities as we shift attention to developing the Inquiry Cycle Map in section 3B of the planner. Decisions you make about the four-part Inquiry Cycle may influence your choices about the Welcome and Wrap-up.

	Physical Space	Virtual Space
Figure 10.2 		

Figure 10.2

Using Space for Interaction and Engagement

	Physical Space	Virtual Space
Turn and Talk	Participants stand up and discuss a question prompt with someone whom they are not sitting next to.	Randomize participants into breakout rooms for brief (1–3 minute) discussions about a question prompt.
Block Party	Participants repeat the above three times and note how their thinking evolves.	Randomize participants into breakout rooms three times in a row to engage them with different perspectives on the question prompt.
Chalk Talk	Write down a key idea, word, or question in the center of a large piece of chart paper. Then ask participants to respond in writing and by reacting to one another's comments and questions.	Have participants respond to a central question in writing using Google Docs or Word 360, then comment on and reply to one another's contributions.
Four Corners	Designate the four corners of the room with four distinct choices *or* a continuum of choices (e.g., Strongly Agree to Strongly Disagree) and invite all to choose one in response to a question prompt. Invite a two-stage conversation: 1. Talk in affinity corners. 2. Talk across corner groups to tease out similarities and distinctions in perspective.	Have participants pick a corner by self-selecting a breakout room or by signing up through any of the following: • Named arrows on a four-quadrant digital whiteboard • Sticky notes on a Jamboard • Typing names into a Google Doc Invite discussion in breakout rooms, then join together to talk across groups to tease out similarities and distinctions in perspective.
Carousel	Have participants stand in two lines and talk with the person across from them in response to a question prompt. Between each question, ask one line of participants to move one spot over so each faces a new partner.	Assign all participants to Group A or B and ask them to add this letter to their screen name. Assign A/B pairs into breakout rooms. At the end of each round, reassign or invite each B to move to the next room.
Continuum Dialogue	Designate two ends of a line on the floor with two poles of a binary topic or two opposite extremes of an issue; ask all to find a place on the line that represents their view. Notice patterns in group trends and discuss.	Have participants pick a position on the line using any of the following: • Named arrows on a line • Sticky notes on a Jamboard • Typing names into a Google Doc • Typing a number (1–10) into the chat Discuss.
Selective Stand	Invite all those who do or agree with approach X to stand up then take turns describing their experience or opinion.	Set Zoom to only show those with live cameras. Have all participants turn their cameras off, then ask them to turn on their camera if they do or agree with approach X and take turns describing their rationale.
Walkabout	Ask participants to get up and walk around together while talking.	Ask participants to call one another and use headphones or a speaker so hands are free (walking optional!).

11

Inquiry Cycle Overview (3B)

Teaching requires an inquiring mind. Because every student is different, every classroom cohort is different, every time of day is different, and every context is different, teachers must make professional judgments about what to teach, when, to whom, and in what way while acknowledging that the results cannot be perfectly predicted. Effective teachers are perpetually curious about how to increase the effect we have on our students' learning. Thus, inquiry is not an add-on; it's just good teaching.

At the same time, we benefit from occasionally moving beyond inquiry as a habit of mind and strategically pursuing more disciplined forms. More perplexing and persistent problems of practice simply require a more focused look. In disciplined inquiry, we seek to make a demonstrable difference by moving methodically through formal stages designed to help us make a strategic change and learn from the results.

The i3PD process for data inquiry (Figure 11.1) has four formal stages:

- **Assess**. We evaluate the status of our outcomes, and we set our sights on what we would like those outcomes to be.
- **Attempt**. We rethink our existing routines as we identify new, informed ways to influence the outcome, and we carry out these practices while monitoring for changes.

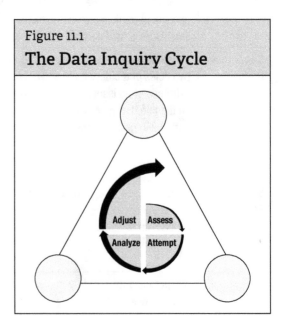

Figure 11.1
The Data Inquiry Cycle

- **Analyze**. We examine evidence of impact to understand what conditions contributed to changes, and we capture new lines of inquiry.
- **Adjust**. We reflect on what systemic changes are necessary and what we will commit to doing about them.

Examine section 3B of your i3PD Planner to familiarize yourself with the key components associated with each of these four stages. As facilitator, you'll use what you know about your participants, the content, and your context to make design choices about each component.

What Does i3PD Look Like?

The four stages of the i3PD process will look slightly different depending on whether you are interrogating a practice gap through a deductive or inductive lens and whether you will be looking at inputs (teaching practice) or outcomes (student learning). When we take a deductive approach and apply what's believed to be known about teaching and its impact to examine teaching practice, we have **knowledge gap inquiry** and when we do the same to examine students' responses to teaching, we have **teaching-learning gap inquiry**. In these cases, we're measuring ourselves against professional standards or established expectations.

On the other hand, sometimes we take an inductive approach, using our collective observations to build theory or to shape collective understandings of what we accept as "quality" or "good enough." In these cases, we pursue **implementation gap inquiry** when we're looking directly at teaching practice, and we pursue **expectations gap inquiry** when we're looking indirectly at teaching practice through student learning products.

Figure 11.2 provides descriptive illustrations of what each of the four models of inquiry might look like. These descriptions allow you to imagine the flow of the work within the professional learning series and to envision how the four stages of inquiry build upon one another to lead to higher-order changes throughout the system.

The i3PD process, as illustrated in Figure 11.1, may be similar in some ways to inquiry models your school already uses, such as instructional walkthroughs, performance evaluation cycles, instructional rounds, lesson study, data cycles, child study protocols, or looking at student work. These all aim to change practice, as does i3PD. The difference is that in i3PD we aim to use what we're learning from changes in practice to also help us understand how to change the system.

i3PD in Your Context

Use the exercise shown in Figure 11.3 to deepen understanding—for both yourself and your participants—about how i3PD compares and contrasts with other familiar

Figure 11.2

Sample Adaptations of Common Inquiry Models to i3PD

🐚 Knowledge Gap Inquiry

Some students are not benefiting from instruction informed by the highest standards of professional knowledge available. *How thorough is our knowledge about this practice?*

	Instructional Walkthroughs	Educator Performance Assessment Process
	Educators visit classrooms to see if they observe predetermined indicators in instruction.	*Educators measure their own or one another's teaching against standards for professional practice.*
Assess: Capture current reality • Standard • Status • Success Target	Starting with a **standard** list of look fors related to implementation of a particular practice or process, groups of educators visit classrooms (live or captured on video) to identify the **status** of whether (and to what extent) each of the observation indicators is in practice. They identify which indicators point to areas in which teachers' professional knowledge is weak or out of date, as well as potential contextual factors that contribute to this pattern. They use results to identify one of the indicators as a **success target** and identify what they will accept as evidence of meeting that target.	Educators begin with a set of professional **standards** that describe what teachers should know and be able to do. They then assess the current **status** of these standards in their practice by examining various forms of data, including observations (by peers, evaluators, or themselves); instructional artifacts (including planning documents, instructional tasks, and assessments); and student products and performances. Taken together, these data identify an area in which their professional knowledge may be weak or out of date, as well as potential contextual factors that contribute to this pattern. They set this standard as a **success target** and identify what they will accept as evidence of meeting that target.
Attempt: Plan and implement changes • Dig • Decide • Do and Document	Educators **dig** for new information that will narrow the gaps in their knowledge about that area of practice, and they use that knowledge to **decide** what they may need to change to update their practice. They will also make a plan to experiment with these changes and to **document** evidence of change in practice and conditions in which the changes occur.	

Analyze: **Examine and interpret evidence** • Identify • Interpret • Infer	Educators review and analyze that documentation in context of their success target to help them **identify** whether the changes they documented represent improvement. They also **interpret** the documentation for patterns that point to conditions that are supporting or limiting changes in practice, and they use this information to draw **inferences** about what they should start and stop doing from now on and what to learn and do next.
Adjust: **Commit to changes** • Structures • Suppositions • Seismic Shift	Educators then broaden their view beyond their individual learning to consider their own and their colleagues' changes in the context of organizational learning needs. By combining the results of their individual lines of inquiry, they identify **structures** that present potential barriers to equity across the system and make **suppositions** about hidden commitments that keep the community from making the changes they say they want to make. They use these analyses to identify and commit to **strategic** moves they will make together to influence the system.

⚙ Implementation Gap Inquiry

Some students are not experiencing instruction that is skillfully implemented.
How skillfully are we implementing this practice?

	Instructional Rounds	**Lesson Study**
	Educators observe and reflect on one another's instruction to develop common understandings about quality teaching.	*Educators codesign a lesson, teach and observe it, and collaboratively analyze the instructional decision making involved.*
Assess: **Capture current reality** • Standard • Status • Success Target	Educators discuss their current student data and their reflections on instruction to agree on a problem of practice related to our i3PD focus: They must identify an observable way in which their practice falls short of the **standards** they have for themselves. They observe classrooms to collect and share descriptive data about this practice, to sync understandings about the **status** of this problem of practice, and to understand where the instructional core is breaking down. This analysis leads to recommendations for next-level work; educators select one recommendation they will pursue in their own practice and identify an appropriate **success target** that describes what quality instruction looks like in that practice.	Educators select a lesson from their curriculum or past practice that employs the practices that serve as the focus of our i3PD experience. This lesson will be a starting point for defining the **standard**. They invite a volunteer from the group to teach this lesson to the rest, and they engage in critical conversation to make predictions about the **status** of the gap between the student responses that would typically result from the lesson as currently taught and their expectations for student responses in the context of skillful practice. In preparation for revising and reteaching the lesson to students, educators then set a **success target**, and, most important, they describe the changes they expect to see in the instructional process.

(continued)

Figure 11.2

Sample Adaptations of Common Inquiry Models to i3PD—(continued)

⚙️ Implementation Gap Inquiry

Some students are not experiencing instruction that is skillfully implemented.
How skillfully are we implementing this practice?

	Instructional Rounds	Lesson Study
Attempt: **Plan and implement changes** • Dig • Decide • Do and Document	Next, educators engage in dialogue to **dig** into one another's funds of knowledge and experience and to share ideas inspired by the classroom-based wisdom they have developed about what works in practice. They help one another **decide** what they might want to do or change to effectively meet their success targets, and they create a plan to make the change. They also arrange to **document** evidence of changes in what they're doing and the effect of those changes on students and conditions in which the changes occur.	Next, educators engage in dialogue to **dig** into research and one another's funds of knowledge and experience. They help one another **decide** how to redesign the lesson to effectively meet their success targets, and they create a plan to make the change. They also arrange to observe the retaught lesson to **document** evidence of changes in what they're doing and the effect of those changes on students and conditions in which the changes occur.
Analyze: **Examine and interpret evidence** • Identify • Interpret • Infer	Educators review and analyze that documentation in context of their success target to help them **identify** whether the changes they documented represent improvement. They also **interpret** the documentation for patterns that point to conditions that are supporting or limiting changes in practice, and they use this information to draw **inferences** about what they should start and stop doing from now on and what to learn and do next.	Educators review and analyze that documentation in context of their success target to help them **identify** whether the changes they documented represent improvement. They also **interpret** the documentation for patterns that point to conditions that are supporting or limiting changes in practice, and they use this information to draw **inferences** about what they should start and stop doing from now on and what to learn and do next.
Adjust: **Commit to changes** • Structures • Suppositions • Seismic Shift	Educators then broaden their view beyond their individual learning to see their own and their colleagues' changes in the context of organizational learning needs. By combining the results of their individual lines of inquiry, they identify **structures** that present potential barriers to equity across the system and make **suppositions** about hidden commitments that are keeping the community from making the changes they say they want to make. They use these analyses to identify and commit to **strategic** moves they will make together to influence the system.	Educators then broaden their view beyond their individual learning to see their own and their colleagues' changes in the context of organizational learning needs. By combining the results of their individual lines of inquiry, they identify **structures** that present potential barriers to equity across the system and make **suppositions** about hidden commitments that are keeping the community from making the changes they say they want to make. They use these analyses to identify and commit to **strategic** moves they will make together to influence the system.

🍳 Teaching-Learning Gap Inquiry

Some students are not being taught in the way that improves their learning processes.
How responsively are we making implementation choices about this practice?

	Data Cycles	LASW Protocols
	Educators drill down from summative to formative data to help them identify where student learning processes are breaking down and how to best help them strengthen them.	*Educators "look at student work" (LASW) to better understand the students' thinking processes and work routines that produced the work.*
Assess: Capture current reality • Standard • Status • Success Target	Educators look at student data from **standards**-based assessments and identify patterns that point to differences between the effect their instructional choices have on individual students' learning and the effect they want it to have. This view reveals the **status** of which students or groups of students are not effectively learning from them, but it doesn't tell us why. Educators then probe for additional knowledge of students to illuminate the students' learning processes. Educators use these data to inform their choice of a student learning standard or an indicator to use as an appropriate **success target**, and, most important, they also describe the changes they expect to see in students' learning processes.	A presenting teacher identifies a student whose work falls below the expected **standard** for performance. They select and examine with colleagues a collection of student work artifacts that provide a window into the student's process of working, such as multiple drafts of a writing project or a video of the student working on a product. Together, they discern the **status** of the students' learning process, reflect on what the student is or is not yet doing to learn, and identify probing questions that help the presenting teacher consider what they are and are not yet doing to meet the student where they are. With commitment to making a shift in their own instructional choices, the teacher sets a **success target** that describes the changes they expect to see in students' work if they are successful in making instructional shifts appropriately.
Attempt: Plan and implement changes • Dig • Decide • Do and Document	Next, educators must **dig** to deepen their knowledge about the student (or student group) and the content standard to make instructional choices informed by a clearer view of what they might expect to see students doing to learn and meet the standard. They **decide** what they need to do or change to effectively coach these students to meet the success target. They also make a plan to **document** evidence of changes in what students are doing and learning and the conditions in which the changes occur.	Next, informed by dialogue with colleagues about what they might expect to see the student doing to learn and meet the standard, the teacher **digs** for new knowledge about the student and the content standard that can help them make instructional choices that will effectively develop students' learning processes. They **decide** what they need to do or change to effectively coach the student to meet the success target. They also make a plan to **document** evidence of changes in what the student is doing and learning and conditions in which the changes occur.

(continued)

Figure 11.2

Sample Adaptations of Common Inquiry Models to i3PD—(continued)

● Teaching–Learning Gap Inquiry

Some students are not being taught in the way that improves their learning processes.
How responsively are we making implementation choices about this practice?

	Data Cycles	LASW Protocols
Analyze: **Examine and interpret evidence** • Identify • Interpret • Infer	Educators review and analyze that documentation in context of their success target to help them **identify** whether the changes they documented represent improvement. They also **interpret** the documentation for patterns that point to conditions that are supporting or limiting changes in practice, and they use this information to draw **inferences** about what they should start and stop doing from now on and what to learn and do next.	
Adjust: **Commit to changes** • Structures • Suppositions • Seismic Shift	Educators then broaden their view beyond their individual learning to see their own and their colleagues' changes in the context of organizational learning needs. By combining the results of their individual lines of inquiry, they identify **structures** that present potential barriers to equity across the system and make **suppositions** about hidden commitments that are keeping the community from making the changes they say they want to make. They use these analyses to identify and commit to **strategic** moves they will make together to influence the system.	

🧑‍🤝‍🧑 Expectations Gap Inquiry

Some students are not supported to meet high expectations.
How authentically are we estimating our effectiveness with this practice?

	Perspective Protocols	Refining Protocols
	Educators look together at student work to gain new insights and perspectives on the effectiveness of supports & accountability for quality work.	*Educators look together at work so teachers can refine or improve the work's alignment with its purpose.*

Assess: **Capture current reality** • Standard • Status • Success Target	Educators examine and describe student work to help one another make observations and interpretations they would not have made of the work on their own. They use these observations to describe the **standards** the work appears to meet. They then compare this observed standard with the expected standard, effectively determining the **status** of whether students have met expectations. This analysis leads participants to identify implications for classroom practice. Educators select a recommendation they will pursue to support students in meeting expectations, and they identify an appropriate **success target** that describes what they expect quality student work to look like in this cycle.	Educators examine one or more teaching or learning artifacts through the lens of a focusing question about the **standards** the work was designed to meet. Participants examine the work and describe the **status** of whether and to what extent the work aligns with its purpose. This analysis leads participants to identify implications for what the presenting teacher might change to improve alignment. They identify an appropriate **success target** that describes what they expect quality student work to look like in this cycle.
Attempt: **Plan and implement changes** • Dig • Decide • Do and Document	Next, educators engage in dialogue to **dig** into one another's funds of knowledge and experience and to share ideas about setting and supporting students to meet high expectations. They help one another **decide** what they might want to do or change to effectively meet their success targets, and they create a plan to make the change. They also arrange to **document** evidence of changes in what they're doing and the effects of those changes on students and conditions in which the changes occur.	Next, educators engage in dialogue to **dig** into research and one another's funds of knowledge and experience. They help one another **decide** how to achieve better alignment between the expectations and the work students are producing, and they create a plan to make the change. They also arrange to **document** evidence of changes in what they're doing and the effects of those changes on students and conditions in which the changes occur.
Analyze: **Examine and interpret evidence** • Identify • Interpret • Infer	Educators review and analyze that documentation in context of their success target to help them **identify** whether the changes they documented represent improvement. They also **interpret** the documentation for patterns that point to conditions that are supporting or limiting changes in practice, and they use this information to draw **inferences** about what they should start and stop doing from now on and what to learn and do next.	
Adjust: **Commit to changes** • Structures • Suppositions • Seismic Shift	Educators then broaden their view beyond their individual learning to see their own and their colleagues' changes in the context of organizational learning needs. By combining the results of their individual lines of inquiry, they identify **structures** that present potential barriers to equity across the system and make **suppositions** about hidden commitments that are keeping the community from making the changes they say they want to make. They use these analyses to identify and commit to **strategic** moves they will make together to influence the system.	

inquiry frameworks. Examine the first two columns to investigate how the components of two popular inquiry frameworks serve purposes similar to the four stages of the i3PD framework. Then analyze inquiry routines from your context in the last column.

Once completed, you can use this page as a planning tool to help you build on existing routines instead of replacing them as you design an inquiry cycle focused on interrogating inequity. You can also share this figure with your participants to help them explore how your inquiry cycle will be familiar but distinctive.

In the four chapters that follow, you will think deeply about each of the four stages of the i3PD inquiry cycle in turn and capture ideas about how to enact each in your context. Within each chapter, find and focus on the section that addresses the model of inquiry that you aim to pursue. Use the guidance provided to help you develop section 3B of the i3PD planner. Make decisions about implementation as you read, capturing notes about what you will do and how long you might need for each step in the planner. Don't forget to consider what participants can do independently or in small groups between sessions. Also, be sure to use what you know about your content, participants, and context as you plan out each stage.

	Data Wise	NBPTS Architecture of Accomplished Teaching	My Local Framework (Add your own here.)
Assess Capture current reality <ul><li>Standard</li><li>Status</li><li>Success Target</li></ul>	<ul><li>Create data overview.</li><li>Dig into student data.</li></ul>	<ul><li>Your students: Who are they? Where are they now? What do they need and in what order? Where should I begin?</li><li>Set high worthwhile goals appropriate for these students, at this time, in this setting.</li></ul>	
Attempt Plan and implement changes <ul><li>Dig</li><li>Decide</li><li>Do and Document</li></ul>	<ul><li>Examine instruction.</li><li>Develop action plan.</li><li>Plan to assess progress.</li><li>Act and assess.</li></ul>	<ul><li>Implement instruction designed to attain those goals.</li><li>Evaluate student learning in light of the goals and the instruction.</li></ul>	
Analyze Examine and interpret evidence <ul><li>Identify</li><li>Interpret</li><li>Infer</li></ul>	<ul><li>Create data overview.</li><li>Dig into student data.</li></ul>	<ul><li>Reflect on student learning, the effectiveness of the instructional design, and particular concerns and issues.</li></ul>	
Adjust Commit to changes <ul><li>Structures</li><li>Suppositions</li><li>Seismic Shifts</li></ul>			

Figure 11.3

Inquiry Cycle Comparison

Sources: Adapted from *Data Wise: A Step-By-Step Guide to Using Assessment Results to Improve Teaching and Learning,* by K.P. Boudett, E.A. City, and R.J. Murnane, 2005, Cambridge MA: Harvard Education Press; and from National Board for Professional Teaching Standards. (2016). *Architecture of Accomplished Teaching.* Retrieved from www.accomplishedteacher.org/resource/the-architecture-of-accomplished-teaching/

Note: A fillable PDF version of this figure is available as part of the Digital Tool Collection. See Appendix A for more information.

12

Inquiry Stage One: Assess (3B)

In the **Assess** stage, we evaluate the current status of our outcomes and set our sights on what we would like those outcomes to be. To accomplish this, participants will need to sync their understandings of the **standard** to use in this cycle, describe the current **status** of the gap and context, and establish a **success** target.

The Inquiry Cycle Map in section 3B of the i3PD planner identifies the three guiding questions for the Assess stage as follows:

- **Standard**: How will participants define the professional standard of this instructional practice?
- **Status**: How will participants identify the gap between this standard and their current practice, and how will they identify what contextual factors might contribute to that gap?
- **Success Target**: How will participants establish a target for improved practice?

In earlier chapters, you decided on a model of inquiry. Now, with section 3B of the i3PD planner in hand, skip ahead to the section of this chapter that addresses your model of inquiry and review the suggestions on how to guide participants in establishing the standard, the current status, and the success target for your inquiry cycle.

Figure 12.1 provides an overview of the key questions from the Assess stage in language that can help you more clearly compare and contrast how the work of capturing current reality is approached differently across the four models of inquiry.

Figure 12.1

Inquiry Stage One: Assess

	Knowledge Gap Inquiry	Implementation Gap Inquiry	Teaching-Learning Gap Inquiry	Expectations Gap Inquiry
Standard	What does **the professional standard** suggest **teachers** should be doing?	What do **we believe** **teachers** should be doing?	What does **the professional standard** suggest **students** should be doing?	What do **we believe** **students** should be doing?
Status	What is the gap between this standard and my current practice?			
	What contextual factors might be contributing to the gap?			
Success Target	By the end of this cycle, what will look different if we succeed in improving our **knowledge of this instructional practice**?	By the end of this cycle, what will look different if we succeed in improving the **implementation quality of our instructional practice**?	By the end of this cycle, what will look different if we succeed in improving our **students' learning processes**?	By the end of this cycle, what will look different if we succeed in improving our **students' work products**?

Knowledge Gap Inquiry: Standard, Status, Success Target

This model of inquiry addresses the need for participants to extend their professional knowledge base beyond what they already know and can do about a specific instructional practice.

Standard

What does the professional standard suggest teachers should be doing with regard to this practice?

To begin, you'll want participants to synchronize their understandings and develop shared language about the instructional practice that will be the focus of inquiry. If your school or district does *not* already have standards describing this practice, visit the work of relevant professional associations, research collaboratives, or other education partners to identify research-informed descriptions of the practice. Identify professional literature such as books, articles, podcasts, or YouTube videos or draw upon those participants might offer. Then, identify conversation protocols that you can provide to support participants in having discussions that lead to shared language and understanding. For example, explore the book *Meeting Goals* (Van Soelen, 2021) or the website of School Reform Initiative for ideas.

Look for a research-informed rubric, a performance checklist, or any other articulation of implementation quality for this practice; if you don't find one, participants can use their research to draft one.

If the practice is new to participants, build in time for activities that will help them unpack this new practice and understand how it relates to other areas of their practice. Establishing the standard is the most important phase of knowledge gap inquiry, and you should plan to spend plenty of time here.

Status

What is the gap between this standard and their current practice, and what contextual factors might be contributing to that gap?

To prepare to support participants as they establish the status of the gap, decide how you will have them measure themselves against these practice standards. Considering the type of practice targeted and the logistics of your context, you might propose a quick self-reporting survey; organize a classroom walkthrough (live or on video); or have participants collaboratively examine instructional artifacts (including planning documents, instructional tasks, and assessment tools) to help them identify patterns in how their current practice does and doesn't align with the standard. They will use this data to name the practice gap.

Although this cycle will focus on what participants need to change to close the knowledge gap in their instructional practice, a variety of contextual conditions also contribute to the gap. These include both collective mindsets (explored in section 1D) and systemic routines and processes (explored in section 2D). Decide here whether you will engage participants in the Immunity Map exercise from section 1D, or simply share the examples you previously identified of collective mindsets that could potentially get in the way of the changes they seek. What self-protective commitments keep us from being active consumers of our professional knowledge base? This is a chance to hear participants' views on these mindsets (or others they identify) and for them to hear how you've designed this experience to be a safe space to question these mindsets.

Similarly, determine whether you will take time to collaborate with participants in deciding which systemic structures and policies you'll keep your eyes on during the inquiry cycle (section 2D and Figure 9.1), or whether you will simply suggest a few systems for participants to focus their attention on. What local structures and policies make it challenging for us to be active consumers of our professional knowledge base? Build in as much time as you can to agree upon the collective mindsets and systemic structures and policies that may threaten your efforts to close your knowledge gap, then hypothesize together about how these key contextual factors keep you from closing that gap.

Success Target

What will look different by the end of this cycle if we succeed in improving our instructional practice?

Here you will help participants articulate what they will accept as evidence of improvement in this inquiry cycle. Remember, the cycle aims to *change practice*. Even though we expect changes in practice to make a difference for student learning, participants' goals should describe what, specifically, they expect to see change in practice and how they will know the change is an improvement. This may require multiple forms of evidence.

Chapter 7 shared some ideas about different types of evidence to which teachers might look, and you did some initial brainstorming about ways to collect evidence of impact in section 2B. Plan to use your ideas as examples and prepare to share strategies for collecting these forms of evidence.

Invite participants to revisit their earlier thinking about the standard of practice to help them point to what they would look at to see that the changes are *improvements*. In some cases, you may have to commit time to further refinement of the descriptors so that they are specific enough to serve as success targets. This is a worthwhile exercise that can further deepen understanding and shared language.

Implementation Gap Inquiry: Standard, Status, Success Target

This model of inquiry supports participants to develop skillful implementation of a particular instructional practice.

Standard

What do we believe teachers should be doing with regard to this practice?

Plan to start your investigation of skillful implementation by synchronizing the understandings about this practice among the professionals in the room. This model of inquiry assumes participants have basic knowledge about this practice but fall short in putting that knowledge into practice. You may want to gather articles and other resources that participants can reference as they define the practice and refine implementation standards together. In this first step, participants will collaboratively articulate the standards of practice they fall short of.

To activate what participants know about the practice and engage them in thinking together about what makes quality implementation, you can engage them, for example, in screening lesson artifacts (such as videos and lesson plans) and discerning together which are examples of high-level practice. This shared experience will provide a strong foundation for the work of articulating an implementation standard. Next, challenge participants to create a list of "look-fors" that describe their conceptions of high-level practice, or develop a rubric that describes practice at multiple levels. They will test and further develop these draft standards throughout the inquiry cycle.

Status

What is the gap between this standard and their current practice, and what contextual factors might be contributing to that gap?

In the next step, provide an opportunity for participants to measure themselves against the draft standards they have collaboratively established. This might involve observing one another's instruction (live or by video); conducting environmental walkthroughs; or exploring instructional artifacts, such as lesson plans, student assignments, and units of study. It should also involve evidence of students' responses, such as observations of student work, observations of students at work, or student interviews. Participants should use these data to be as specific as possible in describing what the gap looks like in their own practice.

Although this cycle will focus on what participants need to change to close the skill gap in their instructional practice, a variety of contextual conditions also contribute to the gap. These include both collective mindsets (explored in section 1D) and systemic routines and processes (explored in section 2D). Decide here whether you will engage participants in the Immunity Map exercise from section 1D, or simply share the examples you previously identified of collective mindsets that could potentially get in the way of the changes they seek. What self-protective commitments keep us from doing what we need to do to improve the quality of our implementation? This is a chance to hear participants views on these mindsets (or others they identify) and for them to hear how you've designed this experience to be a safe space to challenge these mindsets.

Similarly, determine whether you will take time to collaborate with participants in deciding which systemic structures and policies you'll keep your eyes on during the inquiry cycle (section 2D and Figure 9.1), or whether you will simply suggest a few systems as the focus of their attention. What local structures and policies work against our efforts to become skillful practitioners? Build in as much time as you can to agree upon the collective mindsets and systemic structures and policies that may threaten your efforts to close your implementation gap and hypothesize together about how these key contextual factors keep you from closing that gap.

Success Target

What will look different by the end of this cycle if we succeed in improving our implementation of instructional practice?

Participants have already thought together about their shared definition of high-level practice. Now they will think individually about their own success target. Because this cycle aims to change practice and participants are each on their own improvement journey, you will want to build in time—within your sessions or between them—for participants to describe what they expect to see themselves doing more skillfully and describing what that would look like. They can draw directly from the "look-fors" or rubrics they have created as they articulate what they will accept as evidence of improvement in this inquiry cycle.

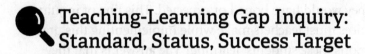

Teaching-Learning Gap Inquiry: Standard, Status, Success Target

This model of inquiry pursues the challenge of implementing instructional practices responsively so that they effectively improve what and how students learn.

Standard

What does the professional standard for this practice suggest students should be doing?

You've already identified an instructional practice as the focus of this inquiry. What, exactly, are we expecting this instructional practice will do for students?

It's worthwhile to begin by ensuring participants all have the same idea of what the practice is. You can support participants to develop shared understanding and language about this practice and what it means to do it skillfully by having them read and discuss a key article, explore relevant resources, or watch and analyze videos of the practice in action. Any instructional practice has decision points. That is, teachers have choices to make about timing, process, pace, materials, and other factors as they implement the practice in a way that is responsive to students. Invite participants to unpack their definition by identifying (listing or describing) the many discretionary points within the practice. These will become important later as your participants inquire about why the practice might not be having the expected impact on students.

Next, turn participants' attention to how this practice is meant to engage students with content and what one might see if it did. Focus on both the products and the processes of students' work. Most content areas have state or national standards that set expectations for what students should be producing. Decide together which sets of standards are most relevant for your line of inquiry. There is less clear guidance for teachers on the processes students must develop and demonstrate to be effective at learning. Support participants to tap professional literature that can help them to identify the range of deeper learning competencies, information-processing routines, executive functioning skills, and work habits we must teach students to employ independently for this instructional practice to have the intended impact on student's work. (See for example Hammond, 2014; McTighe & Silver, 2020; Newhall, 2014; Noguera, 2017.)

Status

What is the gap between this standard and their current practice, and what contextual factors might be contributing to that gap?

Have participants select a particular student (or group of students, such as Spotlight Students who share a similar learning profile) whose response to this instructional practice is not what they would have hoped or expected. This line of inquiry asks: What instructional choices must teachers make while implementing this practice so that it effectively supports these students' learning? The answer is that they need to implement the practice with greater responsiveness to the student. There is a gap between what we believe this instructional practice can do for students and what it is currently doing.

To describe the gap, participants should think about the ways they expected this practice to shape the interactions that happen between students and content and reflect on what is getting in the way. To do so, it is ideal to watch the student doing the work (live or on video). Participants can then use what they see the student doing or not doing to help them to hypothesize which aspects of practice they were not implementing strategically or appropriately for these students. Where observation is not possible, students' work artifacts, their reflection logs, or conferencing conversations can help participants to home in on the gap.

Although this inquiry cycle will focus on what participants need to change to close the gap in the responsiveness of their instructional practice, a variety of contextual conditions also contribute to the gap. These include both collective mindsets (explored in section 1D) and systemic routines and processes (explored in section 2D). Decide here whether you will engage participants in the Immunity Map exercise from section 1D, or simply share the examples you previously identified of collective mindsets that could potentially get in the way of the changes they seek. What self-protective commitments keep us from implementing instructional practices with responsiveness? This is a chance to hear participants' views on these mindsets (or others they identify) and for them to hear how you've designed this experience to be a safe space to challenge these mindsets.

Similarly, determine whether you will take time to collaborate with participants in deciding which systemic structures and policies you'll keep your eyes on during the inquiry cycle (section 2D and Figure 9.1), or whether you will simply suggest a few systems for participants to focus their attention on. What local structures and policies make it challenging for us to effectively be responsive to students' individual needs? Build in as much time as you can to agree upon the collective mindsets and systemic structures and policies that may threaten your efforts to close your teaching-learning gap and hypothesize together about how these key contextual factors keep you from closing that gap.

Success Target

What will look different by the end of this cycle if our changes in instructional practice succeed in improving students' learning processes and products?

Charge participants with identifying the specific student learning standards that they aim to support their Spotlight Students to acquire with this instructional practice during this inquiry. And, more important, challenge them to identify and name the requisite deeper learning competencies, learning dispositions, information-processing habits, executive functioning skills, or work habits they expect to see students demonstrating if they have implemented the instructional practice effectively. We're interested in both what and how students are learning.

Expectations Gap Inquiry: Standard, Status, Success Target

This model of inquiry explores the challenge of how to recognize and raise low expectations so that we hold ourselves accountable for the impact of the instructional practice on students' work.

Standard

What do we believe students should be doing in the context of this practice?

As the facilitator, you would like to assume that participants have some basic knowledge about what the practice is, can implement it skillfully, and can implement it effectively, but you don't know that for sure. Before you focus your participants' attention on predicting the student work expectations of that practice, take time to synchronize understandings about what the targeted instructional practice is and how it is expected to influence students' learning. You can do this by having them read and discuss a key article, explore relevant resources, or watch and analyze videos of the practice in action.

Turning your attention next to the expected impact of this practice on students, provide participants with time and structure to collaboratively articulate their expectations. Rather than turning to content standards and process objectives that have been established externally, invite participants to collect and examine relevant artifacts from their classrooms in search of their own shared language that describes the impact they expect this instructional practice to have on their students. They might inspect student work samples, live classroom observations, video-recorded student performances, instructional artifacts, or other objects as they debate what "success" looks like and push each other's thinking about how to establish a high standard.

Status

What is the gap between this standard and their current practice, and what contextual factors might be contributing to that gap?

Next, participants should look more closely at their own work and characterize the gap between what they see and the standard set above. Make time for participants to share their characterizations with one another. They can help one another make astute observations and deeper interpretations about how student work measures up to the standard. You want them to come away with a rich description that clearly describes the gap between the impact they expect this instructional practice to have on their students and the impact it has been demonstrated to have.

Although this inquiry cycle will focus on what participants need to change to close the gap in their student work expectations, a variety of contextual conditions also contribute to the gap. These include both collective mindsets (explored in section 1D) and systemic routines and processes (explored in section 2D). Decide here whether you will engage participants in the Immunity Map exercise from section 1D, or simply share the examples you previously identified of collective mindsets that could potentially get in the way of the changes they seek. What self-protective commitments keep us from maintaining high expectations for student work? This is a chance to hear participants' views on these mindsets (or others they identify) and for them to hear how you've designed this experience to be a safe space to challenge those views.

Similarly, determine whether you will take time to collaborate with participants in deciding which systemic structures and policies you'll keep your eyes on during the inquiry cycle (section 2D and Figure 9.1), or whether you will suggest a few systems for participants to focus their attention on. What local structures and policies make it challenging for us to effectively establish and maintain high expectations for student work? Build in as much time as you can to agree upon the collective mindsets and systemic structures and policies that may threaten your efforts to close your expectations gap and hypothesize together about how these key contextual factors keep you from closing that gap.

Success Target

What will look different by the end of this cycle if our changes in instructional practice succeed in improving the quality of students' learning processes or products?

Your cycle will support participants as they make changes in practice that help them to recognize when they are not holding students to high expectations or sufficiently supporting them to meet those expectations. What might this look like? Guide participants in setting their own targets for what they will accept as evidence of improvement in this inquiry cycle. Their target should describe how, specifically, they expect to see student work improve if they are successful in making the needed changes to their practice.

Pulling It Together

Use the space in section 3B of your i3PD planner to plan how you will engage participants in each requirement of this stage: syncing understandings of the **standard** to use in this cycle, describing the current **status** of the gap and the context, and establishing a **success** target.

Note that some of these components require synchronous collaboration time, whereas others can happen asynchronously before or between sessions. You can revisit the tips on timing provided earlier in this chapter after mapping out each stage of the process.

13

Inquiry Stage Two: Attempt (3B)

In the **Attempt** stage, we rethink our existing routines as we identify new, informed ways to influence the outcome, and we carry them out while monitoring for changes. To accomplish this, participants will need to **dig** for new information that can help them **decide** what to change. Then they will **document** the changes they make and the effects of these changes on students as they occur.

You'll find the three key planning questions for this stage in section 3B of the i3PD planner and in Figure 13.1. The three key components of the Attempt stage (dig, decide, and do and document) have only subtle differences across the four inquiry models. Your moves as facilitator are similar regardless of your model. Use what you know about your content, participants, and context, together with the suggestions that follow, to plan out this stage.

Dig

How will participants gain new knowledge to assist them in closing the gap and meeting the success target?

If your participants already knew what to do, when to do it, and how to do it well, they would surely already be doing it. They need to do something different, and we should not assume they know *how* to make this change.

You will have to determine to what extent this will be a teacher-directed or learner-directed activity. Based on your own professional knowledge, the resources available to you, the knowledge participants bring, and the time you have with them, you might decide to provide new information; engage participants in finding new information or sharing their expertise; or do something in between, such as providing vetted options from which participants can choose. Following are some ideas for how to elevate new knowledge relative to each inquiry model.

Figure 13.1 **Inquiry Stage Two: Attempt**				
	Knowledge Gap Inquiry	**Implementation Gap Inquiry**	**Teaching-Learning Gap Inquiry**	**Expectations Gap Inquiry**
Dig	How will I gain new knowledge to apply to close the gap between the **standard of knowledge on this topic and the knowledge informing my current practice?**	How will I gain new knowledge to apply to close the gap between our **shared expectation for quality implementation and my current implementation in practice?**	How will I gain new knowledge to apply to close the gap between the **standard of what my students need to do and what my current practice engages them in doing?**	How will I gain new knowledge to apply to close the gap between our **shared expectation for quality student work and the work my current practice produces?**
Decide	What will I start doing, continue doing differently, and stop doing?			
Do and Document	How will I track what I actually do, the effect of these changes, and contextual factors that matter?			

For a Knowledge Gap Inquiry

In the Assess stage we sought to define the practice. Now we want to dig deeper to learn how it works and what conditions are known to be important in decisions about implementation. For this inquiry model, new knowledge about the topic may come from professional associations, education publishers, education research clearinghouses, or other education partners. If we're interested in equity, we should be committed to making sure the decisions we make for our students are informed by the latest advances in pedagogy, the science of learning, and other fields relevant to our inquiry. Identify articles, books, and other tools you can share or explore together with participants.

You might start with education research clearinghouses, such as the U.S. Department of Education's What Works Clearinghouse or Regional Educational Laboratories; some states have their own, such as the Ohio Evidence-Based Clearinghouse. You might also investigate the websites of professional associations. The National Board for Professional Teaching Standards (NBPTS) has standards for accomplished teaching in 31 subject areas and developmental levels (n.d.). Other associations may serve as rich sources of information in specific areas. See, for example, the National Council of Teachers of Mathematics; the International Reading Association; TESOL International Association (formerly Teachers of English to Speakers of Other Languages); the National Association of Special Education Teachers; and Learning for Justice (formerly Teaching Tolerance). A search in Google Scholar or within the catalogues of relevant publishers of education materials can also be fruitful.

For a Teaching-Learning Gap Inquiry

For this inquiry model, participants aim to become more skillful at implementing a practice in a way that helps students interact with content effectively. They may need to do some digging to deepen both their knowledge of the student and their knowledge of the content.

Invite participants to share and research ways of deepening their knowledge of students both as individuals and as learners. Two resources that may be useful starting points are the book *Yardsticks: Child and Adolescent Development Ages 4–14* by Chip Wood (2018) and the free, downloadable NBPTS standards for accomplished teaching available from www.nbpts.org. Each of these 31 sets of standards (for each content area and grade level) begins with "Knowledge of Students." Participants can use these two sources to consider the many dimensions they might compile in a student profile, including evidence of students' intellectual, social, physical, ethical, or emotional development.

To support teachers to hone their knowledge of the content, consider some of the ideas shared in the knowledge gap inquiry section above. Create time and space for participants to share what they already know and what they are learning as many teachers will have favorite curricular resources to recommend. Teachers frequently turn to the internet; decide if you need to offer a cautionary minilesson on vetting resources.

For Implementation and Expectations Gap Inquiries

For these two inquiry models, colleagues look to one another for new knowledge. The goal is to share our own expertise and experiences and push one another's thinking about what we'll accept as "skillful teaching practice" or "quality student work." Our expertise and experience are, of course, influenced by the knowledge base, but because we're interested in equity, we also want to remain vigilant in considering perspectives and voices the knowledge base has failed to include. Historically, researchers and publishers of best practices have been a rather homogeneous group that mirrors neither the teaching workforce nor the student population served by U.S. schools.

By taking time to tap the wisdom emerging directly from our colleagues, this model provides access to grounded knowledge in service of our students.

Although each model of inquiry seeks to close a different kind of gap, the repertoire of moves you might employ to help participants dig through this new knowledge and make sense of it together is the same. In this stage of inquiry, colleagues might be reading and using text-based discussion protocols, teaching one another directly, or forming study groups to extend their knowledge about how to more effectively employ the instructional practice that is the target of their shared inquiry.

How will they know when they're done? Participants are done when they have discovered

- New aspects of the target practice they were previously unaware of or new understandings of aspects they were already familiar with, which drives them to want to try out these new ideas in practice.
- New understandings about the variations of the practice and the conditions under which the practice is most appropriate, which drives them to want to identify or create the appropriate conditions for implementing the practice for maximum effect.
- New perspectives on what is considered quality implementation of the practice, which drives them to want to meet that bar.
- New ways of evaluating the effect of this practice, which can open their minds to ancillary impacts of the practice, such as on school culture or family engagement.

Decide

How will participants decide what they will start doing, continue doing differently, and stop doing entirely?

Although your participants are all focused on the same general professional practice, they may have established unique success targets as part of the Assess stage of the inquiry cycle. In addition, they each have unique characteristics regarding their current context and their Spotlight Students. Thus, they have to work individually to decide how they will test their new knowledge in service of their success target. They have to decide what kind of change they will make in practice.

If the change involves implementing a practice or strategy, participants should review their upcoming unit plans and consider appropriate opportunities to experiment with that change. If the new idea involves an approach or a perspective, they may want to do some reflective writing to think through ways this approach calls for changes in practice. In either case, they should also consider ways in which existing practices and perspectives may no longer be necessary or may conflict with the proposed change and prepare to pause them.

Working as community, participants can help one another create and strengthen their plans for change. The following are examples of approaches they might use to do so.

Deep dive. Participants with similar targets can collaborate to map out the benefits and limitations of various options and make decisions together.

Quick chat. In small groups, participants can generate and explore additional options to help them look past the immediate hunch.

Online efforts. After participants work individually to identify a change they believe they should make and their rationale for making it, they can share this information electronically and respond to one another with probing questions to help colleagues consider possibilities and avoid blind spots.

Quick chat or online efforts. Invite participants to calculate the costs of experimenting with various changes in practice. These are high-impact changes, and we want to consider the proper scope for this experiment so that the pros will be sure to outweigh potential cons.

- Invite participants to brainstorm factors that contribute to the cost of trying this, such as time, effort, imposing on others, opportunity costs, wasted materials, reputation risk, and so on.
- For each proposed experiment, identify ways to scale it down to reduce the cost—for example, by involving fewer people, collaborating to reduce effort, or reducing the scope of the experiment.
- Post each factor with scaled-down ideas to a discussion thread, an online bulletin board, or using online sticky notes.

Knowing *what* they will change doesn't necessarily mean they are *ready* for the change, but they do already have two reasons to embrace the challenging work of changing their practice: The change aligns with shared values and commitments of their school, and the change seeks to make a demonstrable difference to targets that are important to them. Some participants may also have two more reasons to lean in to this change: Digging in the literature may have given them a sense of optimism about their plan, and collaborating with colleagues may have provided an encouraging view of ways this practice has worked for others in their very own context.

Once participants are feeling confident about the change they plan to make in their practice to influence their success target, they will need to develop an action plan that can help them coordinate implementation of the changes with other individuals involved, secure resources, and align with other actions underway in the school. Figure 13.2 shows an Action Planning Template that you can offer your participants.

As part of that plan, participants should brainstorm intermediate indicators of change to look for while pursuing the success target. There's no sense waiting until the end to find out if we're making a difference. In addition, they should also

Figure 13.2			
Action Planning Template			
Action Plan			
Action Steps What will you do?	**Individuals Involved** Which colleagues and students are involved? With whom do you need to coordinate?	**Resources** What resources are needed (e.g., people, time, training, materials)?	**Timeline** On what day and at what time will this step occur? Provide start and end dates.
Observation Alerts			
Indicators of Change What intermediate indicators of change will you look for while pursuing the success target? (Be sure to observe your Spotlight Students.)		**Contextual Conditions** How will you document contextual conditions that might support or limit impact?	

Note: A fillable PDF version of this figure is available as part of the Digital Tool Collection. See Appendix A for more information.

be deliberately attentive to any contextual conditions that might support or limit impact. (Revisit Figure 9.1 as necessary.) They might assess these informally, such as by observing the level of trust within a team, reviewing existing data on parent involvement, or tracking the opportunities teachers have for professional interaction with colleagues. Or they might assess the context formally, such as by conducting a survey of colleagues, interviewing students, or doing a comprehensive audit of instructional materials. If participants are all in the same context, they can narrow down the contextual conditions to ones that are important enough to the success target to warrant attention and develop agreements about how to document them together. Whether collected individually or together, these data will come in handy in context of the fourth stage of inquiry: Adjust.

Do and Document

How will participants decide how to track what they actually do, the effect of these changes, and the contextual factors that matter?

At this point, participants should begin to implement their action plans. But even the best-laid plans are subject to change. Perhaps the resources you expected to use turned out to be unavailable, the students you wanted to reach were absent, or the first steps you took helped you recognize an oversight in your planning. Because we're interested in changing practice and understanding the effect of that change, we need to know what the change actually *was*, not just what we planned for it to be. For this reason, it's important for participants to track what they actually do.

Adjustments to the plan offer a rich opportunity for reflection because assumptions can lurk here. We commonly use the passive tense—"changes were made"—which obscures who made the change and why. The phrase belies assumptions that participants hold about what is in their control. Facing up to these assumptions may prompt participants to consider alternate ways to exert greater control.

Figure 13.3 offers a template for an Implementation Log, which participants can adopt or adapt to suit their work style and plan. They can use this tool to track what they actually do, the effect of these changes, and contextual factors that matter.

Figure 13.3

Implementation Log

Date	Implementation Steps *What did you do?*	Plan Adjustments *What adjustments were made, by whom, and why?*	Indicators of Change *What indicators of change were observed? (Be sure to observe your Spotlight Students.)*	Contextual Conditions *What observations were made of contextual conditions supporting or limiting the effect?*

Note: A fillable PDF version of this figure is available as part of the Digital Tool Collection. See Appendix A for more information.

14

Inquiry Stage Three: Analyze (3B)

In the Analyze stage, participants will examine the evidence they have collected in the previous Attempt stage to **identify** the effect of the tested change and **interpret** what that evidence says about the conditions under which the tested change makes a difference. After reflection, they will **infer** next steps about what they need to do or learn.

You'll find the three key planning questions for this stage in section 3B of the i3PD Planning Map and in Figure 14.1. Use what you know about your content, participants, and context, together with the suggestions that follow, to plan out your Analyze stage.

Identify

How will participants characterize the effect of the change they have made?

Participants established a success target in the Assess stage, so you do want to hold them accountable for judging whether they have met that target. Depending on the inquiry model you were pursuing together, ask participants one of the following questions:

- What evidence shows how your new knowledge informed your practice?
- What evidence shows changes in the quality of your practice?
- What evidence shows that you changed how students were doing their work?
- What evidence shows that you changed what students were producing?

Phrasing the questions in these ways avoids a simple yes or no response and pushes participants to consider *the evidence* that they were successful at meeting the target. If appropriate, consider challenging participants to estimate *the extent* of the change using percentages or a scale from 1 to 10.

Figure 14.1				
Inquiry Stage Three: Analyze				
	Knowledge Gap Inquiry	**Implementation Gap Inquiry**	**Teaching-Learning Gap Inquiry**	**Expectations Gap Inquiry**
Identify	Were you able to change what you were doing?	Were you able to change how well you were doing it?	Were you able to change how students were doing their work?	Were you able to change what students were doing?
Interpret	What does the evidence say about the conditions under which the attempted actions make a difference?			
Infer	What have I learned, and what might I need to learn next?			

Although participants had a particular success target in mind, you should also encourage them to consider unintentional ways in which their changes may have had a positive (or negative) effect. For example, they may note changes in their own thinking or attitudes; in their students' behaviors, interests, or engagement; in student–teacher or collegial relationships; or in their understanding of the context.

Adult learners can be in different places developmentally, with some seeking external validation of success and others embracing the notion that they can set their own standards and evaluate their own success. Participants on both ends of the spectrum benefit from having their colleagues' eyes on the judgments they've made about the effect of their efforts. Opening their work to external review helps the box checkers see that they can create their own boxes; at the same time, it helps the more self-authoring knowers consider perspectives beyond their own.

Following are a few examples of how to engage participants in collaborative evaluations of evidence:

Deep dive. Arrange participants in two lines or concentric circles with each participant facing a partner. Ask a member of the pair to take one minute to share the percentage they've assigned to their degree of success and their evidence of that success. Ask the other member of the pair to take one minute to explain, based on what their partner has just told them, the conditions under which they might assign a *lower* percentage. Switch roles and repeat. Then rotate to new partner pairs and have one partner repeat the percentage they assigned to their level of success and their evidence supporting that percentage. This time, ask the other member of the pair to take one minute to explain, based on what their partner has just told them, the conditions under which they might assign a *higher* percentage. Switch roles and repeat. End the activity with time for participants to reflect individually on the percentage they assigned and whether it needs adjustment.

Quick chat. Invite participants to prepare posters that display their data and the conclusions they have drawn. Have them bring these posters to the session. Then invite participants to do a gallery walk and use sticky notes to attach comments, questions, and suggestions to colleagues' posters.

Online efforts. Participants might post to an online thread the answers to three questions: What was the result of the change you implemented? What percentage of your target did you reach? What is your evidence? Assigned partners can reply to that thread with probing questions for their colleagues' consideration.

Interpret

How will participants interpret what the evidence says about the conditions that have supported or limited their change in practice?

Participants believed that making a certain change in practice would have a certain result. Whether it did or didn't, there's much to learn about the conditions that are required for this change to take place. Two sets of questions can help participants tease out the conditions under which the tested change makes a difference. Concerning a *change in your practice,*

- Did you implement the change? If not, why not? If so, what helped?
- Did you implement it fully and well? If not, why not? If so, what helped?
- Did you implement it differently than planned? If so, why?

Concerning a *change in the outcome,*

- Did you achieve the outcome? If not, why not? If so, what helped?
- Did you achieve the outcome fully and well? If not, why not? If so, what helped?
- Did you achieve outcomes other than those you expected? If so, which ones and why?

The notes participants have captured in their Implementation Logs will be invaluable for providing thoughtful, evidence-informed answers to these questions. Participants can reflect on these questions in a self-directed way, respond in writing, or discuss with colleagues who had similar targets.

This thinking exercise can prepare participants to make some judgments about the conditions that seemed to support or limit the results of the tested change. They can create a two-column chart listing supporting and limiting conditions, or they can create a four-quadrant chart that separates the conditions within their control from those systemic factors that seem beyond their control. The *x*-axis would address the question, How important is this condition in terms of results? Whereas the *y*-axis would address the question, To what extent can I influence this in my current role?

Be sure to remind participants to include in their analysis the structures and policies they identified earlier as a focus for our collective inquiry. In the fourth and final Adjust phase, we will want to look across the participants' inquiry cycles to see what we can discern about the need for systemic improvements.

Infer

How might participants determine what they have learned and might need to learn next?

We wanted to do more than see if this change works just once; we wanted to use this experience to elevate teachers' decision making in an ongoing way. To quote our outcome-based objectives, we expect participants to draw on what they've learned to *routinely* do one of the following:

- Make decisions informed by a wider breadth of the knowledge and skill base for this instructional practice.
- Engage in higher-quality implementation of this instructional practice.
- Strategically and appropriately employ this instructional practice to strengthen students' learning processes.
- Recognize and raise artificially low expectations about what they accept as quality student work products in context of this instructional practice.

In this stage, we ask participants to reflect on whether and how this experience has helped them accomplish one of these objectives. Although some participants may make the leap from what they experienced in this cycle to what they will do differently from now on, others may need support, and all will benefit from capturing their thoughts in writing. Doing so will enable them to begin thinking about what success in that objective will take and what they might need to learn next.

Following are several ways you can support participants to reflect on how this experience has helped them meet the objective:

Deep dive. Use the Microlab protocol, in which participants in pairs or triads each answer three questions with the other participant or participants in the grouping serving as focused listener(s).

- Round One (one minute per participant): What was your target? Why was it important to you at this time?

- Round Two (two minutes per participant): What did you learn from this cycle about this instructional practice and the conditions for employing it effectively?
- Round Three (three minutes per participant): What areas of your practice might these lessons influence directly and indirectly? What new questions do you have?
- Reflect in writing: All participants should now take time to capture key ideas in writing, considering implications for their learning. Perhaps this inquiry has made them curious about another type of practice gap or sparked their interest in a new instructional practice to examine through inquiry.

Quick chat. Thinking through what something will take can sometimes help it to happen. Have participants form small groups and invite them to think through how to sustain and extend the implications of their inquiry cycles, capture new questions that arise, and use those questions to brainstorm potential new cycles. Ask participants to brainstorm answers to the question that follows that is relevant to your inquiry model. They can do this during or in advance of your session.

- Under what conditions might you sustain the changes in practice you made in this inquiry cycle? That is, has that change become part of your knowledge base?
- Under what conditions might the key ideas from this inquiry cycle enable you to engage in higher-quality implementation of this instructional practice in an ongoing way?
- Under what conditions might the key ideas from this inquiry cycle help you make better decisions about how to use this instructional practice to meet student-specific needs?
- Under what conditions might the key ideas from this inquiry cycle help you reflect with a growth mindset on the quality of student work your teaching produces?

Online efforts. You might ask participants to engage in any of the following:

- Reflect individually on lessons learned and contribute their thoughts to a community bulletin board, such as Padlet or Jamboard, or to a Mentimeter poll.
- Synchronously or asynchronously browse responses and identify themes that emerge across the lessons.
- Use participant reflections on the bulletin board themes to name one next step they might take for their own learning and one suggestion for the direction of the community's next inquiry cycle.

The purpose of this structured inquiry cycle was to learn how to make better instructional decisions—not once in this cycle, but routinely. By engaging in the suggested activities and reflecting on their learning, participants come to recognize their part in making this happen. At the same time, we've uncovered potential obstacles that are structured into the system, a topic we'll tackle in Part Four of this book.

15

Inquiry Stage Four: Adjust (3B)

In the Adjust stage, we seek to identify necessary systemic changes and commit to action. To accomplish this, participants must identify the **structures** (routines and processes) that our collaborative inquiry cycle has exposed as barriers to equity and dig beneath them to form **suppositions** about the collective mindsets that feed our current inequitable system. Then participants will have the intel needed to collaborate and commit to individual and collective strategic actions that can set off a **seismic shift.**

You'll find the three key planning questions for this stage in section 3B of the i3PD Planning Map and in Figure 15.1. Use what you know about your content, participants, and context, together with the suggestions that follow, to plan your Adjust stage.

Structures

How will participants illustrate the ways that existing structures and policies currently function as systemic barriers to equity?

Chapter 9 introduced you to a list of sample structures and policies, categorized into six domains, that pointed to ways schools and districts may be inequitable by design. In Chapter 12, as you worked on the Assess (Status) stage, you collaborated with participants to create a plan to track some of those contextual factors. And, in Chapter 14, the Analyze (Interpret) stage offered suggestions for analyzing the data. Now in this component, you'll lead participants in synthesizing these results across their diverse lines of inquiry to help them interrogate how existing structures function as barriers to equity.

Figure 15.1 **Inquiry Stage Four: Adjust**				
	📚 **Knowledge Gap Inquiry**	⚙️ **Implementation Gap Inquiry**	🔍 **Teaching-Learning Gap Inquiry**	👥 **Expectations Gap Inquiry**
Structures	How do current structures function as barriers to equity?			
Suppositions	What assumptions have produced our current inequitable system? What collective mindsets have produced our current inequities?			
Seismic Shift	What strategic moves do you need to make to dislodge barriers in your mindsets and in the system?			

Invite participants to use the data from their inquiry cycles to illustrate how specific local structures and policies served as barriers in their efforts to strengthen instructional equity.

Three different ways you might engage participants in this collaborative work are the following:

Deep Dive. Use an affinity protocol to identify salient themes from across participants' data and then create artifacts to communicate the evidence-informed findings.

- Ask participants to write each of their limiting conditions on a different sticky note. Invite groups of three or four participants to combine their notes and sort them into categories. Add in remaining groups until all sticky notes are combined into categories.
- Assign each original group of three or four participants to one of the larger piles of sticky notes. The group should review the examples within this category and articulate how these represent barriers to equity. Challenge the group to produce a product—vignettes, a data display, or other artifact—that will communicate to other school leaders how these routines and processes currently function as barriers to equity.

Quick Chat. Gather vignettes that illustrate common barriers to equity (see Figure 9.1)

- Display the dimensions that you focused on in your inquiry. Ask participants to submit examples of each via an online poll, chat, or interactive doc (Google Doc or Word 360).

- Divide into small groups and assign a dimension to each. Ask each group to discuss and use chart paper to communicate how the examples in their category represent barriers to equity.
- Reconvene to exchange and extend ideas. Record the presentations to capture ideas shared orally.

Producing rich descriptions of how the school structures we have created work against us is invaluable, but it would be naive and shortsighted to use this information to only try to reform those structures. Certain mindsets led us to create them, and those same mindsets will stymie efforts to change them—unless we uproot them. Participants will use these rich descriptions as clues to uncover collective mindsets, which may or may not align with those you have predicted.

Suppositions

How will participants uncover the collective mindsets that have produced our current system of inequitable structures?

We don't see the air we're breathing, and fish don't see the water in which they swim. Similarly, we take for granted certain suppositions that powerfully influence our decision making, both individually and collectively. We've captured a significant contradiction: We say we want equity, but we create systems that work against it. This is a tremendous opportunity to ask ourselves why we're acting this way.

It would be too easy to point the finger at external factors here: The budget is tight, there's not enough time, and so on. Even when money and time *are* tight—in fact, *especially* when money and time are tight—we make tough choices that reveal our priorities and belie our assumptions.

Here, participants should collaborate to dig for the unexamined suppositions driving the decisions in our community and examine them. You can facilitate this process in various ways.

Deep Dive. Look to the "Five Whys" protocol to get to root causes:

- Ask participants to form groups of four to six people and have each group choose one of the structures identified earlier as a barrier.
- Review the documented examples to refresh your understandings of how, specifically, this structure contributes to inequity in your context.
- Ask the following question: Why do we have this routine or process that runs counter to our commitment to equity? Only accept answers that are grounded in fact. Don't allow hypotheses here. Use the documentation you've collected to help. Multiple responses are welcome.
- Record each response and use each one to form the next "why" question. Continue doing so and recording responses until this is no longer productive.

- Have each group do a think-pair-share to reflect on the final response statements.
- Participants should answer the following questions in closing: What do these themes suggest we suppose to be true? How might we be wrong? What if these suppositions were not true?

Quick chat or **online efforts.** Participants can diagram the causes and effects in play as follows:

- Ask participants to review the documentation the group has created to illustrate how key structures—created by people who say they want equity—contribute to inequity.
- Invite each individual to make a diagram that maps out an array of cause-and-effect relationships that have combined to produce this contradiction. This might look like a decision tree or a fishbone diagram. Have participants create these in advance. They should then bring them to the session or post them privately online for participants to review.
- Ask participants to review the collection of diagrams to search for themes.
- Challenge participants individually (in an online post) or collectively (in small groups) to consider the following questions: What do these themes suggest we suppose to be true? How might we be wrong? What if these suppositions were not true?

The suppositions raised by these exercises can be unsettling and make participants feel vulnerable. In fact, if they don't, you might not have gone deep enough. Emphasize that there should be no blame assigned here; this is no one individual's fault. We have identified the effect of our context on us, and this is a powerful victory. It's what we need to plan higher-order changes to shift the system.

Seismic Shift

How will participants identify the strategic moves they need to make to create a seismic shift in the system?

This is not only the final component of the inquiry cycle but also a new beginning for the next one. If this experience is to be transformational, each new cycle must not begin where the last one left off but advance to a new level. We need to budge the deeply rooted assumptions that stand in the way of equity. This step proposes a change in the ground we're walking on. It aims to make a seismic shift.

In fact, the seismic shift is already underway because it starts with convening a committed group of individuals driven by a widely shared goal to engage in dialogue about their work. And you have already accomplished that.

In this step, we're going to use the data, thoughts, and feelings from this inquiry to help us extrapolate ideas about what we need to do to eliminate barriers to equity more broadly. To accomplish this, we'll reflect together on the question that got us started: How might we ensure that students in our classrooms who have historically been marginalized are

- Benefiting from instruction informed by the highest standards of professional knowledge available?
- Experiencing instruction that is skillfully implemented?
- Experiencing improvement in their learning processes?
- Expected to meet high expectations?

Just focus on the one question you've pursued together with your team as you flash forward 10 years into the future using a modified version of the School Reform Initiative's "Back to the Future" protocol shown in Figure 15.2. Imagine your school has accomplished this goal: Students in our classrooms who have been historically marginalized are receiving instruction that meets the objectives we've been working on. The protocol will get your team thinking about what it feels like to have achieved this victory. Participants will look "back" at how things were at the start of this work and consider the changes in systems, policies, and mindsets that were instrumental to success. At the end of this mental time travel, you'll spend time brainstorming action steps and narrowing them down to commitments to work toward making that vision a reality. While your participants engage in this creative thinking exercise, challenge them to reference the data and insights from their inquiry cycles.

Implementation and Timing Notes

Review the chart in section 3B of the i3PD Planning Map ("Inquiry Cycle Map"); this is where you should have captured your planning notes for each inquiry step. If you feel it would be helpful to share this preview with your participants, go back and adjust the language of the process objectives in section 2B of the i3PD planner ("Rigor") to increase the specificity of the descriptions of the inquiry stages. For example, in the template, the first objective currently reads, "Identify gaps in your own instructional practice (your knowledge, implementation, strategic use, or expectations of that practice) that currently contribute to inequitable outcomes." You might, however, embed into that objective some of the details from your Inquiry Cycle Map implementation notes like this, "Identify gaps that currently contribute to inequitable outcomes by assessing your knowledge base on how to design appropriate scaffolds in writing."

Now that the inquiry work is mapped out, think about how to distribute it across the time you have with your participants. As mentioned, you can move the work along in asynchronous ways that can occur between sessions. You'll need to use what you know about your participants, the content, and the calendar to decide which components call for a deeper dive in a session of synchronous interaction with you and what participants will do on their own.

However you split up the inquiry process across sessions, be sure there is a break between the Attempt stage and the Analyze stage to allow ample time for participants to experiment with changes in practice. For example, the cycle would ideally be supported by weekly sessions over eight weeks, allowing for between three and four weeks of testing changes in the Attempt stage. However, it would also be possible—but not ideal—to address the Assess stage through pre-work and use a full-day session to pursue the Attempt stage, followed by a two-week break for participants to test changes in practice, and a final full-day session for the Analyze and Adjust stages.

The Inquiry Cycle Map in section 3B of the planner has a column for your timing notes. Use this to stipulate which component will take place in which session and which components, if any, will fall between sessions. Let's now take a look at your session agendas.

Figure 15.2	
Back to the Future Protocol	
This protocol requires at least 45 minutes. Schedule accordingly.	
Facilitation notes	• Documentation at each step is key to turning ideas into actions. You can do that on chart paper or on a shared Google Doc or Word document. • This protocol may be stretched out from a one-time experience to a continued series of engagements.
Overview	**Explain the protocol and its unique time-travel perspective.** • Congratulations! It's the year [10 years from now], and our school has achieved instructional equity; historically marginalized students are no longer underserved and are performing on par with their peers. • While we're here in the future, we'll reflect on our achievement journey in four stages: We'll describe our future, we'll look back from that future to describe 10 years ago (now), and we'll use that future perspective to both describe how progress was made and identify the challenges and obstacles we encountered. *Remember: We live in this projected future, so the team should engage and speak accordingly, using present and past tense where appropriate.*
Envision the future	**From where you sit in the future, thoroughly describe what it looks, sounds, and feels like having accomplished instructional equity.** • Speak in *present tense* because this has already happened. • Describe this best-case projection. This is not a hope or a wish; this is a description of what is currently in place in your projected future.

(*continued*)

Figure 15.2	
Back to the Future Protocol—(*continued*)	
Envision the future— (*continued*)	• Do not yet describe how it has happened. • Focus on tangible things you see, hear, feel, and know to be true as a result of having accomplished this vision. *Facilitator tips: Write down participant comments on a "We Did It!" poster for all to see. Ask clarifying questions to help participants avoid generalities and provide more specifics.*
Look back	**Look back from your projected future and describe how it looked when you first started working toward equity.** • Speak in *past tense* because this was how it was when you first envisioned your future. • Speak to all aspects, including both the positives and the challenges that were part of the school, community, or organization at that time. • Remain as concrete and explicit as possible concerning such aspects as culture, achievement, conversations, organizational structures, challenging issues. *Facilitator tips: Write down participant comments on a "10 years ago" poster for all to see. Ask clarifying questions to help participants avoid generalities and provide more specifics.*
Describe how progress was made	**Connect the projected future to the past by clarifying how you moved your organization from where it was then to today's accomplishment.** • Speak in *past tense* because this represents actions that occurred in that past. • Directly and explicitly connect the two time periods by noting actions you took to make the future happen. • When listing how you accomplished that future, discuss and chart how it was accomplished and by whom, what took place and when, and with what resources. *Facilitator tips: Write down participant comments on a "How We Got Here" poster for all to see. If comments are too general, ask participants to be more specific: What **specifically** did we do that helped us close that gap? How **specifically** did that help us communicate better with parents?*
Identify challenges and obstacles	**Identify the challenges and obstacles you had to overcome to achieve your projected future.** • On cards or sticky notes, have team members write down some of the most pertinent challenges that existed in accomplishing this vision. • Be honest and be as specific as possible. • Place the obstacle/challenge cards between the "We Did It!" poster and the "How We Got Here" poster. Leave space between the cards to visually represent gaps that enable the team to thoughtfully maneuver through the obstacles.
Next steps	What are the next strategic moves you need to make to dislodge barriers in your mindsets and in the system? • What will you do? • What will we do as a team?

Source: Adapted with permission from *Future Protocol aka Back to the Future*, developed by S. Murphy, 2008, School Reform Initiative. Available at https://www.schoolreforminitiative.org/download/future-protocol-a-k-a-back-to-the-future.

16

Session Agendas (3C)

You're now ready to duplicate the session agenda template (shown in section 3C of the planner) as many times as needed for the number of sessions you have. As you develop your agenda plans, keep the left columns neat so you will be able to copy and share them with participants. Use the right-hand columns to capture implementation details, including notes about how cofacilitation will be shared, if applicable. You can print section 3C to have in hand as you facilitate to help you stay on track, ensure materials are ready, and make necessary midcourse corrections while still ending on time.

Think about each of your session agendas as a sandwich consisting of three parts—the Welcome, the Inquiry Cycle Work, and the Wrap-up (see Figure 16.1). You will make connections to relevance, rigor, and relationships at both the beginning and the end of the session, while focusing on the inquiry cycle in the middle. You've already outlined the inquiry cycle work that makes up the bulk of your session timeline. Transfer these plans into your session agendas by assigning each component to blocks of session time or to prework that participants will complete between sessions. Be sure to review the notes you've left for yourself in section 3A ("Setting the Stage") about how to maximize the time and space available to you.

Remember that the value of pursuing inquiry in a community resides in the opportunity for dialogue—and deep dialogue takes time. Therefore, when building your agendas, do not shortchange participants' time to interact. Use the suggestions provided to build in as much online work or prework as needed to protect the minutes that participants require for deep dialogue.

Be sure to reserve roughly 15 percent of your session time for the Welcome and Wrap-up. For a one-hour session, that might be 10 minutes total—that is, 5 minutes each. For a full-day session, it might amount to 60 minutes total: 40 minutes for the Welcome and 20 for the Wrap-up.

Figure 16.1

Agenda Planning Framework

1. Welcome

- Relevance
- Rigor
- Relationships

2. Inquiry cycle work

Use section 3B of the i3PD Planning Map to plan out the steps and decide how to distribute them across the time you have.

3. Wrap-up

- Relevance
- Rigor
- Relationships

Adjourn

Some participants will benefit from having an organizer in which they can capture the results of each component. And some learning contexts will require a deliverable that demonstrates the work of the cycle. Figure 16.2 features examples of artifacts participants might produce for each stage of the inquiry cycle. A blank version of the same figure is available as part of the Digital Tools Collection (see Appendix A).

Welcome

Now that you've planned out the Inquiry Cycle Map for your sessions, you're ready to return to thinking about how you will welcome participants into the space—whether face-to-face or virtual—in a way that prepares them mentally, emotionally, and socially; and how you will wrap up each session in a way that reinforces what we've learned, what we've done for one another, and why it's all meaningful.

Establishing Relevance

Here are three key moves that you, as facilitator, can make to establish relevance. It's crucial to

- Recenter the purpose.
- Revisit the objectives.
- Reimagine the outcomes.

	Figure 16.2
	Inquiry Cycle Map: Overview and Sample Artifacts

Stages	Key Components	Guiding Questions	Artifacts
Assess Capture current reality	Standard	What is the professional standard or expectation with regard to this practice?	*State the standard (and cite if applicable).*
	Status	What is the gap between this standard and my current practice? What contextual factors might be contributing to this gap?	*Describe the gap using evidence. List key contextual factors.*
	Success target	What will I accept as evidence that my practice has improved sufficiently?	*State your target.*
Attempt Plan and implement changes	Dig	What new knowledge did I gain to assist me in closing the gap and meeting the success target?	*Identify new ideas you want to try or apply.*
	Decide	What will I start doing, continue doing differently, and stop doing?	*Link action plan.*
	Do and Document	What did I actually do?	*Link implementation log.*
Analyze Examine and interpret evidence	Identify	What is the effect of the change I have made?	*Identify evidence of impact.*
	Interpret	What does my evidence tell me about the conditions that support or limit my change in practice?	*List key supporting and limiting conditions.*
	Infer	What might I need to learn next?	*Capture key ideas and implications.*
Adjust Commit to changes	Structures	In what ways did I encounter current structures as barriers to equity?	*Link collaboratively drafted communication materials.*
	Suppositions	What collective mindsets have created our current system of inequitable structures?	*Capture assumptions.*
	Seismic Shift	What strategic moves can I make with colleagues to influence the system?	*Link activation plan.*

Note: A blank fillable PDF version of this figure is available as part of the Digital Tool Collection. See Appendix A for more information.

You've already articulated the purpose and objectives in section 2A of the planner ("Relevance"). Sharing these with participants is not merely informational; it's an opportunity to invite participants to engage with that specific purpose and with those specific objectives, share ownership of the experience, and feel the bond of common commitment to an important goal. Invite participants to connect with the purpose by having them share their own "why" or by providing time for them to collaborate to put the purpose into their own words. Encourage participants to own the objectives with you by asking them to describe ways they see themselves in the objectives already and by taking an inventory of the assets they bring to the table that can help the community move together in this direction.

This professional learning experience will involve hard work. What's the prize at the end? Take time, especially when things are tough, to zoom out and picture the future. Invite participants to dream—to describe what these outcomes will mean for them, what these outcomes will do for their students, and how these outcomes might transform their school context.

Being Transparent About Rigor

In your role as facilitator, three key moves can help you establish rigor. You should

- Review the day's agenda and clarify how what we'll do today will get us where we want to go.
- Review where we've been and remind participants of where today's work falls in the sequence.
- Review exit slip feedback from the previous session (if applicable) and discuss how useful it has been in helping you better meet their needs.

Your purpose is lofty, and the transformation you envision is ambitious. Why should participants believe we could possibly meet these goals? You've worked hard to create a learning sequence strategically designed to bring your participants to a new place in their practice and mindsets. You've described it in general in section 2B of the planner ("Rigor"), and you've planned it out in detail in section 3A ("Setting the Stage"). For participants to suspend their disbelief and agree to take this bumpy ride with you, they need to know what *you* know about the plan, and they need to have a chance to let you know if it's missing something. You'll want to build time into the beginning of your series to share the full learning arc, perhaps even through a graphic organizer that everyone can reference in subsequent sessions to easily see where we are in the process. In this way, participants can gauge progress, weigh in from their perspective on whether we're on track, and proceed with confidence that they're in your good hands during this learning journey.

Attending to Relationships

Finally, four key moves can help you, as facilitator, attend to relationships. It's important to

- Develop and nurture community agreements about norms.
- Support participants' transition into the space by encouraging them to leave prior thoughts behind and be present.
- Bring all voices in the room so each and every participant feels seen and heard.
- Model your willingness to make yourself vulnerable and show your confidence in the safety of this community.

Establishing agreements about how we'll interact with one another provides a solid grounding for the dialogue this work requires and builds confidence in your role as peer facilitator. As noted earlier, those who are not part of the dominant culture usually have to guess what the unspoken community agreements are or risk being seen as negative or disruptive. Taking time to collaboratively develop—and proactively nurture—community agreements gives us the foundation needed to engage everyone in dialogue as equals and with truth.

For participants to see these agreements at work, you'll want to make space for connecting activities. We want to connect participants to one another; participants to you as facilitator; and possibly, but not necessarily, participants to the content. Whether your meetings are face-to-face or virtual, participants are coming to your session from somewhere with its own people, puzzles, and practices. Your connecting activity can help participants leave that behind and be present. Ideally, it brings all voices into the room, giving everyone a chance to hear and be heard and feel the personal regard of their colleagues. Connecting activities also offer you a chance to model the engagement and vulnerability you hope to see—and to make them contagious.

Low-risk connecting activities can help participants become comfortable enough to begin opening up. Once they do, they will naturally want to go deeper and will willingly engage in activities on the higher-risk end of the spectrum. Letting the group languish in low-risk activities can cause them to lose confidence in you as a facilitator and feel disconnected from colleagues—the opposite of what you want to accomplish. So, challenge participants with healthy high-risk activities when you think they're ready. You can always turn down the heat or step it back up a bit throughout the cycle based on their needs.

Wrap-up

At the end of the session, relevance, rigor, and relationships take on new importance. The session has hopefully introduced new perspectives, pushed participants' thinking, and possibly even deconstructed some preconceived ideas in their minds. Before they go, we want them to put the pieces back together but not in the same way as when they came in. We want to ensure they have time to integrate what they've experienced into their thinking and have considered the changes this new thinking suggests for their practice.

Revisiting Relevance

As you wrap up your session, three key moves can help you revisit relevance. Be sure to

- Make learning visible.
- Make thinking visible.
- Zoom out to view where we are now in the context of our purpose.

You've engaged participants in wrestling with important ideas in this session. Take time to make their learning visible to help it stick. Participants may have learned about a new tool or practiced a new skill. Publicly honor that learning. Celebrate the charts around the room and marvel at the data collected. What do they say about us? You will also want to probe for cognitive accomplishments by asking participants what new ideas they're thinking about. You can prompt participants to make their thinking visible with such sentence starters as, "As a result of today, one thing I will consider is _____" or "I used to think _____, and now I think _____."

We're brought together in this work by a common commitment to improving an instructional practice for important reasons. Remind participants of this. Ask them to think about the effects of our hardworking efforts to improve our decision making with this practice. Dream together: What will we be able to accomplish?

Reinforcing Rigor

As facilitator, you can make these three key moves to reinforce rigor. Be sure to

- Review agreements about what each person will do before the next meeting.
- Preview what we'll do next time and how it connects to today's learning.
- Provide time to complete the exit slip.

Each session is one step on the learning path. It's important to help participants see that we accomplished what we set out to—or didn't because of a worthwhile detour—and that it got us closer to where we're headed. By closing the session with a preview of what you've planned next, you're inviting participants to share ownership of those expectations and do what they need to do to be ready. In addition, they may have crucial questions or important suggestions, which can reinforce the strength of the plan.

The exit slip, which we'll address in more detail in Part Four, has a dual purpose in mind. It will solicit feedback on how well today's session met participants' expectations about what they need next. It will also challenge them to reflect on their role in the community. As such, it reinforces rigor with a bit of accountability while compiling the information you need to make adjustments in service of rigor.

Recognizing the Value of Our Relationships

Three moves on your part can help participants recognize the value of our relationships. Be sure to

- Create space for demonstrations of respect and personal regard.
- Show gratitude for members' competence and integrity.
- Celebrate our power as a team.

We are our own greatest resource for learning new content, seeing new perspectives, and holding one another accountable. Before going our separate ways, we want to be sure to celebrate what we've accomplished and send folks off eager to come back for more.

After a session in which we've pushed one another's thinking and possibly one another's buttons, it's worthwhile to engage participants in activities that help them connect human to human. Individuals may have made a difference for one another in the session by posing a provocative question or simply pausing to listen at the right time. Unless you create space for it, we might not lift that up and appreciate one another. Showing gratitude ends the session on a high note and welcomes more growth-oriented pushing in future sessions.

Finally, there's power in pointing to what we've learned together, acknowledging what we've accomplished together, and celebrating who we've become together. We want participants to feel the power and potential of belonging to a collaborative and committed team.

Figure 16.3 provides some examples of activities you can use to wrap up your sessions. Many of these activities advance more than one goal, a feature you can use as leverage to help reinforce a need you've seen in the group. Sharing appreciations, for example, does double duty: It not only provides an opportunity to recognize members for valued expertise they bring, but also reminds the group that this expertise is an asset and a resource for others.

You do not have to lead the Welcome and Wrap Up yourself. In fact, you can foster shared ownership by inviting participants to take turns choosing and leading a connecting activity, recentering the group in the purpose, or leading reflection on the day's learning. When putting your session plans together, include activities that reinforce relevance, rigor, and relationships in any order, but be sure your plan makes space to address all three of these important ingredients for engagement.

Figure 16.3

Sample Closing Activities

Type	Activities	Respect and Personal Regard	Competence and Integrity	Power of Team
Deep Dive	**Charades.** Challenge members to act out a favorite experience we've had together, an agenda item, or an accomplishment. Follow the same rules as Charades: No talking!	X		X
	Happily Ever After. Standing in a circle, pass a ball of yarn. Whoever starts begins with, "Once upon a time, there was a community…" and provides some description of the community. Pass and unroll the ball of yarn, with each member adding some description about the community's work at the start. After everyone has received the ball, invite members to windup the story and the ball by passing it back in the opposite direction as each member describes what the community accomplished. The story should end with a tidy ball and everyone living "happily ever after."	X	X	X
	Time Capsule. At the beginning of the final session, have each member write their name on a brown paper bag and, if desired, decorate it. During the session, invite each member to write each of their colleagues a short, positive note that describes something they learned from or appreciate about them. At the end of the session, invite members to deliver their notes into the others' Time Capsules, then encourage them to bring their own notes home to read later.		X	
Quick Chat	**To Us!** Invite each member to make a toast to our community. Bring sparkling cider (or something else) and special glasses.	X		X
	Appreciations. Standing in a circle, have each member take a turn picking another member, sharing something they appreciate about them, and then sitting down or stepping back. The person who was picked goes next, appreciating someone else who has not yet been appreciated.	X	X	
	Before and After. Invite participants to open their laptops. Challenge them to find two photos in two minutes: One that represents our community when we started, and one that represents our community now. After, do a gallery walk.	X		X

Type	Activities	Respect and Personal Regard	Competence and Integrity	Power of Team
Online Efforts	**Final Flash.** Have everyone type just one word or short phrase that captures how they're feeling about the work into the chat, but ask them not to post it until the count of three. Countdown and submit them together.	X		
	Team Tagging. Ask: What Twitter-style hashtag characterizes our community? (Use popcorn brainstorming to elicit responses.)	X		X
	Awards. Discuss what awards our community deserves and what the award object should be. (Group discussion, pair-share in breakout rooms, or post individually in the chat.)		X	X

Revisiting the Core Components

With your session plan largely complete, it's a good time to look back at Part One of the i3PD Planning Map. You've left notes for yourself about the participants (section 1B); your own hopes as a facilitator or facilitation team (section 1C); and the collective mindsets that might get in the way (section 1D). Review them and adjust your series plan as necessary. If there is more than one facilitator, add notes for yourselves clarifying where each of you will be taking the lead. Be sure you have provided participants with the following:

- Opportunities for engagement and differentiation
- Opportunities for comprehension, representation, and perception
- Opportunities for action, expression, and movement
- Opportunities for participants to learn from one another

In addition, review your purpose and objectives (section 1A.) Does your language give participants an authentic preview of what to expect, inspire willingness to learn, and promote engagement? An annotated version of Part Three of the planner starts on p. 157. Use it to reflect on how past professional development you led or experienced used time and space and to consider how those experiences may have supported both individual and organizational change. You also can use it to help you refine existing or upcoming inquiry cycles or to plan your own i3PD series. Also, don't forget that a sample of a completed i3PD Planning Map is provided in Appendix E as just one example of how a complete plan may look.

At this point, your session plans capture everything you think your participants need to experience. But you might be wrong. In the next section, we'll design feedback loops that enable participants to tell you if they agree and that ensure they're true partners in shaping the learning experience.

The i3PD Planning Map: Part Three—Annotated

PART THREE: Inquiry Cycle & Learning Sequence

3A. Setting the Stage

Time	Space	Insights and Implications
Note the dates and times of this series. How might the timing constrain or support participants' readiness to engage?	*Note the location and venue setup. How might they constrain or support participants' readiness to engage?*	*What insights and implications do you want to return to when planning this professional learning experience?*
Date: Time:	Location: Venue setup:	

3B. Inquiry Cycle Map

Briefly describe the activities and supports you will provide to guide participants through each stage of inquiry.

When will they do this and how much time will be needed?

Stages	Key Components	Implementation Notes	Timing Notes
Assess: Capture current reality	**Standard** How will participants define the professional standard of this instructional practice? **Status** How will participants identify the gap between this standard and their current practice? How will they identify what contextual factors might contribute to that gap? **Success Target** How will participants establish a target for improved practice?		

(continued)

The i3PD Planning Map: Part Three—Annotated—*(continued)*

3B. Inquiry Cycle Map

Stages	Key Components	Implementation Notes	Timing Notes
Attempt: Plan and implement changes	**Dig** How will participants gain new knowledge to assist them in closing the gap and meeting the success target?		
	Decide How will participants decide what they will start doing, continue doing differently, and stop doing?		
	Do and Document How will participants track what they actually do, the effect of these changes, and the contextual factors that matter?		
Analyze: Examine and interpret evidence	**Identify** How will participants characterize the effect of the change they have made?		
	Interpret How will participants interpret what the evidence says about the conditions that have supported or limited their change in practice?		
	Infer How might participants determine what they have learned and might need to learn next?		

Adjust:
Commit to changes

Structures
How will participants illustrate the ways that existing structures and policies currently function as systemic barriers to equity?

Suppositions
How will participants uncover the collective mindsets that have produced our current system of inequitable structures?

Seismic Shift
How will participants identify the strategic moves they need to make to create a seismic shift in the system?

3C. Session Agendas

Using the digital version of this tool, you will be able to COPY these first two columns to create an agenda to distribute to participants.

Duplicate this agenda template for the number of sessions involved.

Indicate key implementation details here. You can PRINT the full agenda with these columns to have with you as you facilitate. This will help you stay on track, ensure all materials are ready, and make necessary midcourse corrections while still ending on time.

If cofacilitating, indicate who is taking the lead in each part.

Time	Key Topics	Minutes	Implementation Notes	Materials and Handouts
--	Prework			
X:00	1. Welcome			
	Relevance			
	Rigor			
	Relationships			

The i3PD Planning Map: Part Three—Annotated—(continued)

Duplicate this agenda template for the number of sessions involved.

3C. Session Agendas

2. Inquiry Cycle Work			
Each session agenda will be informed by your cycle of inquiry plans from 3B.			
3. Wrap-up			
Relevance			
Rigor			
Relationships			
X:30	Adjourn		

Part Four

Preparing for Continuous Learning at Three Levels

In Part Four, you will determine how you will collect and analyze evidence of changes in instructional practice, participant agency, and systemic inequities as well as in your own personal growth as a facilitator, and you will prepare to build on this learning in future cycles.

17

Collecting and Interpreting Evidence (4A & 4B)

We've all been guilty of it: We want to see certain results, so we create a plan to achieve those results, and we implement that plan hoping to get those results. But then we have no idea how to verify if we've succeeded or not. The problem is that we usually don't have the evidence we need to assess our work—unless we've put in the effort up front to collect it.

In the context of education, it's also a moral and ethical problem. When we take action without knowing whether it's working until we're done, we learn the results too late—and possibly at great cost to the students. We owe it to our students to not waste their time on our hunches. When we're making decisions about educating other people's children, we have an obligation to monitor the effects of our efforts throughout our work, not only to learn from them, but also to make midcourse corrections and ensure we stay on track.

We also owe it to ourselves and our colleagues to not waste our *own* precious time. This work is too urgent, and our students are counting on us to get it right. We need ways of monitoring how it's going so we can see whether we're making the right decisions to get the results we're seeking. In i3PD we will do this by preparing to collect and analyze multiple sources of evidence before we even begin the inquiry cycle, guided by Part Four of the i3PD planner.

Research Questions

The three levels of learning involved in i3PD lead us to three questions about impact. We'll refer to these as *research questions* so as not to confuse them with the inquiry question associated with our selected model of inquiry. In fact, our research questions *inquire* about our inquiry questions, and naming these research questions clearly before your inquiry series begins will allow you to be proactive in looking for evidence that can help answer them.

The first is based on the first objective of your i3PD plan. You are trying to bolster participants' abilities to interrogate one of four types of gaps in their instructional practice that pose a threat to instructional equity and to make changes to address them. This is the explicit focus of your inquiry cycle. Therefore, we will want to ask the following:

Research Question 1. In what ways have participants made changes to practice and improved instructional decision making to close those gaps?

Second, you aim to expand your own confidence and competence as a transformational leader who supports participants to assume roles as agents of their own and their schools' organizational learning. You are trying to influence not just *what* they are learning, but *how they think about* their learning. The second question focuses on the outcomes of your efforts as facilitator in this area:

Research Question 2. To what extent have participants demonstrated confidence, commitment, and capacity as agents of their own learning in this series?

The third research question is aligned to your efforts to identify and influence systemic barriers to equity. The aforementioned changes in practice and mindset are likely to be stymied by structural constraints that predate these changes, and in your inquiry cycle you will use evidence and reflections from the inquiry cycle to proactively propose coordinated adjustments. Therefore, we ask:

Research Question 3. In what ways have participants identified systemic barriers to equity and coordinated efforts toward eliminating them?

In addition, a fourth research question is called for to track the progress of your own personal goal, a facilitator move you identified in Section 1C. In what way do you need to explore this goal? The same four questions we used to identify a practice gap for participants are useful here when identifying your practice gap as a facilitator:

- Do I have a sufficient knowledge base about facilitation to make quality decisions?
- Do I need to learn to do this more skillfully?
- Should I work on doing this more responsively?
- Am I overestimating the impact of my facilitation on participants?

You can use the multiple sources of evidence you will collect in service of interrogating inequity to grow as a facilitator as well. Review the following facilitator-focused interpretations of the four i3PD practice gap questions and use them to turn your personal goal into a fourth research question. Once you've done so, be sure to capture it in section 4A of the i3PD planner ("Multiple Sources of Evidence").

 Facilitator Knowledge Base

Do I have a sufficient knowledge base about facilitation to make quality decisions?

This first question challenges you to see if your practice aligns with the knowledge base on good facilitation practice. This base is vast and includes knowledge about the instructional core, immunity to change, design thinking, dialogue in adult learning, building trust, the importance of context in school improvement, data inquiry, conversation protocols, and more.

If you choose this line of inquiry, you might look back over your completed i3PD planner and identify some of the most crucial decisions you've made in developing this plan. Identify one high-leverage decision related to this goal, such as how you framed the purpose of the series, how you decided to balance work across synchronous and asynchronous activities, how you elected to engage participants in reviewing session exit slips. Resolve to dig a little deeper into the relevant knowledge base to help you make stronger decisions.

 Facilitator Skill in Implementation

Do I need to learn to do this more skillfully?

Knowing what to do and how to do it well are different things. Facilitation involves so many different kinds of moves that it would be rare to be effortlessly skillful at all of them.

You've already identified a facilitation move you feel will be worth your attention in this cycle such as communicating with clarity or fostering mutual accountability. Now that you've drafted the series plan, revisit that goal and determine if it still feels like the right choice and that there will be ample opportunities to work on this skill. If so, you might pursue this line of inquiry by reviewing videos or articles that help you refine your understanding of skillful practice, and then resolving to track your own implementation of this move. Self-observation via video and participant feedback via exit slip data will be helpful.

 Facilitator Teaching and Learning

Should I work on doing this more responsively?

In other words, are my well-intentioned, research-informed facilitation decisions successfully nurturing participants to be agents of their own learning?

If you choose this line of inquiry, you might look over your participant list and identify one or two people to monitor a bit closer than the rest. Perhaps you'll choose a "rule follower" for whom agency might be a real challenge or a "rule breaker" who pushes to take the group off course, possibly in a direction it needed to go. Track how your facilitation moves support or limit that participant's ability to be an effective and productive agent of their own learning and a positive influence on others.

Facilitator Expectations

Am I overestimating the impact of my facilitation on participants?

It's so easy (and pleasurable!) to tell ourselves that all is going well. Participants say they enjoy the sessions, report that "time flies by" in their exit slip comments, and may even note that their learning feels relevant and useful. That's all super nice, but your end goal was to have an effect on their work. Did they make changes in practice, and are their claims of improvement professionally credible?

Your participants will be collecting evidence on the results of the changes they have made in the Assess stage of their inquiry cycles, and you won't be in a position to review all of their data. Nor should you. As a peer facilitator, it's not your role to check their work, but rather to support them in having collaborative conversations that help them make their own determinations about whether their work is good. However, for the purposes of your learning, if you choose this line of inquiry, you might identify one or two participants whose changes you'd like to track and whose data you'll be able to review. Study this information to reflect on what aspects of your facilitation have supported or limited their ability to effect meaningful change. Were certain conversations pivotal to deepening their understanding? How did the structures you provided work for them? Holding midpoint and endpoint check-in meetings with these individuals would be especially useful to your inquiry.

Multiple Sources of Evidence (4A)

Chapter 7 discussed various data sources you might tap for each model of inquiry, and in section 2B of the planner ("Rigor"), you identified those you might collect and analyze as evidence of whether your improvement cycle is having the intended results. Review that list now as you prepare to complete section 4A of the i3PD planner.

Including multiple sources of evidence helps us see the situation from different perspectives. When it comes to data, however, more is not necessarily better. Too much data can cause us to lose focus on what we most need to know. We want to be smart by having a specific plan for collecting data—for why, how, and when we will use this information.

In this section of the planner, list potential data sources in the first column. Then use the subsequent columns to indicate which research questions that data source might help to answer as well as when you might collect and review these data. List all sources that seem viable for now; we'll narrow them down later.

Among your potential data sources, be sure to include exit slips and your own reflection journal. Figures 17.1 and 17.2 show templates for both that you can adopt or adapt to suit your own context.

Exit Slips

An exit slip, in the form of a short survey participants complete at the end of each session, is an important tool for ensuring the kind of quality engagement that leads to changes in practice. If designed properly and used to inform planning, it not only provides needs assessment data that are crucial for ensuring the experience is truly useful and relevant to participants, but also strengthens participants' sense of agency as decision makers in the learning experience.

You can use the annotated template provided in Figure 17.1 to design an exit slip. Whether administered on paper or online, the exit slip should be organized around the four research questions. In the template, for each of these four sections the first part provides an opportunity for feedback to the facilitator on the goals via a Likert scale rating from 1 to 6. Note that a six-point scale effectively challenges participants to make a judgment because there is no safe middle option and offers more variation than a four-point scale.

Because your aim as facilitator is to support participants to be agents of their own learning, the time they take at the end of the session to tell you how you are doing is a perfect time for them to also ask themselves how they are doing. That is, they can reflect not only on whether they're learning, but also on what is helping them learn and what they're doing about it. Therefore, the second part associated with each research question provides an opportunity for participants to reflect on their experience as learners.

The end of the exit slip survey includes four more open-response questions that invite participants to provide further information about what's working and what's challenging, which is essential for planning your next steps.

Set aside time to review the exit slip responses you receive from participants soon after each session. These comments will be harder to interpret when the details of that session have faded from your mind. Take note of patterns. Both trends and outliers are important for ensuring every participant receives what they need. Then summarize results by identifying a few highlights and a few changes you aim to make as a result of your analysis. If participants do not feel the work is addressing the stated goals, over time they will begin to lose trust in you as a facilitator. With this exit slip, however, you'll find that out before it is too late. Be sure to share a summary of exit slip results with participants at the start of the next session.

Figure 17.1
Annotated Exit Slip Design Template

1. Content

Our content-focused goal was to strengthen participants' capacity for making changes in practice and making stronger instructional decisions with regard to a particular professional practice.

1a. How are we doing?

To what extent have we advanced this goal today?

```
1         2         3         4         5         6
|---------|---------|---------|---------|---------|
Low                                          High
```

> *Aligns with Research Question 1*
> *You might want to state the specific instructional practice.*

1b. How are you doing?

What factors are contributing to the growth (or lack of growth) in your capacity for stronger instructional decision making? Factors might be of a personal, a social, an environmental nature, and so on.

_____

_____

1c. What are you doing?

In what ways, if any, have you made changes in practice since our last session?

_____

_____

2. Process

Our process-focused goal was to increase participants' confidence, commitment, and capacity as agents of their own learning.

2a. How are we doing?

To what extent have we advanced this goal today?

```
1         2         3         4         5         6
|---------|---------|---------|---------|---------|
Low                                          High
```

> *Aligns with Research Question 2*

2b. How are you doing?

What factors are helping or hindering you from being agents of your own learning? Factors might include course features, facilitator moves, personal factors, school-based factors, and so on.

_____

_____

2c. What are you doing?

In what ways, if any, do you feel you have increased your confidence, commitment, and/or capacity since our last session?

_____

_____

3. Context

Our context-focused goal was to build capacity to identify and eliminate systemic barriers to equity.

3a. How are we doing?

To what extent have we advanced this goal today?

| 1 | 2 | 3 | 4 | 5 | 6 |

|----------|----------|----------|----------|----------|

Low   High

> *Aligns with Research Question 3*

3b. How are you doing?

What factors may be helping you or hindering you from seeing and confronting the systemic barriers to equity? Factors might include understandings, feelings, social dynamics, and political factors.

_____

_____

3c. What are you doing?

In what ways, if any, have you begun to identify and/or worked to eliminate systemic barriers to equity?

_____

_____

4. Facilitator

My facilitation goal is _____.

4a. How am I doing?

To what extent have I advanced this goal today?

> *You set a goal for your own development as a facilitator in section 1C of the i3PD Planning Map. Add that goal here.*

| 1 | 2 | 3 | 4 | 5 | 6 |

|----------|----------|----------|----------|----------|

Low   High

4b. How are you doing?

What is the effect of this goal area on your learning? What feedback, if any, are you able to offer to support my growth?

_____

_____

Optional Questions

5. What specific aspects of today's learning are you most likely to try or continue to think about?

_____

> *This question helps you identify what resonated with participants and enables you to report back to administrators about changes they might encourage and expect to see.*

(continued)

Figure 17.1
Annotated Exit Slip Design Template—(*continued*)

6. What might make it easy or hard to apply today's learning to your work as an educator?

_____   *This question helps you identify cultural or structural supports that*
_____   *participants perceive as important for success, as well as limitations.*

7. What do you still have questions about?

_____   *This question can help guide your next steps for following*
_____   *up with participants and adjusting your plan.*

8. Anything else?

_____

_____

Note: A reproducible PDF version of this figure is available as part of the Digital Tool Collection. See Appendix A for more information.

Facilitator Reflection Journal

We're often exhausted after facilitating professional learning, and the last thing we want to do is write in a journal—but I will make a quick plug for doing so.

First, the small effort you invest now will make your planning and preparation for the next session more effective and efficient. Your head is swimming with feelings, ideas, and action items when the session ends. Why not quickly capture them before they are lost? It will take more time to do this later.

Second, the act of writing encourages reflection. How do you feel, and why? What stories are you telling yourself about what just happened? What did you notice? What do you wonder? What are the implications for next time? Once the pen gets going, the reflections start flowing, and these abstract thoughts and feelings come together as new knowledge that is useful for helping you make smarter instructional decisions as a facilitator.

Finally, your notes will serve as useful formative assessment data. If some participants are not embracing agency of their own learning, you don't want to wait until the end to do something about it. If participants are not making changes, look for patterns that explain why. Simply knowing you're committed to capturing post-session reflections may heighten your attention to looking for evidence that can inform your research questions. Figure 17.2 offers a template for a reflection journal that you can edit to suit your own reflection style.

Figure 17.2
Facilitator Reflection Journal Template

Date:	Session #:

FEELINGS: *Capture your quick reactions.*	
Roses (comfortable feelings)	**Thorns** (uncomfortable feelings)

IDEAS: *Capture observations you made or paraphrase comments you heard that relate to the research questions.*

Research Question 1: In what ways have participants made changes to practice and improved instructional decision making to close specified gaps?

Research Question 2: To what extent have participants demonstrated confidence, commitment, and capacity as agents of their own learning in this series?

Research Question 3: In what ways have participants identified systemic barriers to equity and have coordinated efforts toward eliminating them?

Research Question 4: To what extent have you advanced toward your personal goal?

ACTIONS: *Jot down the obvious to-dos that come up from this session.*

For Next Session	**For Future Sessions**

Note: A fillable PDF version of this figure is available as part of the Digital Tool Collection. See Appendix A for more information.

Note that the exit slip will be an invaluable catalyst for extending your reflection. Plan to peek at the responses after capturing your reflections, even if it's a day or week later, and consider those responses in the context of the reflections you've captured in your journal. Note any new feelings, ideas or actions that occur to you.

Other Data Collection Methods

Here are some examples of additional data collection methods that might prove useful, depending on the focus of your inquiry.

- **Initial and final survey.** If participants must register for your series, take advantage of the opportunity to gather some preassessment information in an initial survey. Among other key information, you can collect data about their expectations for the series, about the prior knowledge they bring (and might share), and about burning questions they have. You can compare initial responses with matched questions from a final survey. You may want to send out the final survey before the last session so that you can review the data with participants at that final session.

- **Midpoint/endpoint check-in.** If your group is small, you may want to conduct individual interviews or conferences in the middle and/or end of the series. If the group is larger, conduct a survey or focus group. Use this as an opportunity to follow up on some of the themes emerging from exit slips and to seek answers to some of the questions you've captured in your journal.

- **Peer observation pairs.** Not all of the data have to come from or through you. In the Attempt stage, participants may engage in peer observation (live or by video) during which they might take low-inference notes and document insights from their post-observation conferences with each other. Ask them to share these data with you.

- **Document review.** You can examine many types of documents collaboratively with participants, such as teachers' lesson plans, artifacts produced for the inquiry cycle, school communication documents, and more. It's a rich exercise to consider together the question of what we're looking for: What will we accept as evidence of effective practice or improvement as we look at these artifacts?

- **Session documentation.** Since one of the research questions investigates your own practice as facilitator, it may be helpful to video record, audio record, or invite an observer to take low-inference notes of your sessions so that you can reflect on the engagement, body language, and dialogue of your participants and your own self.

After you complete section 4A with the potential data sources you could collect, review it to be sure you have multiple sources informing each question.

Analyzing Data (4B)

We don't want to collect a mountain of data without being strategic about what that data can tell us about the effects of our work. We'll need a plan for organizing our multiple sources of data and for ensuring that we'll be able to analyze them to answer our research questions.

Organizing Data for Analysis

Your list of potential data sources may be lengthy. You can narrow it down by thinking about how you would make sense of it if you were to collect all of it. Figure 17.3 illustrates a way to organize (and potentially narrow down) your data sources with future analysis in mind. Using the data collection templates for exit slips and for the facilitator reflection journal, this table illustrates how to track the question each piece of data could answer, and in doing so, it helps the user to check whether certain questions or whole data sources are redundant and unnecessary.

Keep the original four research questions in mind as you complete this exercise, and don't allow yourself to get pulled beyond them. If a data source will not answer one of your four questions, or duplicates answers you can get from other sources, you don't need that data source.

If you also take note here about how you will display the data, it will cue you to think about how to collect it in a way that makes it easy to display.

The Data Analysis Process

Once you have finalized the narrow list of data sources you need, you can prepare to describe the implementation details of your data analysis plan in section 4B of the planner ("Analyzing Data"). You will have some tough decisions to make as facilitator about who will be involved helping to make meaning of the data and drawing conclusions from it. There is much to review, and many stakeholder perspectives would be valuable here, but time is limited on your end and theirs.

Participants must be involved in data analysis. It's their story that the data will tell, and the experience of looking at evidence to make meaning together of their experience of the inquiry cycle will be a powerful one. The extent of their involvement depends on the time you have and their willingness to participate. You might build time into the final session to explore the data for just one research question; schedule an optional meeting to analyze all or part of the data; or organize the analysis as an asynchronous online activity, in which participants use an online form to submit their reactions to a given set of data. You could also pursue a hybrid approach of providing data displays in advance and using session time to discuss them.

In addition, consider how the perspectives of stakeholders beyond your participants—such as other teachers, coaches, school administrators, district administrators,

Figure 17.3
Sample of Organizing Data for Analysis

Research Questions

1. In what ways have participants made changes to practice and improved instructional decision making to close specified gaps?
2. To what extent have participants demonstrated confidence, commitment, and capacity as agents of their own learning in this series?
3. What evidence shows that participants have identified systemic barriers to equity and coordinated efforts toward eliminating them?

Research Question	Data Source	Data Description	**Analysis** *What questions will these data answer?* *How might the data be displayed?*
1	Exit slip	**Answers to Question 1a. How are we doing?** *(Likert scale: 1–6)* • To what extent have we advanced this goal today?	To what extent did participants feel that sessions built capacity for improved instructional decision making? • Display stacked bar chart showing data from exit slip Question 1a.
1	Exit slip	**Answers to Question 1b. How are you doing?** *(Open response)* • What factors are contributing to the growth (or lack of growth) in your capacity for instructional decision making? Factors might be of a personal, a social, an environmental nature, and so on.	What factors did participants feel helped or hindered their growth with regard to instructional decision making? • List open response answers from exit slip Question 1b, possibly culled or categorized.
1	Exit slip	**Answers to Optional Question 5.** What specific aspects of today's learning are you most likely to try or continue to think about? *(Open response)*	What range of changes did participants attempt to implement to make stronger decisions? • Display responses from exit slip Optional Question 5.
1	Facilitator's reflection log	List of notes and quotes from Facilitator's reflection log	What did participants' changes in practice look and sound like? What seemed to support or limit their success?
2	Exit slip	**Answers to Question 2a. How are we doing?** *(Likert scale: 1–6)* • To what extent have we advanced this goal today?	To what extent did participants feel sessions increased their confidence, commitment, and capacity as agents of their own learning? • Display stacked bar chart showing data from exit slip Question 2a over time.

Research Question	Data Source	Data Description	Analysis *What questions will these data answer?* *How might the data be displayed?*
2	Exit slip	**Answers to Question 2b. How are you doing?** *(Open response)* • What factors are helping you or hindering you from being agents of your own learning? Factors might include course features, facilitator moves, personal factors, school-based factors, etc.	What factors did participants feel helped or hindered their ability to be agents of their own learning? • List open response answers from exit slip Question 2b, possibly culled or categorized.
2	Facilitator's reflection log	List of notes and quotes from facilitator's reflection log	What did participants' changes in agency look and sound like? What seemed to support or limit their success?
3	Exit slip	**Answers to Question 3a. How are we doing?** *(Likert scale: 1–6)* • To what extent have we advanced this goal today?	To what extent did participants feel sessions helped them build capacity to identify and influence the systemic barriers to equity? • Display stacked bar chart showing data from exit slip Question 3a over time.
3	Exit slip	**Answers to Question 3b. How are you doing?** *(Open response)* • What factors may be helping you or hindering you from seeing and confronting the systemic barriers to equity? Factors might include understandings, feelings, social dynamics, political factors, etc.	What factors did participants feel helped or hindered their ability to see and confront the systemic barriers to equity? • List open response answers from exit slip Question 3b, possibly culled or categorized.
3	Exit slip	**Answers to Optional Question 6.** What might make it *easy* or *hard* to apply today's learning to your work as an educator? *(Open response)*	What cultural or structural supports made it easy or hard to make changes? • Cull relevant responses from exit slip Optional Question 6.
3	Facilitator's reflection log	List of notes and quotes from Facilitator's reflection log	What did participants' efforts look and sound like? What seemed to support or limit their success?

Note: A blank fillable PDF version of this figure is available as part of the Digital Tool Collection. See Appendix A for more information.

school partners and possibly even students—might enrich the discussion. Plan to share this suggestion with participants and invite them to take the lead on planning a time and place to engage more voices in looking at the data. In what ways are changes in evidence, and what opportunities are there to take things to the next level?

It's not necessary to share all of the data; plan to select a research question that is relevant and informative to discuss with a given group. For example, participants can share what they think they've learned about changes in practice (and what seems to get in the way) with school administrators and coaches to get their perspectives. You can invite additional teachers to help vet the participants' emerging hypotheses about what supports and limits agency among educators. Or, participants might arrange to engage parents and district administrators to weigh in on their conclusions about systemic barriers to equity. Doing so can help build extended ownership of the problems, provide more well-rounded perspective on the conclusions, and result in a more diverse array of potential next steps. You don't have to decide this now before you've begun the inquiry cycle, but brainstorm your ideas now in Section 4B, and build time into your sessions to consult with participants about these possibilities. (Use this as another opportunity to streamline your data collection plans: If there are data sources you're not going to analyze, don't collect them!)

Our purpose in analyzing data is to draw conclusions from it that can inform the next cycle. If the cycle is successful, it will have answered some questions but opened up new ones, and participants will have some fresh mindsets they will be eager to try on for size. Build time into your final session to discuss plans for the next cycle and how it will come together. Be sure to capture your own notes and reflections on the observed changes and negotiated next steps in your Reflection Journal.

Part Four concludes, as the other parts have, with an annotated version of the i3PD planner for this section and a reminder to review the sample completed i3PD planner in Appendix E. Use the annotated map to reflect on the extent to which continuous improvement is currently supported in PD in your context, and revisit it for easy reference as you prepare to build data collection and analysis routines into the design of your learning sequence to ensure you will be able to learn at three levels.

The i3PD Planning Map: Part Four—Annotated

PART FOUR: Continuous Learning

4A. Multiple Sources of Evidence

Using the digital version of this tool, edit as needed and add any additional measures you plan to collect and review. In the boxes under each Research Question, indicate when you will collect the evidence. If possible, add hyperlinks to the Data Sources column for easy access.

Data Sources	Research Question 1	Research Question 2	Research Question 3	Research Question 4	Collection Routine	Review Routine
	In what ways have participants made changes to practice and improved instructional decision making to close those gaps?	To what extent have participants demonstrated confidence, commitment, and capacity as agents of their own learning in this series?	In what ways have participants identified systemic barriers to equity and coordinated efforts toward eliminating them?	To what extent have you advanced toward your personal goal, established in 1C? _____ _____ _____		

(continued)

The i3PD Planning Map: Part Four—Annotated—(continued)

4B. Analyzing Data

Be sure you have a viable plan for analyzing data before collection: Who will you involve in analyzing data? When and how will you do this?

Data Sources	Who	When	How

Note: An editable version of this figure is available in Word format as part of the Digital Tool Collection. See Appendix A for more information.

18

i3PD in Action

If you're intimidated by the challenge this book places before you, it's understandable. The premise is ambitious because the challenge facing schools is so complex. The fact is, we cannot meet the learning needs of each and every student until each and every teacher embraces continuous improvement of their instructional decision making. There's no quick technical fix. We need to develop a culture in which teachers assume agency of their own professional learning, something our schools don't currently have the structures to do. And we need to create new structures that enable new forms of professional interaction, something we don't currently have the collective mindsets to imagine. One could say we're stuck. I say, "Let's get going!"

With some effort, the same balancing forces that currently lock us into stagnation can become reinforcing processes that accelerate our learning and our collective efficacy. The more we learn, the more we will want to learn. The more we make a difference together, the more we will want to make a difference together. We can get this cycle going.

Learning to Share Leadership

In 2010, I had the support of a generous planning grant to design a system through which experienced teacher leaders could design and facilitate leadership development courses for their colleagues. This is neither something I knew how to do nor something I'd seen before, so I decided I'd need an advisory board of teacher leaders and we'd need to learn as we went along.

We collaborated with district leaders to identify a set of formal teacher leader roles that were perceived as having the greatest chance of making a difference for Boston's schoolchildren, and together we analyzed these roles to create a list of the leadership knowledge and skills that teachers would need to succeed in these roles.

Then, we convened a cadre of teachers who held these teacher leadership roles, and I supported them to design graduate-credit-bearing courses with performance-based assessments that provided participants with opportunities to develop, practice, and reflect on their leadership skills. This produced a series of four courses known as the Boston Teacher Leadership Certificate (BTLC) Program.

Inquiry was the engine that drove continuous improvement of our program. As we worked to help participants learn and practice key leadership skills, we collected data that helped us better understand how to teach the core skills, which course components were most useful, and what contextual factors got in the way. As we worked to help peer facilitators learn and practice effective course facilitation skills, we held reflection meetings that helped us gain new insights about course design, facilitation practice, and the role of this work in facilitators' career satisfaction. Emerging from both of these lines of work were observations about structural barriers, such as insufficient time, conflicting conceptions of shared leadership, ambiguity about autonomy, and so on. As we tackled these issues, we grew to recognize assumptions that were commonly built into the mindsets of school and district leaders and we identified structures commonly built into their systems that were working *against* these administrators' stated commitments to teacher leadership. Teacher leaders and administrators were inadvertently working against each other.

To be sure, these realizations caused conflict for many teachers, specifically for those working with school administrators who did not share their same beliefs and assumptions about the role teachers' expertise can and should play in improving their schools. Not to be put off, many of these teachers went on to become the school administrators they wished they had when they were teachers. At the same time, the data from our program helped to grow new knowledge about how contextual conditions commonly support or limit teacher leadership and has led to a new generation of school leaders committed to leading in sync (Berg, 2018).

The BTLC program was a ripple that became a wave, and it was a crucial element in turning the tide. The 200-plus teachers who participated in the program, nearly two dozen of whom served as peer facilitators, came away with new mental models of what professional learning and leadership are and do, teachers' roles and responsibilities within these, and what teachers' professional expertise can do for schools. In schools with a critical mass of participants, these beliefs became contagious and shifted the collective mindset. In schools that went on to become led by BTLC program alumni, these assumptions were embedded in the culture. As such, the BTLC program served as a powerful model of how individuals can learn from their work and transform their organizations by working simultaneously to shift practices, mindsets, and systems.

Multilevel Learning to Increase Equity

In 2018 I had an opportunity to collaborate with educators in the Waltham Public Schools to construct a new professional learning system that could advance equity. As with the BTLC model, the system was built with inquiry as its foundation and multiple levels of learning as its goal.

In this model, four teacher leaders from each of the district's 10 schools joined with 15 school and district administrators to form a 55-member cross-functional network committed to engaging in cycles of inquiry to learn our way toward more equitable schools. Two of our network's four teams focused their lines of inquiry on the effect of school-based teaming practices on equity, specifically student support teams and instructional leadership teams. Two additional inquiry teams set their sights on the effect of districtwide work on equity, specifically support for student-centered teaching and substitute coverage policies. Network members examined data together to identify and visualize the effect of current practices on inequity, proposed and implemented changes in practice, and collected data on expected and unintended outcomes—all while remaining attentive to insights emerging from the data about systemic changes needed.

Collaborative inquiry packed a mighty, multilevel punch. As teacher leaders began experimenting with student-centered teaching in their own classrooms and supporting colleagues on their teams, for example, they made key changes in practice that helped them home in on what each and every student needs. Yet, when they connected in the network, they also discovered common cross-school issues that competed with the commitment to engage in student-centered teaching and threatened its success. Some teachers identified mindsets about teaching that conflicted with student-centered approaches or found districtwide decisions about the instructional materials needed were not yet aligned. Together with school and district partners in the network, these educators were able to recommend strategic changes within the district professional development plan to shift those mindsets, and they convened with the district ELA coach to select new instructional texts.

Similarly, educators who collaboratively interrogated their school support team (SST) practices helped one another plan improvements that would ensure the needs of underserved students are met by their own schools' teams. Then, looking across schools, they wondered about the mindsets that inhibit SSTs from effectively addressing inequitable outcomes. That summer, *SchoolTalk* by Mica Pollack was selected as a districtwide summer read. In addition, the conclusions they drew about district structures and policies led to recommendations for new guidance for SSTs and ongoing cross-school learning.

Notably, as educators in Waltham changed their practices, mindsets, and systems in ways that increased the opportunities for equity, their interactions—and the shared language they developed—helped to expand a new districtwide ethos about meeting the needs of each and every student. In short, it helped them to overcome the inertia of inequity (Berg & Homan, 2021).

The underlying approach of i3PD, then, has proven its power to create the seismic shift needed for systemic change. Today, we need an earthquake to unearth the roots of inequity. Are you ready to shake things up?

Turn Over a Little Soil...

If you're relatively new to leading professional learning or engaging in inquiry cycles, try moving the soil around before digging in. Use the i3PD planner to map a professional development experience you've already had as a facilitator or participant. Think about ways that experience did or didn't welcome participants with relevance, rigor, and relationship building and how that influenced your readiness to engage as an active learner. Recall ways in which the demands for engagement with the core content distributed responsibility for the learning among the participants and, at other times, ceded responsibility to the facilitator. How did that influence the ownership you felt of your professional learning? Reflect on how the experience wrapped up: In what ways were participants supported to walk away with new practices, new feelings about their role in deepening their own practice, and new insights about how systemic barriers might keep us from learning what our students need us to learn?

You might also loosen the soil by testing one component of the i3PD plan in other contexts. Try building relevance, rigor, and relationships into your team meeting routine. Consider adjusting your existing inquiry cycle model by integrating steps from the i3PD Planning Map. Modify and pilot-test the Exit Slip Template (Figure 17.1) to get used to the routine of reporting back to participants at the beginning of each session and to get your colleagues used to viewing exit slips as an opportunity for reflection. Use the list of contextual conditions (Figure 9.1) as a lens for identifying systemic barriers to equity in other areas of school improvement and as clues to help you spot the collective mindsets that enable them to persist.

And Dig Right In!

Our schools produce inequitable results—and were designed to do so. If we're to correct this, we must try something different. We need to *learn* our way toward more equitable schools.

As schools increasingly turn to teachers as leaders of professional learning, however, many teachers are simply reproducing the ineffective professional workshops they used to complain about themselves. With good reason—strong models and guides for teacher-led professional learning did not exist until now. This book provides the design principles and sample tools needed to get you started in creating a professional learning revolution in your school.

We need to stop waiting for a silver bullet solution to drop from the sky. The solution must come from the test kitchens of our own schools, where educators are committed and supported to engage in disciplined collaborative inquiry. In other words, the solution is in your hands. Don't hesitate. Dig in!

Appendixes

Appendix A.
i3PD Digital Tool Collection

The following tools and templates that appear in this book are accessible online at **www.ascd.org/i3PDdigitaltools**. All are provided as fillable PDFs, except for the i3PD Planning Map, which is provided in Word. For the latest tool variations, illustrations of use, and other related resources, you can also visit **www.jhbergonline.com**.

Figure #	Tool/Template	Description	Page #
	i3PD Planning Map	This four-part planning template guides you in planning an effective inquiry-based professional learning series designed to uproot instructional inequity in three ways.	24
5.1	Immunity Map	This four-column thinking exercise, originally developed for individuals wrestling with their own change, is adapted here to support facilitators to predict and prepare for potential challenges of change their participants might experience.	61
8.2	Making Agreements About Community Norms	Community agreements are only as good as participants' shared understanding of them. Use this two-part activity to help your community members get on the same page about what our agreements mean and what we'll do to hold one another accountable for meeting them.	88
11.3	Inquiry Cycle Comparison	In what ways is the i3PD cycle of inquiry similar to and different from other inquiry models familiar to you? Two national models are illustrated as examples for you to compare. Use the space provided to add your own locally familiar frameworks.	115
13.2	Action Planning Template	Adopt or adapt this tool to create a plan with colleagues that identifies action steps, individuals involved, resources needed, and timeline.	131
13.3	Implementation Log	Effective teachers create strong plans but are also prepared to change course to meet their students' needs. Participants can use this tool to track what they actually do as facilitators, the effect of these changes, and contextual factors that matter.	133

(continued)

Figure #	Tool/Template	Description	Page #
16.2	Inquiry Cycle Map: Overview and Artifacts	Each stage in the i3PD inquiry cycle has key components that pose guiding questions. How might participants demonstrate their response to each? Complete this blank version of Figure 16.2 to plan and communicate expectations.	149
17.1	Exit Slip Design Template	Critically review the survey questions included in this template and edit to suit your own and your participants' needs. Be sure to keep the exit slip short and anonymous to increase participation and the usefulness of responses.	168
17.2	Facilitator Reflection Journal Template	Use this template to guide your reflection after facilitating each session.	171
17.3	Organizing Data for Analysis	Edit and add to this table to plan how you might use your data to answer the core research questions of i3PD.	174

Appendix B.
Protocol Families

Protocols are conversation guides. They are structured to help a group of participants to efficiently and effectively reach a shared goal. Therefore, facilitators must take care to select a protocol that is properly matched to the goal. The table below can help.

Protocol Family and Key Phrases	Description of this Protocol Family	Examples from School Reform Initiative (www.schoolreforminitiative.org)
Seeking Perspective • What do others see? • I don't know where to go with it. • I need another perspective. • I need new eyes.	In this protocol family, participants look at student or adult-generated artifacts and gain new insights and perspectives in two ways: (1) because presenters offer little or no context, feedback is less influenced by their perspective, and (2) participants offer feedback on work through three different lenses: literal, interpretive, and evaluative.	• ATLAS • ATLAS with Data • Collaborative Assessment Conference • Examining Assessments • Art Shack
Exploring and Managing Dilemmas • I am stuck. • I've tried X, Y, and even Z. • I keep thinking about it. • I cannot figure it out.	A dilemma is a puzzle, an issue that raises questions or some aspect of a relationship, process, or product that you just can't figure out. Protocols with dilemmas prompt the presenter to think more deeply or expansively about the situation, not to necessarily find *the* or *an* answer. As participants look at student or adult-generated artifacts, different thinking or understandings happen in three ways: (1) presenters offer context and set a focusing question; (2) presenters receive and, in some instances, respond to participants' probing questions and assumptions; and (3) participants temporarily take on the dilemma in response to the focusing question.	• Issaquah • Consultancy • Peeling the Onion • Descriptive Consultancy

(continued)

Protocol Family and Key Phrases	Description of this Protocol Family	Examples from School Reform Initiative (www.schoolreforminitiative.org)
Refining • I have a goal. • There might be a gap. • It is not quite there. • Some of it is good.	In refining work, presenters seek to refine or improve a student work sample, document, or project so it more closely aligns with their goals or purposes. After hearing a detailed history of the work thus far, participants offer specific feedback focused on bridging the gap between the current work and the original goal or purpose.	• Tuning • Slice • Ghost Walk • Gap Analysis • Equity
Generating • I'm stuck (maybe). • I don't know where to start. • I might know it if I hear it. • I'm willing to start over or blow it up.	"Being stuck" is a common characteristic for situations appropriate for a protocol in this family. These processes offer two benefits: (1) participants temporarily take on the issue and generate ideas and possibilities for consideration, and (2) presenters stay silent during the process, removing themselves from the pressure of having to immediately respond to each idea and thereby opening themselves up to recognizing assumptions they hold.	• Chalk Talk • Charrette • Constructivist Protocol • Fears and Hopes • Realms of Concern and Influence • Success Analysis • Wagon Wheel Brainstorming • The World Café
Building Shared Understanding • We don't all understand… • They don't agree about… • We need to learn about… • Building community is a goal.	This family of protocols differs from the others in that one person's work or dilemma is not the focus. *Thus, a presenter is not required in these protocols.* Hearing multiple points of view or ideas around a common question, experience, or other prompt, such as a given text, is a first step toward building shared understanding. These protocols provide processes to capture multiple points of view. Then, through guided discussion, participants arrive at some degree of shared understanding of the issues, challenges, agreements, and opportunities facing the group.	• Affinity Mapping • Block Party • Coffee Talk • Compass Points • Continuum Dialogue • Creating Metaphors • Diversity Rounds • Making Meaning Adapted for Text • Microlabs • Norms Construction • Paseo • ProMISE for Texts about Equity • Q and A (Questions and Assumptions) • Student Profiles • Text Rendering • The Final Word • The 4 As • Text-Based Seminar

Sources: Adapted with permission from *Protocol Families*, developed by G. Thompson-Grove, F. Hensley, and T. Van Soelen, 2017, School Reform Initiative. Available at https://www.schoolreforminitiative.org/download/protocol-families; and from *Meeting Goals: Protocols for Leading Effective, Purpose-Driven Discussions in Schools* (pp. 10-11), by T. M Van Soelen, 2021, Solution Tree. Copyright 2018 by K. Ridinger and T. M. Van Soelen.

Appendix C.
Four Sample Immunity Maps

📚 Knowledge Gap Inquiry

Improvement Goal/ Commitment	Doing/Not Doing	Hidden/Competing Commitments	Big Assumptions
What do our Spotlight Students need us to improve? We are committed to getting better at ensuring these students receive state-of-the-art instruction by expanding our professional knowledge and repertoire.	**What are we doing and not doing that work against our improvement goal?** • We pull strategies labeled as "best practice" from anywhere; we don't vet sources. • We don't stop and question: "Best" for whom and under what conditions? • We don't maintain ongoing links to sources of professional knowledge (e.g., networks, professional associations, research literature). • When we *do* grow our knowledge, we don't follow through and try it out in practice.	**What might be worrisome about doing the opposite of the things in column two?** It's a lot of work to research and vet practices. • We worry we're not prepared to play this role; we don't really know how to find and evaluate professional resources efficiently or effectively; it's embarrassing because we probably should know how to do this. • We worry that if we did vet sources, we would have no time left to do all the other stuff we're more accountable for; basically, we can get away with not doing it. • We are not sure that's our role; we worry that we'll be taking on the role of district leaders and step on toes or cause tension by contradicting them. Seeking out professional knowledge is admitting there are things about my profession that I don't know. • We worry that being a learner exposes our lack of knowledge (to ourselves and others), which is a blow to our egos and our sense of professionalism. • We worry about going beyond our "small pond" and being lost/feeling small, becoming a small fish in a big pond.	**What do our competing commitments suggest about how we might see the world and ourselves (i.e., our collective mindset)?** We assume it is dangerous to reveal one's weaknesses. We assume that educators should know everything, and not knowing is a bad thing. We assume that rocking the boat is categorically a bad thing. We assume we're powerless to influence the seemingly intractable systems and structures in place.

(continued)

191

📖 Knowledge Gap Inquiry—(continued)

Improvement Goal/Commitment	Doing/Not Doing	Hidden/Competing Commitments	Big Assumptions
	• We don't question or investigate how historically marginalized groups have been (and may continue to be) systematically limited from instruction informed by advances in the field.	We have so many systems and structures in place designed to support current practice. • We worry that trying to change them would be really hard and frustrating; it seems futile; we have no sense of efficacy over this. • We worry that we'll miss those current practices and the systems of support that make them easy. • We worry that we won't have allies and that we'll be seen as a lone, antagonistic, aggressive, angry, or rebellious voice. Trying something new is scary because we don't know if it will work. • We worry that if we step outside our comfort zone we'll be uncomfortable and that our students will see that. • We worry that it might jeopardize the control we currently (think we) have in our classroom. Investing time and effort in learning about historical injustices would open a can of worms. • We worry that we'll be blamed or implicated. • We worry that it will be a waste of time; we already get the idea, don't we? • We worry that we should already know this history; it's embarrassing that we don't. **What self-protective, hidden commitments stand behind our worries?** • We are committed to not revealing our professional weaknesses. • We are committed to protecting a certain image of ourselves as professionals. • We are committed to not adding to our plates without taking something away. • We are committed to not stepping on toes. • We are committed to not rocking the boat, especially in ways that will create more work for us. • We are committed to not creating discomfort for ourselves or others.	We assume that the comfort of educators who resist uncomfortable conversations about race is more important than the academic success of students who are being underserved. *How might we test and reverse one or more of the above assumptions in our i3PD sessions?*

Implementation Gap Inquiry

Improvement Goal/ Commitment	Behavior Inventory (Doing/Not Doing)	Hidden/Competing Commitments	Big Assumptions
What do our Spotlight Students need us to improve? We are committed to getting better at ensuring these students experience high-quality implementation of this practice.	**What are we doing and not doing that work against our improvement goal?** • We don't reflect and think critically about the quality of our implementation of this practice. • We don't give one another authentic, growth-oriented feedback. • We don't invite colleagues to observe and provide feedback. • We ignore or argue with others who give us feedback for our benefit. • We give up instead of incorporating feedback and trying again.	**What might be worrisome about doing the opposite of the things in column two?** If we reflect and think critically, the cons may outweigh the pros. • We worry we'll focus on all the things we did wrong and feel bad. • We worry we'll regret all the things we should have done that seem obvious in retrospect. • We worry that the time we take to do these things will draw away from time we might have used to make the next lesson better. We're afraid to give each other authentic feedback. • We worry that we may step on toes or hurt feelings. • We worry that we might be seen as vengeful or jealous. • We're not confident in our suppositions; we worry that we might be wrong and that we'll feel bad for steering colleagues in the wrong direction. If we invite others to observe us, we make ourselves vulnerable to their criticism. • We worry we might hear feedback we don't want to hear. • We worry we may be judged; colleagues may form opinions they don't share with us. • We worry that colleagues may disparage us with other colleagues. If we get good, critical feedback, that means we have a lot of work to do. • We fear that we'll learn about a gap that's larger than we're ready to deal with. • We worry that it means we're not the great teacher we thought we were. • We worry that we won't be able to make the changes needed. • We worry we'll feel bad thinking about all the students who experienced our previous poor implementation of this practice.	**What do our competing commitments suggest about how we might see the world and ourselves (i.e., our collective mindset)?** We assume our worth and value as teachers are tied up in receiving positive feedback, as opposed to how we respond to feedback. We assume that teachers do not have a growth mindset. We assume not all colleagues are committed to agreements about confidentiality and judgement. We assume we know what we need to learn. We assume deficit thinking, that students of color are unmotivated and looking for a chance to act up.

(continued)

⚙️ Implementation Gap Inquiry—(continued)

Improvement Goal/ Commitment	Behavior Inventory (Doing/Not Doing)	Hidden/Competing Commitments	Big Assumptions
		We're unsure we'll be able to implement the practice effectively; it feels especially risky to try it with these students. • We worry about creating classroom chaos or confusion and disturbing the semblance of control we (think we) have. • We worry these students won't have patience with us as learners and will see this as an opportunity to cause trouble. • We worry about being seen as a poor learner (by ourselves, our students, and our colleagues). **What self-protective, hidden commitments stand behind our worries?** • We are committed to not bruising our own egos. • We are committed to not jeopardizing relationships with colleagues. • We are committed to protecting ourselves, not making ourselves vulnerable to backbiting and gossip. • We are committed to not letting others push us further than we're ready to go. • We are committed to not losing control over the classroom. • We are committed to not being judged by our performance with these students.	We assume when students don't learn from us it's their fault. ***How might we test and reverse one or more of the above assumptions in our i3PD sessions?***

Teaching-Learning Gap Inquiry

Improvement Goal/ Commitment	Behavior Inventory (Doing/Not Doing)	Hidden/Competing Commitments	Big Assumptions
What do our Spotlight Students need us to improve?	**What are we doing and not doing that work against our improvement goal?**	**What might be worrisome about doing the opposite of the things in column two?**	**What do our competing commitments suggest about how we might see the world and ourselves (i.e., our collective mindset)?**
We are committed to getting better at making strategic and appropriate decisions about this professional practice that lead these students to strengthen their learning processes.	We are afraid we're not doing the right thing.	We assume that good teaching is better gauged by what the teacher does than by what the student does.
	• We're so focused on what we're doing that we don't pay attention to what students are doing.	• We worry that if we can't prove we did it "right," the low achievement of these students will be our fault.	
		• We worry about being seen as an ineffective or uncommitted teacher.	
	• We're so focused on student learning outcomes that we don't pay due attention to student learning processes.	We don't know what to look for in the student learning process; we're used to looking at outcomes.	We assume that if others see how much we don't know, we will be regarded as unprofessional and incompetent.
		• We worry that we don't know what it might look like to monitor the learning process; we're embarrassed by the fact that we don't know; it seems we should know.	
		• We worry that diverting attention from outcomes may make us look like we're shirking accountability.	
	• We plan lessons without attention to the individual learning needs and styles of these students.	We are afraid of being overwhelmed by the diversity of student learning needs and styles.	We assume that the short-term wins of public achievement targets are more important than longer-term wins of closing achievement gaps.
		• We worry that we can't cater to them all, that we'll let some students down.	
	• We pay more attention to what most students are doing than to what our Spotlight Students are doing.	• We worry that in trying to meet the needs of all, we'll do none of it well.	We assume that the product of student learning is more important than the process of students learning to become independent learners.
		• We worry about whether we understand the role culture should play; as culturally responsive educators, we think we should know.	
		We are concerned about how our focus on a racial, an ethnic, or a linguistic group will be perceived.	
		• We worry that we'll be seen as racist for singling students out.	
		• We worry that these students will feel that we're picking on them.	
		• We worry about our own cultural competency and our ability to manage the potential objections of white parents and colleagues.	

(continued)

🔍 Teaching-Learning Gap Inquiry—(continued)

Improvement Goal/ Commitment	Behavior Inventory (Doing/Not Doing)	Hidden/Competing Commitments	Big Assumptions
		What self-protective, hidden commitments stand behind our worries? • We are committed to simplifying this; we are committed to believing there is a simple solution, technical fix, or strategy that we can get "right." • We are committed to not revealing the gaps in our professional knowledge. • We are committed to not taking on work we're unsure we can do well. • We are committed to not making waves. • We are committed to not risking being seen as racist or culturally incompetent.	We assume that the culture does not value risk-taking in service of learning. We assume there's a lack of consensus in the community that race-based disparities require a race-based lens to address them. ***How might we test and reverse one or more of the above assumptions in our i3PD sessions?***

🕸 Expectations Gap Inquiry

Improvement Goal/ Commitment	Behavior Inventory (Doing/Not Doing)	Hidden/Competing Commitments	Big Assumptions
What do our Spotlight Students need us to get better at? We are committed to getting better at recognizing and raising low expectations of students' work in context of this instructional practice.	**What are we doing and not doing that work against our improvement goal?** • We accept participation in lieu of performance. • We give extra credit for meaningless add-ons. • We don't use formative assessment moves; we learn too late when students are underperforming. • We monitor all students or look at averages, which obscures the experience of these students.	**What might be scary about doing the opposite of the things in column two?** We're not sure whether we can support every student to meet high expectations for performance. • We worry that we won't be able to reach some students, that there will be a demographic pattern in who we don't reach. • We worry that some students can't be reached, that they don't have the intelligence. • We worry that we don't have the pedagogical skills we like to think we have. If we don't accept participation and other add-ons as part of the grade, we fear students of color will be more likely to have low grades. • We worry that these students will have a low sense of efficacy and cause problems in the classroom. • We worry that posting a pattern in which students from historically marginalized groups get low grades might cause others to question whether we're biased or racist. Monitoring student performance formatively is a lot of work. • We worry that it will take more effort than it's worth, especially because we know the outcome anyway. • We worry that it might create more work for us because it might reveal new things we need to make time to do. • We worry that we might not know how to respond to the results effectively and that we probably should know how. It feels risky to look specifically at the performance of these students. • We worry that we won't like the patterns we see; we worry that we're playing a role in creating these patterns, and we're frustrated that we don't know what it is. • We worry that we might jeopardize our pleasant view of how "most" students are doing if we focus on these few students.	**What do our competing commitments suggest about how we might see the world and ourselves (i.e. our collective mindset)?** We assume that it's not okay to call attention to racial patterns. We assume there is a belief that some students cannot meet high expectations. We assume that effective teachers see success with 100 percent of students 100 percent of the time. We assume that our worth as teachers is determined by whether students like us. We assume that other contributors to underperformance will not also be addressed.

(continued)

Expectations Gap Inquiry—(continued)

Improvement Goal/ Commitment	Behavior Inventory (Doing/Not Doing)	Hidden/Competing Commitments	Big Assumptions
		What self-protective, hidden commitments stand behind our worries?	We assume that everyone would prefer good news to the truth.
		• We are committed to not looking for racial patterns in the students we haven't been able to reach.	*How might we test and reverse one or more of the above assumptions in our i3PD sessions?*
		• We are committed to hiding our concern that some students cannot meet our expectations.	
		• We are committed to protecting our image of ourselves as effective, equity-minded teachers.	
		• We are committed to being liked by students.	
		• We are committed to not spending time on something that won't make a difference and to not making more work for ourselves.	
		• We are committed to underplaying our role in student underperformance.	
		• We are committed to making ourselves feel good with a rosy picture of how students are doing.	

Source: Adapted from *Change Leadership: A Practical Guide to Transforming Our Schools,* by T. Wagner et al., 2012, San Francisco: John Wiley & Sons. Copyright 2012 Minds at Work.

Want to learn more? Here are some recommended readings:

• *Change leadership: A practical guide to transforming our schools* (John Wiley & Sons, 2012) by T. Wagner, R. Kegan, L. L. Lahey, R. W. Lemons, J. Garnier, D. Helsing, A. Howell, & H. T. Rasmussen.

• *Immunity to change: How to overcome it and unlock potential in yourself and your organization* (Harvard Business Review Press, 2009) by R. Kegan and L. L. Lahey.

• *An everyone culture: Becoming a deliberately developmental organization* (Harvard Business Review Press, 2016) by R. Kegan and L. L. Lahey.

Appendix D.
Norms Construction:
A Process of Negotiation

Purpose

This is a consensus-building process that uses a series of negotiations to construct norms for a learning community.

Time

Approximately 45 minutes

1. Negotiation with self (approximately 10 minutes)

a. Journaling to know your "self" (5 minutes) *write, list, draw*

Participants have time to reflect on aspects of learning that are important when choosing to work and learn in community. Questions might include the following:

- What do you expect of yourself as a member of this group?
- What do you expect of others?
- What do you remember about a time when you experienced powerful learning in a group?
- What was present in that situation?
- Can you recall feedback and specific language that stood out for you in that experience (e.g., group juggle, feedback, learning from text)?

b. Proposing what *I need* (2 minutes) *circle ideas, highlight, combine*

Based on the insights generated from journaling, negotiate your ideas down to three requests to make of yourself for learning well in this group. For instance, *In order to learn well with this group, I need to...*

c. Proposing what *we need* (3 minutes) *record on three sticky notes*

Participants now translate the three ideas claimed as personal needs (in the previous negotiation with self) to group needs, and they transfer each request to a sticky note. Each sticky note will now "hold" one proposed norm, for a total of three proposed group norms. To support this transfer of ideas from self needs to group needs, offer a prompt such as, *In order to do our best learning together in this community, we need to . . .*

1. (sticky note #1)
2. (sticky note #2)
3. (sticky note #3)

At the conclusion of this step, each participant should have three norms to take forward for additional negotiations.

Participants signal the facilitator when they complete this process. The facilitator will match individuals to form pairs.

2. Negotiation with one other colleague (in pairs) (approximately 10 minutes)

Each person brings to the pair the three sticky notes that represent their proposed norms. The two colleagues work together to renegotiate their proposals (their combined six sticky notes) to a shared three sticky notes.

Participants signal the facilitator when they complete this process. The facilitator will match pairs to form quads.

3. Negotiation among four colleagues (in quads) (approximately 10 minutes)

Each pair brings to the quad their three sticky notes. Members of each quad work together to renegotiate their proposals (their combined six sticky notes) to a shared three sticky notes.

The facilitator knows the groups have completed their negotiations when each group has posted their proposed norms.

4. Negotiations "rest" with the group (approximately 10 minutes)

Each quad posts their three proposed norms for community review. Similar norms can be grouped or combined through community agreement. *The goal is to "see" our proposed needs with no additional conversation.*

The norms are read aloud to the community. *The goal is to "hear" our proposed needs with no additional conversation.*

When the proposed norms are posted and "rest" with the group, group members have the time and space to disassociate from particular norms offered by particular people. These proposed norms now serve as a reference point for continued learning in community.

5. Negotiations achieve consensus and reside with the group (for next meeting)

Although there may be consensus and shared ownership of the norms, the norms language may be a bit messy: a collection of sticky notes with words and phrases in different forms.

Because revising and editing with a large group can become tedious after members have spent so much energy in negotiations, most groups are pleased to have the facilitator or volunteers do the editing necessary to propose a more "polished" version of the norms for the group to consider and refine and ratify at the beginning of the next meeting.

6. Norms revisited (in future meetings)

Group norms continue to "live" for the community. They can be routinely revisited, providing the group a stable starting point for any needed renegotiations.

Facilitation Notes

Preliminary Experiences

Constructing norms through a process of negotiation often takes place after proceeding through a preliminary set of experiences intended to develop understandings about professional collaboration and critique within learning communities. Here's a sampling of preliminary experiences supported by facilitated conversations. The protocols for each are available at www.schoolreforminitiative.org.

- *Group Juggle*. Participants debrief using questions that focus on working together in groups toward shared goals.
- *Microlab or World Café*. These protocols offer time to check in with individuals about their experiences and goals related to collaboration within community.
- *Feedback principles/feedback nightmares*. Participants can use a Chalk Talk or walkabout to identify issues related to giving and receiving feedback.
- *Compass Points*. This approach helps participants identify learning needs based on learning styles.
- *Learning from text*. Participants identify words and ideas in a shared text to help them generate shared language.

Previewing the Work

The group should have a sense of the work they will be doing together *before* offering norms. This will give them a better sense of what they need to effectively collaborate.

Revisiting the Work

Many groups set time in a meeting agenda to review their norms. Questions that encourage "tending to" group norms include the following:

- In what ways are our norms helping us "grow" our thinking?
- Should we change our norms in some way to help us better meet our goals?
- What norms are we using well?
- What norms seem difficult for us?
- What norm will I/we work on today?

Source: Adapted with permission from *Norms Construction: A Process of Negotiation* developed by B. Bisplinghoff, 2017, School Reform Initiative. Available at https://www.schoolreforminitiative.org/download/norms-construction-a-process-of-negotiation.

Appendix E.
Sample Completed i3PD Planning Map

PART ONE: Core Components

1A. Content

Focus of Learning	Practice Gap
Appropriate scaffolding to support students to meet high expectations in writing (grades 2–5)	We will interrogate potential gaps between participants' current practice and (choose one) ☐ Practice informed by the current knowledge base for this practice. ☐ Professional standards for quality implementation of this practice. ☐ Practice that responsively matches teaching to students' learning processes. ☑ Practice that authentically achieves high expectations for students' learning products.

1B. Participants

The Cohort and Their Context	Questions	Insights and Implications
This school-based PD series will involve seven classroom teachers from grades 2–5 (two ESL teachers, two resource teachers, and three specialists including science, music, and technology). This collaborative staff has established significant trust. 40 percent of students are Black, 40 percent are Latinx, 11 percent are white, and 9 percent are multiracial. 12 percent are English language learners, and 9 percent are students with disabilities. Our school has not successfully supported our Black students to independently produce high quality writing.	What is the current understanding these teachers have about the difference between scaffolding and differentiation? Which participants already consider themselves experts with regard to this practice? Teachers are concurrently engaged in a book study about antiracism. What connections, if any, do they see to this work? I'll plan to answer these questions as part of a connecting activity within the first session.	I predict a range of expertise on this topic among the faculty; I'll aim to tap this expertise as an asset in the series, while ensuring everyone is extending their learning. There is an opportunity to help participants connect this series to their book study on antiracist teaching. I'll have to learn more about the current focus and goals of that activity.

(continued)

1C. Facilitators

Your Role	Your Goal(s)	Cofacilitation Notes
The school's Instructional Leadership Team established the vision for this series for our school's upper elementary staff. They asked us to lead because we have a fair amount of knowledge and skill in this topic. We're going to plan the broad arc of this series to ensure we finish in six sessions, but we will respond to participants' input on how they want to shape the details of the learning journey. We will assume responsibility for introducing relevant professional literature and resources but will invite participants to do so, too. Participants will be responsible for keeping up with the work; as facilitators, we will provide the time and structure as well as a culture of mutual accountability to support that.	Facilitator 1: I hope to improve my ability to support participants to stay focused on the goal. We only have six sessions. Although I want to be responsive to participants, it's my responsibility to ensure the work has integrity and results in real changes in practice, so I will need to make sure we don't get sidetracked and run out of time. Facilitator 2: I'm concerned about helping participants see multiple perspectives. It's challenging for me as a facilitator when knowledgeable veterans declare there's only one right answer. I have to manage my own emotions while also being more skillful at helping others to open their minds. We will monitor results by reviewing the exit slips and reflecting together at the end of each session.	Our cofacilitation team has complementary strengths. We teach different grades and have different teaching styles. Facilitator 1 will prepare and facilitate the whole-group discussions, and Facilitator 2 will be responsible for introducing and managing the small-group work. We have not cofacilitated together before. We have agreed to review the exit slips together immediately after each session and to meet on Thursdays before school for a longer meeting to reflect and plan.

1D. Seeing the System: Core Assumptions

Improvement Goal	Behavior Inventory (Doing/Not Doing)	Hidden Competing Commitments	Big Assumptions
1. What do our Spotlight Students need us to improve?	2. What are we doing and not doing that work against our goal of improving our practice for our Spotlight Students?	3A. What might be worrisome about doing the opposite of the things in column two?	4. What do our hidden commitments suggest about how we might see the world and ourselves (i.e., our collective mindset)?
We are committed to getting better at using scaffolding appropriately to support the growth and independence of the disproportionate number of Black and Latinx students in our school who are not yet producing high quality writing.	• We are planning lessons and assignments with one student profile in mind. • We are not deepening or using our knowledge of students to inform decisions about what's appropriate for each student. • We lean heavily on others (e.g., ESL and special ed teachers) to address these students' needs. • We are not removing scaffolding or encouraging students to do so when it is no longer needed. • We are sharing lots of tools but not teaching students to make their own informed choices about when to use them. • We are not disaggregating data by race or looking at student work to make evidence-informed decisions about what we need to change.	• We fear it would be a lot of work to differentiate instruction. — We worry that we don't have the time. — We worry that we don't know how. • We are afraid students won't feel successful and will become a behavior problem we can't handle. — We worry we'll lose control of the class. — We worry they won't be able to make effective choices on their own. • We fear that disaggregating results or LASW might reveal big gaps or disparities. — We worry about what this will do to the image we and others have of ourselves as competent professionals. — We worry that we'll be blamed or called racist. — We worry about opening up a conversation about race in today's climate.	We assume that • Teachers are being judged by others, personally and professionally. • Teachers must appear in control at all times. • We are culturally competent; we don't have more to learn.

(continued)

1D. Seeing the System: Core Assumptions—(continued)

Improvement Goal	Behavior Inventory (Doing/Not Doing)	Hidden Competing Commitments	Big Assumptions
		3B. What self-protective, hidden commitments stand behind our worries?	
		We are committed to not being incompetent or out of control of the class.	
		We are committed to protecting ourselves from being seen as racist or culturally incompetent.	
Insights and Implications	• How might we normalize struggle and the messy path of progress with regard to ourselves and our students? • How might we acknowledge racism's thumbprint on all of us so there's no stigma associated with revealing race-based patterns of underperformance and the learning we need to do? • How might we channel our intense feelings about this issue into a commitment to creating a growth mindset culture together?		

Source: Adapted from *Change Leadership: A Practical Guide to Transforming Our Schools,* by T. Wagner et al., 2012, San Francisco: John Wiley & Sons. Copyright 2012 Minds at Work.

PART TWO: Creating Connections

2A. Relevance

Purpose	Outcome-Based Objectives
• We believe each and every child deserves to gain skills they need to be equipped to meet the challenges of the 21st century. • Teachers' ability to provide appropriate scaffolding is essential to that because scaffolds can provide supportive on-ramps for students' meaningful engagement with content, but when we overscaffold, we give students a false sense of security about their readiness to succeed in life. • Closing this instructional practice gap is important for these specific participants, at this time, in this setting because these teachers have noticed persistent patterns in the writing products of Black and EL students who are currently demonstrating low growth. This change in teachers' practice will help these students to build the toolkits they need to produce high-quality writing.	If this series is successful, 1. Individual participants will (choose one) ☐ close their knowledge gap: They will be able to make decisions informed by a wider breadth of the knowledge and skill base for this instructional practice. ☐ close their implementation gap: They will be able to engage in high-quality implementation of this instructional practice. ☐ close their teaching-learning gap: They will be able to use this instructional practice more strategically and appropriately to strengthen students' learning processes. ☑ close their expectations gap: They will be able to recognize and raise artificially low expectations about what they accept as quality student work products in context of this instructional practice. And 2. Our community of participants will use inquiry results to identify systemic barriers to equity and be able to take action together.

(continued)

2B. Rigor

Process Objectives	Evidence of Impact
As individual participants, you will support one another to • **Assess:** Identify gaps in your own instructional practice (your knowledge, implementation, strategic use, or expectations of that practice) that currently contribute to inequitable outcomes. • **Attempt:** Design a response to the gap and a system for documenting change as you take action to close it. • **Analyze:** Interpret evidence of change, identify challenges to change, and integrate insights into your professional practice. As a community, we will • **Adjust:** Reflect on patterns across our lines of inquiry to identify relevant systemic factors that inhibit equity and organize our efforts to make the changes they require.	We will examine student work products from before and after the inquiry cycle to look for improvements in quality. We will also interview students about how they know their work is good and what they've learned to help them improve the quality of their work. Black and EL students' writing will meet the standards for the upcoming unit. We will compare disaggregated percentages of students meeting the standards in the upcoming unit with the percentages in the last two units.

2C. Relationships

Strengthening Trust: Respect and Personal Regard	Clarifying Role Expectations
Teachers have strong relationships of respect, and we already start all meetings with an opportunity to connect human to human. They have less personal regard when it comes to different life circumstances: Some may feel others don't work as hard or show as much commitment as they do. We will plan to use the Continuum Dialogue at the beginning of each session, with a different dimension or two each time, so participants come to appreciate our differences.	We will distribute copies of Figure 8.1 ("Facilitator and Participant Roles") and use it to discuss what our colleagues can expect from us. Then, we will ask participants to select a bullet that represents the greatest challenge for them and another that represents the greatest relief. We'll compare responses and discuss.

Strengthening Trust: Competence and Integrity	Community Agreements
Teachers have a good sense of one another's strengths and are willing to reach out and respond with help when needed. Some may feel others are less dependable when it comes to follow-through. We will be sure to make expectations that require follow-through explicit and participants' successes in meeting them visible.	Our school has schoolwide agreements. We'll revisit them at the beginning and identify which few will be most important for the work ahead. We could use this prior experience with school agreements to discuss examples of what each looks like.

2D. Seeing the System: Structures and Policies

Contextual Conditions	Local Structures and Policies
Schoolwide expectations and agreements	*We have assemblies that honor attendance and effort but not achievement. This seems like a mixed message when encouraging productive struggle for high expectations.*
Student ownership, engagement, and safety	*We want students to be independent learners and develop the habits of "owning" scaffolds so they know when to use them on their own. However, the structure of our textbook and related assessments provides scaffolding that works against our push for student ownership.*
Materials for curriculum, instruction, and assessment	*Teachers do not have ready access to relevant, high-quality professional materials; they spend a lot of time creating materials on their own instead of vetting provided ones.*

PART THREE: Inquiry Cycles and Learning Sequence

3A. Setting the Stage

Time	Space	Insights and Implications
Dates: First and third Wednesdays in March, April, and May Time: 3:30–5:00 p.m.	Location: School PD Lounge Venue setup: Hollow Square We can also use the hallway, main lobby, and outdoors.	These sessions will be held at the end of busy days and during the final months of the year. I'll need to monitor and proactively manage group energy. I'd like to support participants to document the work in this series to make it easy to pick up next year.

3B. Inquiry Cycle Map

Stages	Key Components	Implementation Notes	Timing Notes
Assess: Capture current reality	**Standard** How will participants define the professional standard of this instructional practice?	We will read an article about scaffolding and discuss it using a text-based protocol. Then, in small groups, we'll apply what we've learned by looking at student work that students produced with the aid of scaffolds. We'll use a perspective protocol (Collaborative Assessment Conference) to identify what students were working on.	Session 1
	Status How will participants identify the gap between this standard and their current practice? How will they identify what contextual factors might contribute to that gap?	We will review results from our school's Instructional Leadership Team's analysis of grades and state assessments to understand why they selected this focus. We'll use this data together with our own experiences to describe our expectations gap.	Session 1
	Success Target How will participants establish a target for improved practice?	Between Sessions 1 & 2, participants will draft success targets: How will they change what they're doing, and how do they expect this to change what students are doing? They should also bring any relevant professional resources they have to share.	Between 1 and 2

Attempt: Plan and implement changes	**Dig** How will participants gain new knowledge to assist them in closing the gap and meeting the success target?	Participants will use sticky notes to brainstorm the questions they have about teachers' current scaffolding practices and how students respond to scaffolding. They will organize the sticky notes into themes and break into teams to answer the questions using available resources that I and participants will provide. We will display findings for all to access and review.	Session 2
	Decide How will participants decide what they will start doing, continue doing differently, and stop doing?	Participants will use the time between sessions to review our notes, read relevant literature, and decide what they will do or change. They will draft an Action Plan.	Between 2 and 3
	Do and Document How will participants track what they actually do, the effect of these changes, and the contextual factors that matter?	Participants will share their plans in triads, give one another feedback on those plans, and help one another develop strategies for tracking what they do and its effect, specifically, on Spotlight Students. Participants will carry out their action plan between Sessions 3 and 4.	Session 3
Analyze: Examine and interpret evidence	**Identify** How will participants characterize the effect of the change they have made?	Participants will work in triads to review data they have collected and brought, compare their success targets, and draw conclusions about the effect of the change.	Session 4
	Interpret How will participants interpret what the evidence says about the conditions that have supported or limited their change in practice?	Participants will use their data to identify key supporting and limiting conditions and discuss the evidence supporting their conclusions.	Session 4
	Infer How might participants determine what they have learned and might need to learn next?	Participants will use the time between these meetings to test their conclusions with additional observations and bring ideas about what might be adjusted to the group next time.	Session 4 through 5

(continued)

3B. Inquiry Cycle Map—(continued)

Stages	Key Components	Implementation Notes	Timing Notes
Adjust: Commit to changes	**Structures** How will participants illustrate the ways that existing structures and policies currently function as systemic barriers to equity?	Participants will compare data with one another, look for patterns in the conditions that supported and limited success throughout the school, and draft a plan that can be used to communicate this new schoolwide problem of practice and engage relevant stakeholders.	Session 5
	Suppositions How will participants uncover the collective mindsets that have produced our current system of inequitable structures?	In small groups, participants will reflect on the problem of practice to identify some of the mindsets that produce it or lock it in place. Between this session and the next, they will look for evidence of these mindsets in our context.	Session 5
	Seismic Shift How will participants identify the strategic moves they need to make to create a seismic shift in the system?	Participants will engage in the Back to the Future protocol and develop an Action Plan with commitments for individual and collective action to make critical shifts of mindsets and systems.	Session 6

3C. Session Agendas

Session 1

Time	Key Topics	Implementation Notes	Minutes	Materials and Handouts
--	Prework	Complete the Pre-series Survey		
	1. Welcome		20	
3:30	**Relevance** • Purpose • Objectives	Use Sections 2A and 2B to share the significance of the work we're about to launch together and to clarify what participants can expect to do and produce.	5	Slides with the purpose and objectives
3:35	**Rigor** • Series overview • Today's agenda	Provide an overview of the plan for our six sessions and review today's agenda.	5	series plan today's agenda

Time	Section / Activity	Min	Description	Materials
3:40	**Relationships** • Community agreements • Connecting activity	10	Review schoolwide norms and identify connections to this specific work. Connecting activity: Continuum Dialogue [See http://schoolreforminitiative.org/doc/continuum_dialogue_youth.pdf]	Copy of schoolwide norms
	2. Inquiry Cycle Work	60		
3:50	**Standard**	30	We will read an article about scaffolding and discuss it using a text-based protocol. Then, in small groups, we'll apply what we've learned by looking at student work that students produced with the aid of scaffolds. We'll use a perspective protocol (Collaborative Assessment Conference) to identify what students were working on.	article protocol student work samples copies of the protocol
4:20	**Status**	30	We will review results from our school's Instructional Leadership Team's analysis of grades and state assessments to understand why they selected this focus. We'll use this data together with our own experiences to describe our expectations gap.	ILT data analysis results
	3. Wrap-up	10		
4:50	**Relevance**	2	Revisit objectives and what we did to meet them. Revisit the series overview: where we are in the process and what's coming next.	
4:52	**Rigor**	4	Share the QR code for the exit slip. Review the plan and prework commitments for next time.	exit slip
4:56	**Relationships**	4	Closing activity: Appreciations (Discuss the purpose of the closing activity and ask for a volunteer to lead this in the next session.)	
5:00	Adjourn			

(continued)

3C. Session Agendas — Session 2

Time	Key Topics	Minutes	Implementation Notes	Materials and Handouts
—	**Prework** **Success Target**		Participants will draft success targets: How will they change what they're doing, and how do they expect this to change what students are doing? They should also bring relevant professional resources they have to share.	
3:30	**1. Welcome**	10		
3:30	**Relevance** • Purpose • Objectives	2	Review the purpose and objectives.	
3:32	**Rigor** • Exit slip review • Today's agenda	2	Review exit slips from the last session and the adjustments made to today's agenda in response. Review today's agenda in the context of the plan for our six sessions.	agenda exit slip data
3:34	**Relationships** • Community agreements • Connecting activity	6	Review schoolwide norms. *Connecting activity:* Continuum Dialogue with two new attributes (Discuss the goals and ask for a volunteer to lead it next time)	
3:40	**2. Inquiry Cycle Work**	70		
3:40	**Dig**	70	Participants will use sticky notes to brainstorm questions they have about what teachers do and how students respond to scaffolding. They will organize the sticky notes into themes and break into teams to answer the questions using available resources (that I and participants will provide). We will display findings for all to access and review.	sticky notes
4:50	**3. Wrap-up**	10		
4:50	**Relevance**	2	Revisit objectives and what we did to meet them: We did lots of "digging." What's one thing you discovered?	
4:52	**Rigor**	4	Share the QR code for the exit slip. Review the plan and prework commitments for next time.	exit slip
4:56	**Relationships**	4	Closing activity led by a participant (Ask for a volunteer to lead this in the next session.)	
5:00	Adjourn			

3C. Session Agendas — Session 3

Time	Key Topics	Minutes	Implementation Notes	Materials and Handouts
—	**Prework** Decide		Participants will use the time between sessions to review our notes and decide what to do or change. They will draft the Action Plan.	
3:30	**1. Welcome**	10		
3:30	**Relevance** • Purpose • Objectives	2	Review the purpose and objectives.	
3:32	**Rigor** • Exit slip review • Today's agenda	2	Review today's agenda in the context of the overview of the plan for our six sessions. Review exit slips from the last session and the changes made in response.	agenda exit slip data
3:34	**Relationships** • Community agreements • Connecting activity	6	Review schoolwide norms. Continuum Dialogue with two new attributes (Ask for a volunteer to lead a new connecting activity next time)	
3:40	**2. Inquiry Cycle Work**	70		
3:40	**Document**	30	Participants will share their plans in triads and give one another feedback on the Action Plans they have developed and brought today.	feedback protocol
4:10	**Document II**	40	Participants will help one another develop strategies for tracking what they do and its effect, specifically, on Spotlight Students.	progress monitoring suggestions
4:50	**3. Wrap-up**	10		
4:50	**Relevance**	2	Revisit objectives and what we did to meet them: How did your colleagues' feedback help enhance your plans? Revisit the series overview: where we are in the process and what's coming next.	
4:52	**Rigor**	4	Share the QR code for the exit slip. Review plan and prework commitments for next time.	exit slip
4:56	**Relationships**	4	Closing activity led by a participant (Ask a volunteer to lead this in the next session.)	
5:00	Adjourn			

(continued)

3C. Session Agendas		Session 4		
Time	Key Topics	Minutes	Implementation Notes	Materials and Handouts
--	Prework		Participants will carry out their Action Plan. (Ideally 2–4 weeks)	
	1. Welcome	10		
3:30	**Relevance** • Purpose • Objectives	2	Review the purpose and objectives.	
3:32	**Rigor** • Exit slip review • Today's agenda	2	Review today's agenda in the context of the overview of the plan for our six sessions. Review exit slips from the last session and the changes made in response.	agenda exit slip data
3:34	**Relationships** • Community agreements • Connecting activity	6	Review schoolwide norms. New connecting activity (Ask for a volunteer to lead a new connecting activity next time)	
	2. Inquiry Cycle Work	70		
3:40	**Identify**	30	Participants will work in triads to review data they have collected and brought, compare their success targets, and draw conclusions about the effect of the change.	data review protocol
4:10	**Interpret**	40	Participants will compile their list of key supporting and limiting conditions and discuss the evidence supporting their conclusions.	
	3. Wrap-up	10		
4:50	**Relevance**	2	Revisit objectives and what we did to meet them: How is your thinking about scaffolding changing? Revisit the series overview: where we are in the process and what's coming next.	
4:52	**Rigor**	4	Share the QR code for the exit slip. Review plan and prework commitments for next time.	exit slip
4:56	**Relationships**	4	Closing activity led by a participant (Ask a volunteer to lead this in the next session.)	
5:00	Adjourn			

3C. Session Agendas | Session 5

Time	Key Topics	Minutes	Implementation Notes	Materials and Handouts
—	**Prework** Infer	10	Participants will use the time between these meetings to reflect on what they have learned and bring key ideas and implications next time.	
3:30	**1. Welcome**			
	Relevance • Purpose • Objectives	2	Review the purpose and objectives.	
3:32	**Rigor** • Exit slip review • Today's agenda	2	Review today's agenda in the context of the six sessions. Review the exit slips from the last session and the changes made.	agenda exit slip data
3:34	**Relationships** • Community agreements • Connecting activity	6	Review schoolwide norms. New connecting activity (Ask for a volunteer for next time)	
	2. Inquiry Cycle Work	70		
3:40	**Structures**	40	Participants will compare data, look for patterns in the conditions that supported and limited success throughout the school, and draft a plan to engage relevant stakeholders with findings.	sticky notes
4:20	**Suppositions**	30	In small groups, participants will reflect on the problem of practice to identify some of the mindsets that produce it or lock it in place. Between this session and the next, they will look for evidence of these mindsets in our context.	chart paper or padlet
4:50	**3. Wrap-up**	10		
	Relevance	2	Revisit objectives and what we did to meet them. Invite reflection on changes in thinking: "As a result of today, one thing I will consider is ____." Revisit the series overview: where we are in the process and what's coming next.	

(continued)

3C. Session Agendas—(continued)   Session 5

Time	Key Topics	Minutes	Implementation Notes	Materials and Handouts
	3. Wrap-up—(continued)	10		
4:52	Rigor	4	Share the QR code for the exit slip. Review plan and prework commitments for next time.	exit slips
5:56	Relationships	4	Closing activity led by a participant. (For next time, the final session, facilitators will lead it)	
5:00	Adjourn			

3C. Session Agendas   Session 6

Time	Key Topics	Minutes	Implementation Notes	Materials and Handouts
--	Prework		Complete the final survey.	
	1. Welcome	10		
3:30	Relevance • Purpose • Objectives	2	Review the purpose and objectives.	
3:32	Rigor • Exit slip review • Today's agenda	2	Review today's agenda in the context of the overview of the plan for our six sessions. Review exit slips from the last session and the changes made in response.	agenda exit slip data
3:34	Relationships • Community agreements • Connecting activity	6	Review schoolwide norms. New connecting activity	
	2. Inquiry Cycle Work	60		
3:40	Strategies	60	Participants will engage in the Back to the Future protocol and develop an Action Plan with commitments for individual and collective action to make critical shifts of mindsets and systems.	protocol chart paper

	3. Wrap-up	20		
4:40	Relevance	5	Revisit objectives and what we did to meet them. Revisit the series overview, then invite responses: "I used to think _____ and now I think _____."	
4:45	Rigor	5	Share the QR code for the exit slip.	exit slip
4:50	Relationships	10	Closing activity: Share and discuss key findings from the surveys. Identify personal commitments and our commitments to each other in the context of our work.	
5:00	Adjourn			

PART FOUR: Continuous Learning

Data Sources	Research Question 1	Research Question 2	Research Question 3	Research Question 4	Collection Routine	Review Routine
	In what ways have participants made changes to practice and improved instructional decision making to close those gaps?	To what extent have participants demonstrated confidence, commitment, and capacity as agents of their own learning in this series?	In what ways have participants identified systemic barriers to equity and coordinated efforts toward eliminating them?	To what extent have you advanced toward your personal goal established in 1C? _support participants to stay focused on the goal._		
Initial and final survey	✓	✓	✓		Pre- and post-series	Before first session and before final session
Exit slip	✓	✓	✓	✓	Every session	At the end of every session
Facilitator's reflection journal		✓		✓	Every session	Mid-series and end of series
Document review	✓		✓		After the Analyze and Adjust stages	After the Analyze and Adjust stages
Participant conferences	✓			✓	mid-series	Facilitators will meet once with each participant

4B. Analyzing Data

Data Sources	Who	When	How
Initial and final survey	Session participants and facilitators	During the final session	Facilitators will collect the final survey data before the final meeting and prepare a display that compares pre- and post-data for each participant (anonymously).
			Facilitators and participants will review these displays and interpret them together.
Exit slip	Facilitators	After each session	Formulas will auto-calculate average scores for the Likert scales for easy comparison over time.
			Facilitators will meet to review the exit slips, read comments, and identify themes to report back in the subsequent session.
Facilitator's reflection journal	Facilitators	Before the mid-series conferences and at the end of the series	Facilitators will meet to share reflections and identify themes and questions to raise in participant conferences.
Document review	All	In sessions after the Analyze and Adjust stages	Facilitators and participants will collaborate in analyzing the data from the inquiry cycles as part of our session activities.
Participant conferences	All	Mid-series	Facilitators will meet with participants individually to gather data regarding Research Question 2 and conference with them about themes or questions that have come up.

References

Alliance for Resource Equity. (2019). *The education combination: 10 dimensions of education resource equity to unlock opportunities for every student.* Retrieved from https://www.educationresourceequity.org/documents/education-combination.pdf

Alvarez, A., & Bachman, R. (1997). Predicting the fear of assault at school and while going to and from school in an adolescent population. *Violence and Victims, 12,* 69–86.

Angulo, A. J. (Ed.). (2016). *Miseducation: A history of ignorance-making in America and abroad.* Johns Hopkins University Press.

Avolio, B. J., & Bass, B. M. (2002). *Developing potential across a full range of leadership cases on transactional and transformational leadership.* Mahwah, NJ: Lawrence Erlbaum Associates.

Ball, D. L. (2018). *Just dreams and imperatives: The power of teaching in the struggle for public education.* AERA 2018 Presidential Address, Annual Meeting of the American Educational Research Association, New York.

Bass, B. M., & Riggio, R. E. (2006). *Transformational leadership* (2nd ed.). Mahwah, NJ: Lawrence Erlbaum Associates.

Berg, J. H. (2018). *Leading in sync: Teacher leaders and principals leading together for student learning.* Alexandria, VA: ASCD.

Berg, J. H., & Gleason, S. C. (2018). Come together for equity. *The Learning Professional, 39*(5), 24–27.

Berg, J. H., & Homan, E. C. (2021). Overcoming the inertia of inequity. *Educational Leadership, 78*(6), 80–81.

Bisplinghoff, B. (2017). *Norms construction: A process of negotiation.* Houston, TX: School Reform Initiative. Retrieved from https://www.schoolreforminitiative.org/download/norms-construction-a-process-of-negotiation

Blankstein, A. M., Noguera, P., & Kelly, L. (2016). *Excellence through equity: Five principles of courageous leadership to guide achievement for every student.* Alexandria, VA: ASCD.

Boudett, K. P., City, E. A., & Murnane, R. J. (2005). *Data Wise: A step-by-step guide to using assessment results to improve teaching and learning.* Cambridge, MA: Harvard Education Press.

Bryk, A., & Schneider, B. (2002). *Trust in schools: A core resource for improvement.* New York: Russell Sage Foundation.

Chapman, C., Chestnutt, H., Friel, N., Hall, S., & Lowden, K. (2016). Professional capital and collaborative inquiry networks for educational equity and improvement? *Journal of Professional Capital and Community, 1*(3), 178–197.

Cochran-Smith, M., & Lytle, S. L. (2001). Beyond certainty: Taking an inquiry stance on practice. In A. Lieberman & L. Miller (Eds.), *Teachers caught in the action: Professional development that matters* (pp. 45–58). New York: Teachers College Press.

Cochran-Smith, M., & Lytle, S. L. (2009). *Inquiry as stance: Practitioner research for the next generation.* New York: Teachers College Press.

Cohen, D. K., & Ball, D. L. (1999). *Instruction, capacity, and improvement.* CPRE Research Report Series (RR-43). University of Pennsylvania: Consortium for Policy Research in Education.

Collinson, V., & Cook, T. F. (2007). *Organizational learning: Improving learning, teaching, and leading in school systems.* Thousand Oaks, CA: Sage Publications.

Darling-Hammond, L., Hyler, M. E., & Gardner, M. (2017). *Effective teacher professional development.* Palo Alto, CA: Learning Policy Institute.

Dorn, E., Hancock, B., Sarakatsannis, J., & Viruleg, E. (2020, December 8). COVID-19 and learning loss—disparities grow and students need help. Retrieved from https://www.mckinsey.com/

industries/public-and-social-sector/our-insights/covid-19-and-learning-loss-disparities-grow-and-students-need-help

Duffy, F. M. (2014). Paradigms, mental models, and mind-sets: Triple barriers to transformational change in school systems. *Educational Technology, 54*(3), 29–33.

EdBuild. (2019). Nonwhite school districts get $23 billion less than white districts despite serving the same number of students. Retrieved from https://edbuild.org/content/23-billion/full-report.pdf

Eller, J. (2004). *Effective group facilitation in education: How to energize meetings and manage difficult groups.* Thousand Oaks, CA: Corwin Press.

Elmore, R. F. (1996). Getting to scale with good educational practice. *Harvard Educational Review, 66*(1), 1–26.

Equity. (1989). In the *Oxford English Dictionary* (2nd ed.). New York: Oxford University Press.

Fullan, M. (2007). *The new meaning of educational change* (3rd ed.). New York: Teachers College Press.

Goldin, C. (1999). *A brief history of education in the United States.* (NBER Historical Paper No. 119). Cambridge, MA: National Bureau of Economic Research.

Hammond, Z. (2014). *Culturally responsive teaching and the brain: Promoting authentic engagement and rigor among culturally and linguistically diverse students.* Thousand Oaks, CA: Corwin Press.

Hargreaves, A., & Fullan, M. (2015). *Professional capital: Transforming teaching in every school.* New York: Teachers College Press.

Hattie, J. (2009). *Visible Learning: A synthesis of over 800 meta-analyses relating to achievement.* London: Routledge.

Hawkins, D. (2002). *The informed vision: Essays on learning and human nature.* New York: Algora Publishing.

Jeynes, W. H. (2007). *American educational history: School, society, and the common good.* Thousand Oaks, CA: SAGE.

Johnson, S. M. (2005). The prospects for teaching as a profession. In L. V. Hedges & B. Schneider (Eds.), *The social organization of schooling* (pp. 72–90). New York: Russell Sage Foundation.

Johnson, S. M., Kraft, M. A., & Papay, J. P. (2012). How context matters in high-need schools: The effects of teachers' working conditions on their professional satisfaction and their students' achievement. *Teachers College Record, 114*(10), 1–39.

Kegan, R., & Lahey, L. L. (2009). *Immunity to change: How to overcome it and unlock the potential in yourself and your organization.* Boston: Harvard Business Review Press.

Kegan, R., & Lahey, L. L. (2016). *An everyone culture: Becoming a deliberately developmental organization.* Boston: Harvard Business Review Press.

Knowles, M. C. (1990). *The adult learner* (4th ed.). Houston, TX: Gulf Publishing.

Kochanek, J. R. (2005). *Building trust for better schools: Research-based practices.* Thousand Oaks, CA: Corwin Press.

Kraft, M. A., Simon, N. S., & Lyon, M. A. (2020). Sustaining a sense of success: The importance of teacher working conditions during the COVID-19 pandemic. (EdWorkingPaper: 20-279). Retrieved from Annenberg Institute at Brown University at https://doi.org/10.26300/35nj-v890

Leithwood, K., Harris, A., & Hopkins, D. (2019). Seven strong claims about successful school leadership revisited. *School Leadership & Management, 40*(4), 1–18.

Lindsay, C. A., Blom, E., & Tilsley, A. (2017). Diversifying the classroom: Examining the teacher pipeline. Urban Institute. Retrieved from https://www. urban. org/features/diversifying-classroom-examining-teacher-pipeline.

Loughland, T., & Nguyen, H. T. M. (2016). Using the instructional core to implement a professional learning programme for primary science teachers in Australia: Teacher learning and student skill outcomes. *Teacher Development, 20*(4), 498–520.

Love, N. (2009). *Using data to improve learning for all: A collaborative inquiry approach.* Corwin Press.

Mann, H. (1855). *Lectures on education.* Boston: Ide & Dutton.

Massachusetts Consortium for Innovative Education Assessment (MCIEA). (2018). School quality measures framework. Retrieved from https://www.mciea.org/uploads/1/2/0/7/120788330/mciea-sqm-framework-short-2018.pdf

McTighe, J., & Silver, H. F. (2020). *Teaching for deeper learning: Tools to engage students in meaning making.* Alexandria, VA: ASCD.

Metzger, W. P. (1987). A spectre is haunting American scholars: The spectre of "professionalism." *Educational Researcher, 16*(6), 10–21.

Mezirow, J. (1981). A critical theory of adult learning and education. *Adult Education, 32*(1), 3–24.

Morgan, I., & Amerikaner, A. (2018). Funding gaps 2018: An analysis of school funding equity across the U.S. and within each state. *Education Trust*. Retrieved from https://edtrust.org/resource/funding-gaps-2018/

Murphy, S. (2008). *Future protocol aka Back to the future*. Houston, TX: School Reform Initiative. Retrieved from https://www.schoolreforminitiative.org/download/future-protocol-a-k-a-back-to-the-future

National Board for Professional Teaching Standards. (n.d.). National Board Standards. Accessible from http://www.nbpts.org/standards-five-core-propositions/

National Board for Professional Teaching Standards. (2016). *Architecture for Accomplished Teaching*. Accessible from http://accomplishedteacher.org/resource/the-architecture-of-accomplished-teaching/

National Research Council. (2000). *How people learn: Brain, mind, experience, and school: Expanded Edition*. Washington, DC: National Academies Press.

National Research Council. 2002. *Scientific Research in Education*. Washington, DC: The National Academies Press. https://doi.org/10.17226/10236/scientific-research-in-education.

Newhall, P. W. (2014). *Executive function: Foundations for learning and teaching*. Prides Crossing, MA: Landmark School Outreach Program.

Noguera, P. (2017) Taking deeper learning to scale. Palo Alto, CA: Learning Policy Institute.

Quinn, N. (2005). How to reconstruct schemas people share. In N. Quinn (Ed.), *Finding culture in talk: A collection of method* (pp. 33–81). New York: Palgrave Miller.

Quintero, E. (2017). *Teaching in context: The social side of education reform*. Boston: Harvard Education Press.

Rincón-Gallardo, S., & Fleisch, B. (2016). Bringing effective instructional practice to scale: An introduction. *Journal of Educational Change, 17*(4), 379–383.

Romme, A. G. L., & Van Witteloostuijn, A. (1999). Circular organizing and triple loop learning. *Journal of Organizational Change Management, 12*(5), 439–454.

Rury, J. (2004). *Education and social change: Themes in the history of American schooling*. New York: Routledge.

Sarason, S. B. (1996). *Revisiting "The culture of the school and the problem of change."* New York: Teachers College Press.

Schon, D. A. (1987). *Educating the reflective practitioner: Toward a new design for teaching and learning in the professions*. San Francisco: Jossey-Bass.

Senge, P. M. (2006). *The fifth discipline: The art and practice of the learning organization*. New York: Crown Business.

Stelitano, L., Doan, S., Woo, A., Diliberti, M. K., Kaufman, J. H., and Henry, D. (2020). The digital divide and COVID-19: Teachers' perceptions of inequities in students' internet access and participation in remote learning. Retrieved from https://www.rand.org/pubs/research_reports/RRA134-3.html.

Tosey, P., Visser, M., & Saunders, M. N. (2012). The origins and conceptualizations of 'triple-loop' learning: A critical review. *Management learning, 43*(3), 291–307.

Tschannen-Moran, M. (2014). *Trust matters: Leadership for successful schools*. San Francisco: Jossey-Bass.

University of Chicago Consortium on School Research. (n.d.). *The 5essentials framework*. Retrieved from https://uchicagoimpact.org/sites/default/files/5eframework_outreach%26marketing%20%281%29.pdf

U.S. Department of Education, Institute of Education Sciences (IES), National Center for Education Statistics (NCES), & National Assessment of Education Progress (NAEP). (2011a). *Classroom context: Emphasis on algebra*. Retrieved from https://www.nationsreportcard.gov/math_2011/context_2.aspx?-subtab_id=Tab_3&tab_id=tab2#chart

U.S. Department of Education, IES, NCES, & NAEP. (2011b). *Writing 2011*. Retrieved from https://www.nationsreportcard.gov/writing_2011/summary.aspx

U.S. Department of Education, IES, NCES, & NAEP. (2015). *2015 reading assessments*. Retrieved from https://www.nationsreportcard.gov/reading_math_2015/#reading?grade=4

Van Soelen, T. M. (2021) *Meeting goals: Protocols for leading effective, purpose-driven discussions in schools*. Bloomington, IN: Solution Tree Press.

Vella, J. (2002). *Learning to listen, learning to teach: The power of dialogue in educating adults*. San Francisco: Jossey-Bass.

Wagner, T., Kegan, R., Lahey, L. L., Lemons, R. W., Garnier, J., Helsing, D., Howell, A. & Rasmussen, H. T. (2012). *Change leadership: A practical guide to transforming our schools*. San Francisco: Wiley & Sons.

Wood, C. (2018). *Yardsticks: Child and adolescent development ages 4–14* (4th ed.). Turners Falls, MA: Center for Responsive Schools.

Index

Note: Page references followed by an italicized *f* indicates information contained in figures.

Action Planning Template, 130, 131*f*
action research projects, 12
adjust
    about, 13, 13*f*, 76, 107, 140, 141*f*
    adaptations to inquiry models, 109*f*, 110*f*,
       112*f*, 113*f*
    Back to the Future Protocol, 144, 145*f*–146*f*
    implementation and timing notes, 144–145
    inquiry cycle comparison, 115*f*
    seismic shifts, 141*f*, 143–144, 145*f*–146*f*
    structures, 140–142, 141*f*
    suppositions, 141*f*, 142–143
adult learners, 36–37
aequus, 8
agency, 164
analyze
    about, 13, 13*f*, 76, 107, 134, 135*f*
    adaptations to inquiry models, 109*f*, 110*f*,
       112*f*, 113*f*
    identify, 134–136
    infer, 137–139
    inquiry cycle comparison, 115*f*
    interpret, 136–137
Appreciations, 154*f*
assess
    about, 12, 13*f*, 75, 106, 116, 117*f*
    adaptations to inquiry models, 108*f*, 109*f*,
       111*f*, 113*f*
    expectations gap inquiry, 123–125
    implementation gap inquiry, 119–121
    inquiry cycle comparisons, 115*f*
    knowledge gap inquiry, 117–121
    teaching-learning gap inquiry, 121–123
assumptions, big, 61*f*, 63
ATLAS, 21
attempt
    about, 12, 13*f*, 75, 106, 126, 127*f*
    adaptations to inquiry models, 108*f*, 110*f*,
       111*f*, 113*f*
    decide, 129–132, 131*f*
    dig, 126–129

attempt—(*continued*)
    do and document, 132, 133*f*
    Implementation Log, 132, 133*f*
    inquiry cycle comparisons, 115*f*
Awards, 155*f*

Back to the Future Protocol, 144, 145*f*–146*f*
Before and After, 154*f*
behavior inventory, 61*f*, 62
big assumptions, 61*f*, 63
blaming the victim, 11
block party, 105*f*
Boston Latin School, 9

carousel, 105*f*
chalk talk, 105*f*
change, 15–16, 58–63
Charades, 154*f*
check-ins, midpoint/endpoint, 172
classism, 11
Collaborative Assessment Conference, 21
collaborative inquiry, 12, 13–14, 18–21, 19*f*
collective mindsets, 15–16, 59
community agreements, 86–87, 88*f*–89*f*,
  199–202
connections
    about, 90
    context matters, 90–91
    identifying dimensions of system to explore,
      91–95
    sample structures and policies, 92*f*–94*f*
content
    about, 35
    expectations gap inquiry, 42–43
    implementation gap inquiry, 41
    instructional core and adult learning, 36–37
    knowledge gap inquiry, 40–41
    learning focus, 38–39
    Planning Map annotated, 66
    student-led inquiry, 43–44
    teaching-learning gap inquiry, 42

continuous learning (i3PD)
   about, 161
   evidence collection and interpretation,
      163–176
   Planning Map annotated, 177–178
continuum dialogue, 105f
core assumptions
   about, 58–59
   behavior inventory, 61f, 62
   big assumptions, 61f, 63
   hidden competing commitments, 61f, 62–63
   immunity to change, 59–63, 61f
   improvement goal, 60–62, 61f
   mindset shifts, 63–65
   Planning Map annotated, 68
   worldview, 63
core components (i3PD)
   content, 35–44, 45f
   core assumptions, 58–65, 61f
   facilitators, 52–57, 55f
   participants, 46–51
   Planning Map annotated, 66–68
   revisiting, 155–156
COVID-19, 2, 104
creating connections for a productive learning
   environment (i3PD), 69
   connections in context, 90–95, 92f–94f
   Planning Map annotated, 96–98
   relationships, 80–87, 88f–89f
   relevance, 71–74
   rigor, 75–79
culture and climate supports, 92f

data, 14
   analyzing, 173–176, 174f–175f
   sources, 166–172, 168f–170f, 171f
decide, 127f, 129–132
deep dive, 130, 135–136, 137–138, 141, 142–
   143, 154f
designing your inquiry cycle & learning cycle
   (i3PD)
   about, 99
   adjust, 140–145, 145f–146f
   analyze, 134–139, 135f
   assess, 116–125, 117f
   attempt, 126–132, 127f, 131f, 133f
   inquiry cycle map, 106–114, 108f–113f, 115f
   Planning Map annotated, 157–160
   session agendas, 147–156, 148f, 149f,
      154f–155f
   time and space, 101–104, 103f–104f, 105f
Dewey, John, 13
difference, 82
dig, 126–129, 127f
digital tool collection, 187–188
dilemmas, exploring and managing, 189

disorienting dilemma, 58–59
disruption, 58–59
do and document, 132, 133f
document review, 172
double-loop learning, 14–15, 16

education system, US, 9–10, 11
equality, 8–9
equity
   versus equality, 8–9
   inquiry stance into, 10–14, 13f
evidence collection and interpretation
   about, 163
   analyzing data, 173–176, 174f–175f
   data sources, 166–172, 168f–170f, 171f
   exit slips, 167, 168f–169f
   facilitator reflection journal, 170, 171f
   Planning Map annotated, 177–178
   research questions, 163–166
evidence of impact, 76–79
exit slips, 167, 168f–169f
expectations gap inquiry
   about, 19f, 21
   adaptations to i3PD, 112f–113f
   adjust stage, 141f
   analyze stage, 135f
   assess stage, 123–125
   attempt stage, 128–129
   facilitator growth, 166
   Immunity Map, 197–198
   interrogating decisions about whether we're
      doing it effectively, 42–43, 45f
   rigor issues, 78–79
expertise, 13

facilitators
   about, 36–37, 52
   assessing progress, 164–166
   cofacilitating, 56
   leaders versus, 53–54, 55f
   learning expectations, 54
   Planning Map annotated, 67
   reflection journal, 170, 171f
   role, 52–54, 84f
family perspectives, 102
Final Flash, 155f
four corners, 105f

generating, 190

Happily Ever After, 154f
Hattie, John, 21
hidden assumptions, 60, 61f
hidden competing commitments, 61f,
   62–63
homogeneity, 10–11

i3PD. *See also specific components*
    about, 21–23
    defined, 3
    digital tool collection, 187–188
    inquiry cycle map, 106–114, 108*f*–113*f*
    leadership sharing, 179–180
    multilevel learning, 181–182
    Planning Map, 24–32
    Planning Map annotated, 66–68, 96–98,
        157–160, 177–178
    Planning Map completed, 203–221
    protocol families, 189–190
    revisiting core components, 155–156
    testing out, 182–183
identify, 134–136
Immunity Map, 60, 61*f*, 191–198
immunity to change, 59–63
impact of teaching, 20–21
implementation gap inquiry
    about, 19*f*, 20
    adaptations to i3PD, 109*f*–110*f*
    adjust stage, 141*f*
    analyze stage, 135*f*
    assess stage, 119–121
    attempt stage, 128–129
    facilitator growth, 165
    Immunity Map, 193–194
    interrogating decisions about how to do it
        well, 41, 45*f*
    rigor issues, 77
Implementation Log, 132, 133*f*
improvement goals, 60–62, 61*f*
individual learning, 16–17
individual mindsets, 15
inductive approach, 107
inequity
    COVID-19 and, 2
    overview of approaches to, 2–4
    roots of, 1–2
infer, 137–139
inquiry. *See also specific inquiry stages*
    about, 10–11
    inquiry cycle map, 106–114, 108*f*–113*f*, 115*f*
    power of, 13–14
    stages of, 12–13, 13*f*
instructional core. *See* core components (i3PD)
instructional observations, 77
interaction and engagement, 105*f*
interpret, 136–137
interviews, stakeholders, 78–79
interviews, students, 78

knowledge gap inquiry
    about, 18–20, 19*f*
    adaptations to i3PD, 108*f*–109*f*
    adjust stage, 141*f*

knowledge gap inquiry—(*continued*)
    analyze stage, 135*f*
    assess stage, 117–121
    attempt stage, 127–128
    facilitator growth, 165
    Immunity Map, 191–192
    interrogating decisions about what to do,
        40–41, 45*f*
    rigor issues, 76–77

leaders, school
    leadership sharing, 179–180
    leadership supports, 94*f*
    and organizational learning, 17–18
learning
    individual, 16–17
    learning supports, 93*f*
    multilevel learning, 181–182
    organizational, 17–18
learning community norms construction,
    199–202
looped learning, 14–16

Mann, Horace, 9
Massachusetts colony, 9
mental models, 58–59
mindsets
    collective, 15–16
    individual, 15
multilevel learning, 181–182

National Board Certification, 12
Native Americans, 10
natural justice, 8–9
negotiation, 199–202
norms construction, learning community,
    88*f*–89*f*, 199–202

observations of students at work, 78
observations of teaching, 77
online tools, 104, 130, 136, 138, 143, 155*f*,
    187–188
oppression, 11
organizational learning, 17–18
outcome, change in, 136

participants
    about, 37, 46
    assessing progress, 163–164
    communication and planning, 49–51
    data collection, 46–48
    engagement, 47, 49–50
    Planning Map annotated, 66–67
    roles, 84*f*
    trust, 80–83
peer observation pairs, 172

personal regard, 82
Planning Map
    about, 24–32
    annotated, 66–68, 96–98, 157–160, 177–178
    completed, 203–221
policies and structures
    about, 90
    context, 90–91
    identifying dimensions of system to explore,
        91–95
    sample structures and policies, 92f–94f
power structures, 11
practice, change in, 136, 164
professional capacity, 93f
professional development, 16–18
project-based learning, 12
protocol families, 189–190
Puritan values, 9

quick chat, 130, 136, 138, 141–142, 143, 154f

racism, systemic, 2, 11
refining, 190
reflection journal, 170, 171f
relationships
    about, 80
    community agreements, 86–87, 88f–89f
    role expectations, 83–86, 84f
    in session agenda, 151, 153
    trust, 80–83
relevance
    about, 71
    outcome-based objectives, 74
    purpose, 72–74
    in session agenda, 148–150, 152
respect, 82
result patterns, 14–16
rigor
    about, 75
    evidence of impact, 76–79
    expectations gap inquiry, 78–79
    implementation gap inquiry, 77
    knowledge gap inquiry, 76–77
    process objectives, 75–76
    in session agenda, 150, 152–153
    teaching-learning gap inquiry, 77–78
role expectations, 83–86, 84f

sameness, 81
seeking perspective, 189
selective stand, 105f
session agendas
    about, 147–148
    Agenda Planning Framework, 148f
    welcome, 148–151
    wrap-up, 151–154

session documentation, 172
sexism, 11
single-loop learning, 14
Slice, 21
space, 102–104, 105f
stakeholder interviews, 78–79
standards
    in assess stage, 116, 117f
    expectations gap inquiry, 123–124
    implementation gap inquiry, 119–120
    knowledge gap inquiry, 117–118
    teaching-learning gap inquiry, 121–122
status
    in assess stage, 116, 117f
    expectations gap inquiry, 124
    implementation gap inquiry, 120
    knowledge gap inquiry, 118–119
    teaching-learning gap inquiry, 122–123
structural supports, 93f
students
    blaming for lack of learning, 11
    interviews, 78
    learning processes, 77–78
    observations of, 78
    student artifacts, 77
    triangulated student work, 78
    work, 78
success targets
    in assess stage, 116, 117f
    expectations gap inquiry, 125
    implementation gap inquiry, 121
    knowledge gap inquiry, 119
    teaching-learning gap inquiry, 123
surveys, initial and final, 172
systemic barriers, 2, 164
systems-level learning, 17–18

teaching
    artifacts, 77
    complexity of, 11
    diminishment of, 11
    instructional observations, 77
    observations of teaching, 77
    self-reports and reflections, 77
    student artifacts, 77
    teaching logs, 77
    teaching supports, 92f
teaching-learning gap inquiry
    about, 19f, 20–21
    adaptations to i3PD, 111f–112f
    adjust stage, 141f
    analyze stage, 135f
    assess stage, 121–123
    attempt stage, 128
    facilitator growth, 165–166
    Immunity Map, 195–196

teaching-learning gap inquiry—(*continued*)
    interrogating decisions about how to do it
      responsively, 42, 45*f*
    rigor issues, 77–78
Team Tagging, 155*f*
time, 102, 103*f*–104*f*
Time Capsule, 154*f*
To Us!, 154*f*
triangulated student work, 78
triple-loop learning, 15, 16
trust, 80–83

Tuning, 21
turn and talk, 105*f*

understanding, building shared, 190
uniqueness, 82

values, shared, 81
vulnerability, 85

walkabout, 105*f*

About the Author

Jill Harrison Berg, EdD, is a leadership coach, school improvement consultant, researcher, and writer specializing in teacher leadership, school transformation, and instructional equity. As such, she helps education leaders strengthen their capacities for creating powerful, coordinated systems that maximize teachers' leadership potential and that enable schools to accelerate student success.

Berg began her career in the classroom, teaching in international, independent, and public school settings. Since leaving the classroom in 2001, she has supported scores of school and district administrators as a leadership coach and strategic planning partner and has been tapped by various local, state, and national institutions and organizations to enrich special projects.

Most recently, Berg played a key role in the Boston Public Schools and Boston Teachers Union's collaborative effort to research the status of teacher leadership in the district and to construct a strategic plan for teacher leadership that is coherent, equitable, and sustainable. She is currently a research collaborator in WestEd's work with the KnowledgeWorks REMIQs project, a five-state study designed to identify the characteristics of high schools that are successful in serving students from historically marginalized groups. In addition, she is a curriculum design consultant and an inquiry coach for Zaretta Hammond's Culturally Responsive Education by Design Professional Learning Community.

In her more than 30 years working in educational practice, research, and policy, Berg has written many articles on teacher leadership, teaching quality, leadership development, and school improvement. Her regular column, "Leading Together," in ASCD's *Educational Leadership* magazine, heightens readers' attention to the complementary roles that teacher leaders and administrators can play as they coperform leadership to improve their schools. Berg is the author of two previous books: *Improving the Quality of Teaching through National Board Certification* (Christopher Gordon Press, 2003) and *Leading in Sync: Teacher Leaders and Principals Working Together for Student Learning* (ASCD, 2018).

Berg earned her doctoral degree in learning and teaching at the Harvard Graduate School of Education, her master's degree in education from Lesley University, and her bachelor's degree from Harvard University. In 1998, she was one of the first teachers in Massachusetts to achieve National Board Certification.

Related ASCD Resources

At the time of publication, the following resources were available (ASCD stock numbers in parentheses):

Building Equity: Policies and Practices to Empower All Learners by Dominique Smith, Nancy Frey, Ian Pumpian, and Douglas Fisher (#117031)

Coherent School Leadership: Forging Clarity from Complexity by Michael Fullan and Lyle Kirtman (#118040)

Creating a Culture of Reflective Practice: Capacity-Building for Schoolwide Success by Pete Hall and Alisa Simeral (#117006)

Creating the Opportunity to Learn: Moving from Research to Practice to Close the Achievement Gap by A. Wade Boykin and Pedro Noguera (#107016)

Culture, Class, and Race: Constructive Conversations That Unite and Energize Your School and Community by Brenda CampbellJones, Shannon Keeny, and Franklin CampbellJones (#118010)

The Equity and Social Justice Education 50: Critical Questions for Improving Opportunities and Outcomes for Black Students by Baruti K. Kafele (#121060)

Excellence Through Equity: Five Principles of Courageous Leadership to Guide Achievement for Every Student by Alan M. Blankstein, Pedro Noguera, and Lorena Kelly (#116070)

Fighting for Change in Your School: How to Avoid Fads and Focus on Substance by Harvey Alvy (#117007)

Five Practices for Equity-Focused School Leadership by Sharon I. Radd, Gretchen Givens Generett, Mark Anthony Gooden, and George Theoharis (#120008)

The Innocent Classroom: Dismantling Racial Bias to Support Students of Color by Alexs Pate (#120025)

Leadership for Learning: How to Bring Out the Best in Every Teacher, 2nd Edition by Carl Glickman and Rebecca West Burns (#121007)

Leading Change Together: Developing Educator Capacity Within Schools and Systems by Eleanor Drago-Severson and Jessica Blum-DeStefano (#117027)

Leading In Sync: Teacher Leaders and Principals Working Together for Student Learning by Jill Harrison Berg (#118021)

The Learning Leader: How to Focus School Improvement for Better Results, 2nd Edition by Douglas B. Reeves (#118003)

Personalized Professional Learning: A Job-Embedded Pathway for Elevating Teacher Voice by Allison Rodman (#118028)

Strengthening and Enriching Your Professional Learning Community: The Art of Learning Together by Geoffrey Caine and Renate N. Caine (#110085)

Success with Multicultural Newcomers & English Learners: Proven Practices for School Leadership Teams by Margarita Espino Calderón and Shawn Slakk (#117026)

For up-to-date information about ASCD resources, go to www.ascd.org. You can search the complete archives of *Educational Leadership* magazine at www.ascd.org/el.

For more information, send an email to member@ascd.org; call 1-800-933-2723 or 1-703-578-9600; send a fax to 1-703-575-5400; or write to Information Services, ASCD, 1703 N. Beauregard St., Alexandria, VA 22311-1714 USA.

WHOLE CHILD
TENETS

1 HEALTHY
Each student enters school healthy and learns about and practices a healthy lifestyle.

2 SAFE
Each student learns in an environment that is physically and emotionally safe for students and adults.

3 ENGAGED
Each student is actively engaged in learning and is connected to the school and broader community.

4 SUPPORTED
Each student has access to personalized learning and is supported by qualified, caring adults.

5 CHALLENGED
Each student is challenged academically and prepared for success in college or further study and for employment and participation in a global environment.

THE **WHOLE** CHILD

The ASCD Whole Child approach is an effort to transition from a focus on narrowly defined academic achievement to one that promotes the long-term development and success of all children. Through this approach, ASCD supports educators, families, community members, and policymakers as they move from a vision about educating the whole child to sustainable, collaborative actions.

Uprooting Instructional Inequity relates to the **challenged** tenet.

For more about the ASCD Whole Child approach, visit **www.ascd.org/wholechild.**

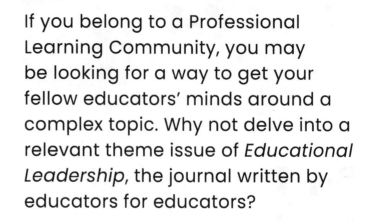

CPSIA information can be obtained
at www.ICGtesting.com
Printed in the USA
LVHW021119110723
752021LV00048B/877